B
U
P

edited by

Stefano Caselli · Stefano Gatti

CAPITAL MARKETS

Perspectives over the Last Decade

Typesetting: Laura Panigara, Cesano Boscone (MI)
Cover: Cristina Bernasconi, Milan

EGEA S.p.A.
Via Salasco, 5 - 20136 Milano
Tel. 02/5836.5751 – Fax 02/5836.5753
egea.edizioni@unibocconi.it – www.egeaeditore.it

First edition: April 2023

ISBN Domestic Edition	979-12-80623-11-9
ISBN International Edition	978-88-31322-85-0
ISBN Digital Domestic Edition	978-88-238-8622-3
ISBN Digital International Edition	978-88-31322-86-7

Print: Logo srl, Borgoricco (PD)

Table of Contents

List of Figures

Chapter 1

Chapter 2

Chapter 3

Chapter 4

List of Tables

Chapter 3

Chapter 4

List of Abbreviations

ABB	Accelerated book-building
ABS	Asset-backed security
AIM	Alternative Investment Market
AMF	Autorité des Marchés Financiers
BaFin	Bundesanstalt für Finanzdienstleistungsaufsicht
CAGR	Compounded Average Growth Rate
CMU	Capital Markets Union
CONSOB	Italian Companies and Exchange Commission (Commissione Nazionale per le Società e la Borsa)
DCM	Debt Capital Market
DEBRA	Debt-Equity Bias Reduction Allowance
EBIT	Earnings Before Interest and Taxes
EBITDA	Earnings Before Interests Taxes Depreciation and Amortization
ECB	European Central Bank
ECM	Equity Capital Market
ESG	Environmental, social and governance
GDP	Gross domestic product
GFC	Global Financial Crisis
HY	High Yield
IB	Investment Bank
IG	Investment Grade
IPO	Initial public offering
IRAP	Regional production tax (Imposta regionale sulle attività produttive)
IRES	Corporate income tax (Imposta sul reddito delle società)
ISTAT	Italian National Institute of Statistics (Istituto Nazionale di Statistica)
M&A	Mergers & Acquisitions
MBS	Mortgage-backed security
MEF	Ministry of Economy and Finance (Ministero dell'Economia e delle Finanze)
MiFID	Markets in Financial Instruments Directive
NPLs	Non-performing loans

NRRP	National Recovery and Resilience Plan
OECD	Organization for Economic Co-operation and Development
OPS	Public offer of subscription (Offerta pubblica di sottoscrizione)
OPSV	Public offer of subscription and selling (Offerta pubblica di sottoscrizione e vendita)
OPV	Public offer of selling (Offerta pubblica di vendita)
PIR	Piani Individuali di Risparmio
QE	Quantitative Easing
SBP	Social Bond Principles
SEO	Seasoned equity offering
SMEs	Small and medium-sized enterprises
S.p.A.	Joint-stock company (Società per azioni)
SPAC	Special Purpose Acquisition Company
S.r.l.	Limited liability company (Società a responsabilità limitata)
TESG	Technical Expert Stakeholder Group on SMEs
TUF	Italian Consolidated Law on Financial Intermediation (Testo Unico della Finanza)

Foreword

by *Andrea Vismara*

2023 marks a very special year for Equita as we celebrate our 50th anniversary. A remarkable milestone for a financial institution that, over the years, has been able to set itself apart as the leading independent investment bank in Italy, as well as an innovative player for the entire Italian financial system.

Since its establishment in 1973 as "Euromobiliare," Equita and its professionals have committed to improving financial markets and promoting corporate finance transactions to foster companies' growth and innovation. And as strong evidence of how capital markets are so important for the system and for us, Equita itself has been listed twice – first as Euromobiliare and then as Equita – on both the SME growth market and the regulated market.

In 2013, our DNA as an independent investment bank and our focus on capital markets led us to develop a partnership with Bocconi University, an institution which has capital markets at its heart, just like we do. Since the very beginning, the aim of the partnership between Equita and Bocconi was to study the Italian capital markets, which have historically been under-developed, considering the size of our economy and in comparison with all major OECD countries. And it is well known that this gap has significantly harmed the ability of Italian corporates to invest and innovate in their businesses, as well as their ability to compete on a global basis.

The reasons for the unsatisfactory development of our capital markets, which was very clearly described in a specific report published by OECD in 2020, range from the over-reliance on bank lending by Italian corporates, to the small number of domestic investment banks and institutional investors, such as pension funds, to the exceedingly complex regulatory framework. But ultimately, the main reason has been the historical lack of interest in capital markets of our own governments and regulators: government debt and bank lending have always been the key priorities, and Italian industrial policies have never focused on the need for efficient capital markets for the benefit of companies and investors.

Looking at what we have done in the past ten years jointly with Bocconi, we are honored to see that all our efforts – in terms of research and financial publications – have been reworked and summarized in a book to celebrate our partnership. At the same time, we feel really proud of what has been done in the past decade to promote capital markets, financial education, and human capital.

I would like to mention, for instance, the award for the best strategies on capital markets we hand out each year within the partnership (with the sponsorship of Borsa Italiana – Euronext Group) to companies that have accelerated their growth by accessing equity and debt capital markets. Another key element of the partnership I would love to recall are the scholarships with which Equita has supported students since 2013 (not limited to Bocconi but including several other schools and universities), as well as the initiatives to promote gender equality in finance, such as the "Bocconi Awards for Women," with which we sponsor scholarships for deserving female students majoring in finance and Executive MBA candidates.

Coming back to our joint research, since the very beginning of the partnership, thanks to the academic contribution of Centro BAFFI-CAREFIN we have analyzed the ongoing condition of capital markets, focusing from time to time on intermediaries, investors, companies, and their reasons to go public. We have carried out a thorough comparison with more developed models, such as the UK's model, and analyzed the performance reported by securities issued by Italian companies over the last decade. And we have always integrated this analysis with recommendations for regulatory improvements and system-wide initiatives.

Over time, encouraging improvements have emerged which also show a growing awareness of the importance of our capital markets for companies and investors.

Among the positive initiatives, we can certainly mention the pieces of legislation passed by the Italian Government to promote the introduction of PIR funds (individual savings plans) and ELTIFs (European Long Term Investment Funds), which have subsequently been further improved with the so-called "PIR Alternativi." The PIR funds for instance – whose main aim was to overcome the lack of liquidity for small and mid-caps by incentivizing the investments of long-term retail investors in such growth listed companies – benefit from tax exemption on capital gain and financial income if certain conditions are met. The same is true for the PIR Alternativi, but with a slight difference on their primary purpose because these funds are aimed at channeling Italian savings toward both public and private Italian SMEs, as it is the case in UK and France for instance. The introduction of tax credits on listing expenses for SMEs completing an IPO is another market-friendly initiative that took a significant step in encouraging Italian companies to go public.

More recently, the listing process has been simplified, following the recommendations of the task force coordinated by the Ministry of Economy and Finance (summarized in the so-called "Libro Verde"). Government representatives have also announced a wider-ranging piece of legislation which should address a number of regulatory issues regarding our capital markets.

This is in line with a renewed effort also at European level to modernize the regulatory framework and to enhance the appeal of its capital markets, as clearly shown by the work of the Technical Expert Stakeholder Group on SMEs (or TESG, a group of experts – which included Equita) promoted by the European Commission, and the Listing Act proposal published in late 2022.

In Italy, CONSOB has adopted simpler approval procedures, aligned the time limits for prospectus approval to the European standards and granted the possibility to draft prospectuses in English. On the same side, Borsa Italiana has simplified the documentation requirements, the extent of its role in the review process of listings and the responsibilities of listing agents.

All of these initiatives point out the concrete commitment of regulators to ensure faster and easier access to capital markets for issuers, and enhance the overall attractiveness of debt and equity markets, as a way to accelerate growth and diversify funding sources for European companies. Equita and Bocconi have been at the forefront of all of these developments, deeply involved in all the policy discussions and drafting of the main pieces of legislation.

However, in the last decade, prior to this recent collective effort, regulation had gone in the opposite direction, mainly as a result of new European directives, which overcomplicated the entire framework when unnecessary. I am referring to MiFID II, introduced in January 2018 with the aim of increasing transparency, protecting investors, and improving growth markets dedicated to SMEs, or the Market Abuse Regulation (MAR), entered into force in July 2016 to contrast market abuse and promote market integrity.

Whilst the regulator's purposes were noble, a number of mistakes were made, and the introduction of MiFID II and MAR resulted in significant unintended consequences, first of all an increasing level of complexity that have compromised the willingness of companies to access capital markets, especially for mid and small caps.

And nothing has been done to make sure that investment banks and investors (particularly the ones focusing on smaller companies) can prosper and guarantee efficient capital markets for European companies. Quite the opposite, with initiatives such as the MiFID II directive, which demands the completely unnecessary unbundling of the cost of research from trading fees. These rules are destroying the research industry, increasing concentration, cutting the research coverage of European companies, especially on mid and small caps, and making it impossible for weaker research institutes to survive. Within the recent Listing Act proposal, the European Commission has clearly stated that MIFiD II had a very negative impact on research coverage and is now considering some major adjustments.

In summary, some progress has been made but, as the book clearly shows, there are still a number of important issues to be addressed. In order for capital markets to function properly in Italy, initiatives must still be taken on different fronts so that the whole ecosystem made of investment banks, investors, companies, taxes and regulatory framework makes our capital markets attractive for companies and investors.

For example:

- Rules must be simplified so as to make it less burdensome for companies to go public and remain listed over time.
- Incentives must be put in place to develop a healthy research industry, after years of decreasing coverage and disappearing investment banks.
- Taxes such as the FTT that create a competitive disadvantage for the Italian equity markets must be removed.
- Local investors must be further developed, with a clear commitment from pension funds, insurance companies, banks and banking foundations to contribute actively to our capital markets.
- The Government, CONSOB and Bank of Italy must all make it their objective to find ways to develop the markets and cooperate actively with all the stakeholders.

In sum, an effective industrial policy must be put in place to foster the development of capital markets and reduce the gap with the ones of the main OECD countries and the effort should be coordinated by a dedicated team, across ministries and institutions, to take ownership of this important task.

Introduction

by *Stefano Caselli* and *Stefano Gatti*

Almost ten years ago, at the beginning of 2012, Bocconi University and Equita teamed up with the objective to produce and disseminate high-quality applied research on the role of capital markets for the European and Italian economies that could be useful for policymakers, scholars, and students. The idea was to develop a real "culture of capital markets" in academia and professional circles.

The time was ripe for such cooperation. The lack of a robust financial infrastructure of capital markets, the need to strengthen the investor base, and flaws in the intermediation structure of capital markets were clear factors of competitive disadvantage for Italy vis-à-vis other European countries.

During the past ten years, the joint efforts of the Bocconi University researchers and Equita produced a series of reports that were presented at annual conferences and discussed with policymakers and professionals. In addition, the data collected to prepare these research reports became the basis for the Annual Observatory on Italian capital markets.

Well before the outbreak of the COVID-19 pandemic, the overall evidence showed that capital markets in Italy were still underdeveloped. In fact, the past decade was characterized by serious weaknesses in the structure and functioning of these markets, what we define as the *three gaps*:

1. Italy lacks a strong base of domestic investors able to absorb debt and equity instruments issued by domestic companies (the *investor gap*).

2. The overwhelming dominance of traditional bank lending has reinforced the dependence of companies, particularly small and medium-sized firms (SMEs), on bank lending, which still represents the foremost source of financing for Italian companies (the *financing gap*).
3. For large segments of Italian companies, the investment banking business is dominated by large international intermediaries, with only a minor role played by domestic investment banks/integrated financial intermediaries (the *intermediation gap*).

After ten years, it was time to return to the published research reports, to update and present them comprehensively in an organic framework. An update was also made necessary by a changed financial and macroeconomic scenario that marked a break with the time when the original reports were prepared.

In fact, after the beginning of quantitative easing by the ECB, the past decade was characterized by financial repression and low or even negative interest rates. The results of our analyses were heavily influenced by a macroeconomic scenario where growth and public and private financing were strongly supported by an ultra-expansive monetary policy.

Starting from 2022, the financial and macroeconomic scenario has dramatically changed. The geopolitical tensions brought about by the Russian-Ukrainian war, the new inflationary scenario and the quantitative tightening of central banks worldwide have put an end to a period of inflated prices on almost all financial assets. The effects on Italian capital markets have been immediate, and rather painful.

As of this writing, the FTSE Mib Index has lost 13.3% year-on-year, and market capitalization has dropped to about €620 billion from €757 billion at year's end 2021. At present, the ratio of the Italian market capitalization to GDP stands at 33.9%, compared to 43% at the close of 2021. The trend of new admissions on the different segments of the Italian stock exchange has been equally bleak: 2022 registered 30 new admissions (down from 49 in 2021), four of them on Euronext Milan, and the others on the Euronext Growth Milan. That same year, total fundraising was only €1.45 billion, without taking into account nine capital increases for €4.7 billion.

Market performance, in terms of prices and volumes, is not the only thing that was unsatisfactory: 2022 will probably be remembered as the year of delistings.[1] In fact, we saw 19 tender offers for an amount of about €3 billion, and 21 delistings, 13 on the main market and 8 on the Euronext Growth Milan. The result was lost capitalization of about €28 billion, of which €19 billion alone was represented by the Atlantia deal.[2]

However, against this backdrop, the changed macroeconomic scenario offers a unique possibility to reimagine and rebuild the capital market infrastructure, securing a foothold for Italy and the EU on the path toward a full postpandemic recovery. Compared to the context of the past decade, two developments could trigger a real relaunch of capital market circuits in Italy: first, the MEF Green Book and the proposed EU Listing Act; second, the National Recovery and Resilience Plan (NRRP).

The MEF Green Book and the proposed EU Listing Act

The European Union has intensified efforts to strengthen capital market circuits, with a special focus on SMEs (Technical Expert Stakeholder Group (TESG) on SMEs, 2021). In an increasingly polarized geopolitical scenario, now more than ever the European Union is considering capital markets and market-based corporate finance as the keys to relaunching the Eurozone (High Level Forum on the Capital Markets Union, 2020). This recognition of the importance of capital markets has led to the creation of a task force coordinated by the Italian Minister for Economy and Finance, along with the publication of a Green Book on the competitiveness of the Italian capital markets as a form of support for growth (MEF, 2022).

---

[1] The delisting process has been driven by anchor shareholders and by sponsored private equity buyouts. A major cause of this retreat from the stock exchange is that key shareholders believe that prices in the market do not reflect the fair value of the listed companies. If, on one hand, delistings reduce size and strength of equity capital markets, on the other, these deals draw attention to a renewed need for capital market efficiency, so as to properly price the fundamentals of listed companies.

[2] While the delisting trend has been particularly severe in Italy, also other markets in continental Europe, notably Germany, have suffered the same situation. See Storbeck (2022).

A further push toward the creation of the Capital Markets Union (CMU) is the EU proposal of the Listing Act EU, with the objective of harmonizing listing rules in the European Union. The measure does not foresee a perfectly unified capital market infrastructure with a single supervisory authority and a European Prospectus that is automatically recognized by each member state. But at least in the short term, the Listing Act is a further step toward the simplification of information requirements and a reduction of listing costs for IPOs and seasoned equity offerings. A cheaper, streamlined, less bureaucratic listing process, particularly for SMEs, is vital for reversing the trend of delisting and attracting more firms to stock exchanges.

The effects of this renewed attention to capital market circuits are material and encouraging. Here are a few:

1. The prospectus will be shorter (maximum 300 pages), with a standardized format, sequence of sections and information. It will be prepared in English, without the need for publication in the language of the issuer's country, and made available online in electronic format.
2. For *follow-on offers*, firms will be exempted from the requirement to publish the prospectus if the securities being issued are similar to those already listed.
3. The process for controlling and approving the prospectus by supervising national authorities will be simplified.[3]
4. Lastly, the minimum free float will be reduced from 25% to 10%, giving more flexibility to issuers whose anchor shareholders want to maintain control stakes in their firms.

---

[3] As a recent example of the already visible effects of the simplification of the control and approval of prospectuses, we can cite the exemption for firms from the requirement of submitting to CONSOB the document of procedures for transactions by related parties, and information about the independence of Board Members. See CONSOB (2023).

The National Recovery and Resilience Plan (NRRP)

In 2021, the Italian Government launched the NRRP (Equita, 2021a, 2021b) and established the main guidelines for relaunching the Italian economy in a postpandemic scenario. The Italian NRRP can count on a substantial budget: including about €13.5 billion from the React-EU Plan, total available resources exceed €235 billion. Of this figure, €62 billion is earmarked for the Ministry of Infrastructure and Sustainable Mobility alone, the lead actor in reducing the infrastructure gap in the country.

The impact of the NRRP has produced significant effects on Italian capital markets, albeit not always in the direction foreseen by the reforms cited above. In fact, 2022 was the year of large transactions, often sponsored by private equity in the transportation, energy, and telecommunication sectors.

According to the KPMG Report on Mergers and Acquisitions (M&A) in Italy, private equity investors sponsored 131 deals for over €19 billion, up from €12.1 billion in 2021. The largest transactions were indeed targeting infrastructure investments, among others the €8 billion acquisition of ASPI-Autostrade per l'Italia by Holding Reti Autostradali (the consortium formed by Cassa Depositi e Prestiti, Blackstone and Macquarie), and the €1.3 billion acquisition of 41% of the Daphne 3 vehicle, which controls 30.2% of Inwit – Infrastrutture Wireless Italiane – by a consortium of investors led by Ardian.

While these deals do not contribute directly to the development of capital market circuits, they will definitely produce positive effects on the ecosystem, opening opportunities in the M&A business also to Italian intermediaries and advisors.

* * *

In this scenario characterized by lights and shadows, Italian capital markets are being presented with an unmissable occasion to become a catalyst for the postpandemic recovery.

In this book, the reader can understand the reasons why Italian capital markets have never taken off, and at the same time why the scenario is hopefully changing.

The chapters represent each key component of an ideal ecosystem. Chapter 1 by Gimede Gigante focuses on intermediaries and the structure of the investment banking industry in Europe and Italy. Chapter 2 by Marta Zava is dedicated to investors, analyzing the attractiveness of Italian capital markets and assessing whether an investment in these markets has paid off in the past decade. Chapter 3 by Carlo Chiarella explores equity capital markets, paying specific attention to the motivations behind the listing process of Italian issuers and their shareholder base. Chapter 4 by Giulia Negri looks at Debt Capital Markets (loans and bonds) and the drivers of the cost of funding for Italian issuers.

As we've said, this book marks the 10th anniversary of the collaboration between Bocconi University and Equita, but also the 50th anniversary of Equita. As a summary and an organic presentation of the results of the past decade of research, we truly hope that it can help shed light on the structural features of the financial structure of Italian capital markets.

Only by knowing the history of a market can professionals, policymakers, students, and scholars understand its weaknesses and find ways to improve and relaunch it.

References

Caselli, S., Gatti, S., Chiarella, C., Clerici, M., & Marchi, M. (2022). *Infrastructure, capital markets and opportunities for the real economy in the post-pandemic landscape.* Bocconi University/Equita Quarterly Columns Series on Capital Markets, n. 4. Available at: equitalab.eu

CONSOB (2023). *Vigilanza sul governo societario e sulle operazioni con parti correlate nell'ambito dei prospetti di offerta e ammissione alle negoziazioni – Richiamo di attenzione n. 1/23 del 13 gennaio 2023.* Available at: consob.it

Equita (2021a). The National Recovery & Resilience Plan (NRRP): Mission possible.

Equita (2021b, July 26). Utilities – Sector update.

High Level Forum on the Capital Markets Union (2020, June). *A new vision for Europe's capital markets: Final report of the high-level forum on the Capital Markets Union.* Available at: finance.ec.europa.eu

MEF (2022). *La competitività dei mercati finanziari italiani a supporto della crescita.* Available at: dt.mef.gov.it

Storbeck, O. (2022, December 22). Porsche and the decline of the German stock market. *Financial Times.*

Technical Expert Stakeholder Group (TESG) on SMEs (2021). *Empowering EU capital markets for SMEs: Making listing cool again.* Available at: commission.europa.eu

1 Investment Banking: Intermediaries as Infrastructure of Capital Markets

by *Gimede Gigante*

Innovation and Corporate Entrepreneurship Center (ICE), SDA Bocconi School of Management

---

The aim of this chapter[1] is to introduce the investment banking industry both in Europe and in Italy, and to analyze what are the main players operating in the segments of Equity Capital Markets (ECMs), Debt Capital Markets (DCMs), and Mergers & Acquisitions (M&A). A trend that has recently been observed in Europe is the predominance of US banks, especially in the M&A and the ECM sectors, where size is a crucial factor to secure the largest and most remunerative deals. In terms of volumes and number of deals, 2021 was an exceptional year in all the segments, while the situation has deteriorated in 2022, mainly because of the rise in interest rates and the unstable international political situation. Italy remains a market with its own peculiarities: Most of M&A are domestic, the market capitalization of the Milan Stock Exchange is still small compared to the Italian GDP and Italian companies, which have a relatively small size, remain reluctant to address public markets. However, recent interventions from the Italian government have incentivized both bond issues and new listings in the Euronext Growth segment.

Investment banks play a role of paramount importance within capital markets as they provide a range of services that facilitate the smooth functioning of these markets. First and foremost, a key role is that investment banks act as intermediaries between investors and companies in need of funding. They do this offering different services, that stem

[1] The author of the chapter thanks Francesco Toti and Giulia Zanetello for their support as research assistants.

from ECMs, to DCMs and Leveraged Finance. They indeed help corporations, organizations, and sovereign institutions raise capital by underwriting and issuing securities, such as stocks, loans, and bonds. Moreover, investment banks act as advisors in complex transactions such as mergers, joint ventures, and restructuring operations, that fall under the general definition of M&A. By supporting companies' external growth, investment banks enable them to reach the critical mass which is needed to successfully tap capital markets and adequately diversify their sources of financing.

In these respects, the role of investment banks is incredibly dependent on two key aspects of this industry that are often neglected when dealing with it. The first is related to the network requirements of being the epitome of financial deals. Indeed, to raise funds and find new business opportunities, to be a market maker and to better understand how financial markets will move, it is necessary to have a powerful network and be its pivot. Indeed, this gives privileged access to market participants and more information on the market itself, two aspects that are crucial in a world of limited knowledge. On a practical note, this is likely to be translated into a greater size and broader global presence, which is in many cases hardly achieved by European and Italian banks, as this chapter will argue. In addition, the importance of the network of each bank should be studied also in relation to its network of potential clients.

The second aspect under analysis is the ability to manage complex transactions: The image that the bank offers to the external world is a naïve, yet faithlessly accepted proxy of it. A bank needs to be well respected by the market for it to thrive, otherwise markets may fear it will crush, (possibly) causing its effective crush.[2] And as long as they seem profitable and involved in deal-making activities, banks that are deemed too big to fail will survive in the market.

In summary, investment banks are a crucial and pivotal, yet delicate component of capital markets, providing a range of services that facilitate and enhance the efficient functioning of these markets. In light of this, the scope of this chapter is to provide a better understanding of

---

[2] For the basis of the mechanism at the core of this, see Diamond & Dyvbig (1983).

the evolution of the investment banking sector in Europe, with a specific section dedicated to Italy, in order to highlight the key trends that are shaping the industry and what are the implications for the economy, the policymakers and all the companies operating in it. Investment banks play a central role in the economy: They are intermediaries that connect companies to investors, promoting an efficient flow and allocation of capital. By enabling firms to access capital markets and investors, investment banks promote their growth and the development of the economic area in which such companies operate. For this reason, a well-functioning investment banking system should be a crucial political priority for Europe, as an impoverishment of it will undermine the growth potential of European companies and the European economic area. Bearing this in mind, regulators and policymakers need to implement the most effective measures in order to support the investment banking system, especially in consideration of the narrowing gap that has emerged between US and European banks, as it will be discussed further on. This chapter will thus study and provide evidence on the role of investment banks within these markets, aiming at showing what is the actual situation in Europe and in Italy given what the future ahead is likely to look like.

The chapter is structured as follows. The first section introduces the investment banking system in Europe, analyzing the recent trends that are shaping the market and the main players operating in it. Then, to deeper understand the market dynamics, we will break down the analysis into the three main segments of the investment banking industry: ECMs, DCMs, and M&A. For each of them, its structure and its evolution over time will be analyzed, in order to highlight the most relevant trends both on the supply side, that is, the types and sizes of the financial instruments offered by firms and also on the advisory side, looking at the different broker categories and their ranking. The second section will implement the same analysis but limited to Italy. Then, a concluding paragraph presents final considerations and remarks.

1.1 Investment Banking in Europe: Recent Trends

This section is aimed at discussing the main developments in the investment banking industry in Europe. In particular, an analysis of the trends that are currently characterizing the market and how they can potentially impact the brokerage services provided by banks to corporates will be conducted.

The investment banking industry in Europe is facing some significant trends and developments that are shaping the industry as a whole. In particular, the consequences of the Global Financial Crisis (GFC) are still visible both on the equity and bond markets, despite several years having now passed. First, the regulatory framework created after the crisis, especially an increased capital absorption derived from different Basel guidelines, has made financial intermediaries more cautious, undermining their ability to provide liquidity to traders and investors. Moreover, the injection of a huge amount of cash in the markets through the Quantitative Easing program has increased a lot the size of capital markets and simultaneously reduced their volatility, making investments banks reluctant to provide market-making services.

In such an environment, a rise of alternative investments such as private equity and private debt was experienced, which have registered a steady growth in the past two decades. Within ten years from now, asset owners will place 20% of their assets in private markets, from the current proportion which is near 14% (Willis Towers Watson, 2021). In light of this, a potential risk of market illiquidity arises, thus affecting the stability of the global financial system as a whole (*Reuters*, 2019). 2022 in particular saw a remarkable change in the capital markets, with a rise in both inflation and interest rates. This dual increase, together with a spiking volatility caused by geopolitical tensions and the Russia–Ukrainian conflict, has severely impacted the business of investment banks. The sector has indeed, especially in the M&A segment, experienced a significant slowdown during 2022.

Another trend that is shaping the investment banking industry in Europe is the growing importance of sustainable finance. As concerns about environmental, social, and governance (ESG) issues have risen, there has been an increasing demand for investment products that take these issues into account. This has led to the development of a range of sustainable finance products and services, and many investment banks are now placing a greater emphasis on ESG in their operations.

On top of these trends, that are common to the whole industry, some other trends are peculiar to the European landscape. An ageing population combined with a lower depth of capital markets might turn into lower investments through a lower saving rate (Bloom et al., 2010), with potentially serious consequences not only on the investment banking industry but also on other economic sectors. This waterfall effect might even be amplified by the high degree of interconnectedness of the European business and financial landscape due to the EU Single Market. Lastly, the effects of Brexit are undoubtedly causing troubles in the financial industry. Regulatory issues and organizational issues are only a few of the problems that top management teams of these institutions need to overcome to minimize as much as possible these costs. However, these trends are likely to continue to evolve in the coming years, and it is important for investment banks to adapt and stay up to date in order to remain competitive in this dynamic industry.

Investment banks in Europe seem to be also facing what could be labelled "insider paradox." European investment banks have a consistently lower market share than their US counterparts (see the last paragraph of Section 1.1.3), in spite of having Europe as their core business areas. The reasons behind this paradox are many and hard to detect. What surely matters is the size of the network of investors that a bank can have and, in this respect, US banks have a considerably larger network because of their global scope. Moreover, the size of the bank per se is a key determinant of the scope and complexity of the deals that a bank can work on. However, this picture is only partly complete. To expand into a foreign market, any activity requires a sufficiently large scale of operation for it to be profitable. And the investment banking business is in no way different. As this section will show, US bulge bracket banks are those top performers that erode the market share of European banks. It is thus important to study in detail the reasons for these phenomena to better understand this industry and to try to draw some novel insights. The following sections will analyze the industry by breaking it down into its three main components, namely, ECMs, DCMs, and M&A advisory, focusing on the different deals that fall under these three categories. In order to do so, all deals in the aforementioned areas completed between 2010 and 2022 and involving only European companies were retrieved from Refinitiv Workspace.

To analyze ECMs in Europe, two different datasets provided by Refinitiv were used: Volume Analysis data and League Table data. In this way, it is possible to look at both the supply side, in terms of size of issues and number of IPOs, and at the brokering side, with a focus on who are the main underwriters. The same logic is followed when discussing DCMs, even though for the sake of a better analysis a distinction between bonds and loans was made, in order to highlight possible differences both in terms of selection and size. Finally, data for the M&A League Table contained all the deals involving only Europe-based targets and acquirors. Advisors were ranked based on Rank Value, a measure computed by subtracting from the transaction value the value of any liabilities assumed in a transaction and by adding the target's net debt.

Each subsection will focus on different measures of the relevant market to give an overview of the segment and to pave the way for some of the topics that will be dealt with within the following chapters. In particular, it will try to build a bridge between what will be under analysis in the remainder of the book and what are the major, overall trends that the industry is facing at the moment. The goal is to offer the reader an exhaustive but comprehensive characterization of the investment banking phenomenon in Europe, in order to assess whether its size and structure are adequate to support the economy by creating the conditions for an efficient flow and allocation of capital. Therefore, the analysis is constructed at the deal level, focusing on primary market activities and advisory services dedicated to M&A and to the placement of newly issued financial instruments in both public and private markets.

1.1.1 ECM

ECM is, within investment banks, the practice that deals with all the activities concerning the financing of a company that involve capital markets, for example derivatives, issuing or selling shares via IPO, as well as accelerated book offers and block trades. The analysis is focused only on Initial Public Offerings (IPOs), that is when a private company decides to access the stock market for the first time. Listed shares can be offered both to private and to institutional investors, depending on the company's will and the market conditions. Investment banks play a crucial role in the process, as they usually offer underwriting services. Sometimes, the bank that act as underwriter is also the book-builder, responsible of gauging the interest of potential investors and collecting their orders. Since the IPO process is very long and complex, there are typically many investment banks involved, playing the role of co-underwriters, global coordinators, or selling banks.

Other ECMs operations include Follow-ons, or Seasoned Offerings, that occur when already listed firms offer additional new shares on the market. In Europe, issuers are obliged to address existing shareholders before offering shares to new investors, in order to avoid dilution: This process is called a right issue. Finally, an Accelerated Book Building (ABB) occurs when a large portion of a listed company is sold on the market in a very short time period. Given the strict timelines, ABB is usually targeting qualified institutional investors, and thus, the bank's existing network plays a crucial role in this process.

The reason why the focus of this subsection is exclusively on IPOs is twofold. On the one hand, IPOs do represent a key, distinctive feature of this industry, and trends that characterize IPOs are usually reflected in SEOs and ABBs. On the other hand, it mirrors the underlying business environment, in particular when put in comparison with the M&A sector. Indeed, differential trends among the two do capture firms and investors' preferences that have evolved over the years, both in terms of capital allocation decisions and varying risk profiles.

The numbers of the Equity Market in Europe

As a first step to get a picture of the size of ECMs in Europe, attention should be paid to how many and how big, in terms of volumes, the IPO deals are.

Figure 1.1 shows these two quantities together, breaking them down for each year under analysis. Two major facts can be noticed. First, there is a clear trend of decreasing new IPOs after 2015. Second, 2021 is marked by a peak in both the number and the volumes. Focusing on this second aspect, several reasons might explain this unprecedented surge. Whereas a restart from slowdown of the initial period of the COVID-19 pandemic is surely a reason behind this, economic and fiscal aid measures that were put in place by governments and by the European Union should also be kept into consideration. Indeed, macroeconomic aid packages and similar programs might have played a paramount role in pushing capital markets in 2021, thus contributing to explaining part of – if not all –

Figure 1.1 **IPOS: volumes (left-hand scale) vs. number of issues (right-hand scale)**

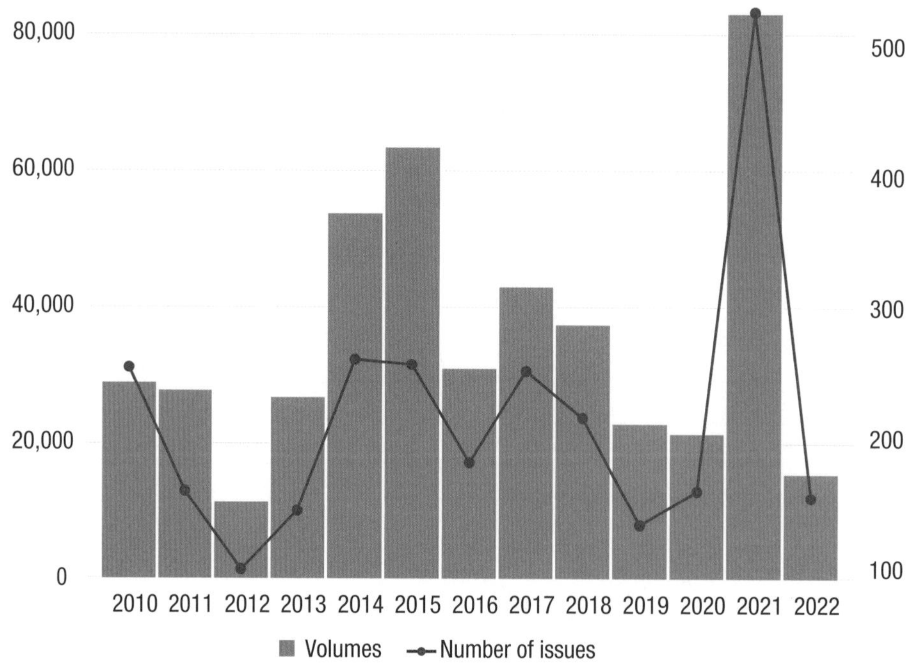

Source: author's elaboration of Refinitiv data.

the surge in IPOs. Another phenomenon that may help to understand the overperformance of 2021 is the SPACs' euphoria, led by the presence of too much capital to be deployed in the market. This trend was completely inverted in 2022, when the number of new SPACs has been incredibly low. This dramatic decline coincided with a broader IPO slowdown and rising interest rates as investors lost their appetite for risk.

2022 might be instead labelled as *annus horribilis* as the situation has changed dramatically. European ECM has been lagging, and issues registered the lowest level in a decade, with new issues which were down by 81% compared to the previous year. Moreover, it is interesting to notice how the "gap" between volumes and number of issues is narrower than in other years, pointing at a possible underperformance of these IPOs vis-à-vis similar IPOs in other years.

A concomitance of factors played a role in the incredibly low numbers shown by the graph. Among these factors, a stricter monetary policy and higher levels of inflation in the Eurozone were for sure two leading causes. The reduction of money supply by Central Banks has determined an increased in volatility, which is well reflected by the surge in the VIX index[3] at the beginning of 2022. During the first semester of 2022, average volatility was around 24, while pre-COVID, its level was around 16. The perceived uncertainty in the markets can be explained looking at the tensions still unsolved between Russia and Ukraine, at the solid inflationary drive and at the change of prime minister in the UK occurred in early September. An increase in implied volatility has a major influence on the number of companies who tap capital markets for the first time, and only the prospect of a future recovery of the business cycle will be able to drive a surge of new equity.

The general slowdown of the Equity market, also reflected in the underperformance of the Euro Stoxx 600 that lost around 10% in 2022,[4] is

[3] VIX is the ticker symbol for the Cboe Volatility Index, which is widely used by investors to anticipate future market volatility. Sometimes referred to as the "fear index," VIX is a reflection of investor uncertainty and expected future price fluctuations across the broader financial market.

[4] Please refer to the StoXX Europe 600 Index performance factsheet as of December 2022. Available at: stoxx.com.

not only a European phenomenon, as the same dynamics are impacting all markets worldwide. In fact, 2022 registered a 66% drop in transactions at a global level, with a marked reduction in the United States and Japan, while the Middle East/Africa represented the only exception to this negative market outlook.

Another interesting analysis concerns the breakdown of European Capital Markets by nationality, looking at the local performance of Equity Markets. In terms of geography, the top European Market by number of IPOs remains the UK, despite Brexit and the unsolved political tensions within its government. Germany, France, and the Netherlands follow up in the rankings. However, in terms of size, the order is totally different: while UK and French listing are characterized by a relatively small size, in the range of €80–100 million, in the German and Dutch markets an average quotation of around €500 million is found. This aspect suggests the fact that the market in Germany and in the Netherlands is less attractive for small and medium-sized enterprises (SMEs) than the Alternative Investment Market (AIM) London and Euronext Growth Paris markets, offering less growth potential for the firms operating in such territories.

To conclude on this section, it is worth mentioning that the European Equity Market is concentrated in terms of nationality, with the countries that rank among the first five, UK, Germany, France, Italy, and Netherlands, accounting for around 60% of all the deal volume.

The main players in the sector: A closer look at League Tables

Another major step into the study of European ECM is the analysis of who are the major players of this sector. To do so, it is important to take a closer look at the so-called "League Tables," which represent a list of all major investment banks, ranked by fees revenues or deal sizes. League Tables are usually produced once a year and they provide different rankings based on the business, namely, M&A, ECM, and DCM. The aim of such tables is to give a comprehensive overview of investment banks' overall performance, of which fees and number of deals are considered a valid proxy. Over the years, the importance of League Table has grown a lot, and nowadays they are the most used tool to evaluate the reputation and the prestige of different investment banks. For this reason, there is fierce competition between banks in order to assure a good positioning in the leagues.

A common trend that emerges clearly from the League Tables and their evolution over time is how European investment banks have been losing market share with respect to their US peers. **Figure 1.2** shows the average market share of European and US IBs for what concerns the IPOs of European firms. As anticipated in the previous paragraphs, there is a stark difference between US and European banks in this respect. US banks have indeed, throughout all the years, a market share that is around 4% higher than European banks. This finding is further reinforced also by **Table 1.1**, which shows the top 10 banks which have appeared at least once in the list of top 25 banks by ECM deals in Europe. Out of these, six are US banks and only four are European ones.

Figure 1.2 ECM: average market share of a US vs. European IB

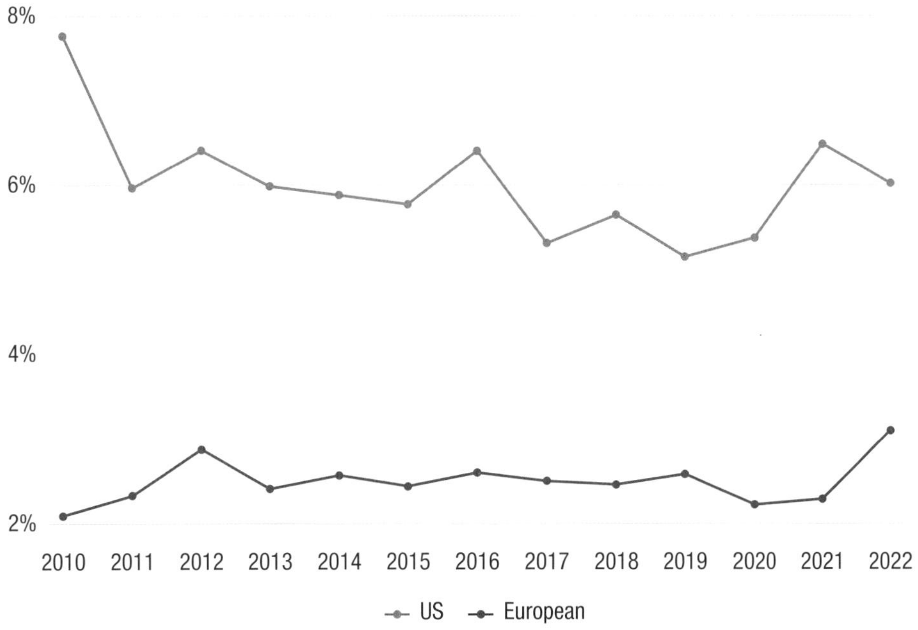

Source: author's elaboration of Refinitiv data.

What is however most striking is how the ranking is dominated by Bulge Bracket banks. This may however will be well explained by the size requirements of being the manager underwriter: The bigger you are, the easier it is for you to make a good deal happen for your client. And here European banks show that there is still some road ahead. In fact, so far a tendency for European banks to scale down their operations has been observed, in order to become smaller but keep positive profits. On the other hand, the strategy of US banks has been the opposite: They have grown in size, especially through capital increases, and this has enabled them to better position across all deal types and geographies, achieving higher fees. The losers of this shift were, inevitably, European banks: Over the last decade, the gap between European and US banks has always been very wide, as the graph shows. This is immediately clear also looking at the League Tables: Even if the top 10 banks by ECM deals, as shown in **Table 1.1**, are almost equally split between European banks and US banks, the latter systematically outrank EU

Table 1.1 Top 10 banks by ECM deals

Managing underwriters	Number of times in top 25	Country	Type
Citi	13	US	Bulge Bracket
Goldman Sachs & Co	13	US	Bulge Bracket
Barclays	13	Europe	Bulge Bracket
Deutsche Bank	13	Europe	Bulge Bracket
JP Morgan	13	US	Bulge Bracket
BofA Securities Inc	13	US	Bulge Bracket
Credit Suisse	13	Europe	Bulge Bracket
Morgan Stanley	13	US	Bulge Bracket
UBS	12	Europe	Bulge Bracket
Jefferies LLC	11	US	Boutique and Middle Market

Source: author's elaboration of Refinitiv data.

banks at the top. Since 2014, the first three positions of the League have been systematically occupied by American banks, and from 2019 onwards, the situation is even worse, as no European bank has been able to position itself also among the top five.

In light of this, the conclusion is that the largest and more remunerative deals in terms of fees are now a privilege that is reserved only to few US Bulge Bracket banks, leaving European banks to compete for smaller and less remunerative deals. This has resulted in an increased polarization of the ECM, where few US banks are able to secure a conspicuous part of the market share for themselves, at the expense of their subscaled Europeans peers.

1.1.2 DCM

DCM practice is related to the advisory and financial services that Investment Banks offer to clients to find the best way to raise debt capital in different situations. They are usually divided into two segments, namely, bonds and loans, which can be further subdivided into Investment Grade and High Yield depending on the credit quality. The issuance of Investment Grade bonds pertains to the DCM division of investment banks, while a niche segment, the Leveraged Finance division, is devoted to the advisory, underwriting and placement services of HY Instruments, mainly Leveraged Loans and High Yield Bonds.

Another distinction that is worth mentioning is the one between publicly traded bonds and private placements. In fact, more recently there has been a rapid expansion in the market for private placements of unrated bonds, especially by smaller issuers looking for financing alternatives after the credit crunch that followed the GFC. The main motivations for firms to tap private markets are a high level of confidentiality, flexibility, and simplicity, as there are few regulatory requirements to fulfil and no public rating is needed.

The subsection that follows will show and discuss the major trends of European DCM in terms of volume and deal numbers.

Trends shaping the European Debt Market

Starting the analysis of the DCMs, the first thing to be observed is that such markets present different patterns once bonds and loans are considered separately. Indeed, **Figures 1.3** and **1.4** differ a lot both in size and pattern. Bonds are characterized by a greater size in terms of both volumes – expressed in millions of euros – and number of deals. Indeed, whereas in all the years under analysis the number of bonds' deals is always greater than 4,000, in no year the number of loans' deals is greater than 2,500. However, what strikes the most is how bonds and loans differ in terms of pattern of deals.

Figure 1.3 Bonds: volumes (left-hand scale) vs. number of issues (right-hand scale)

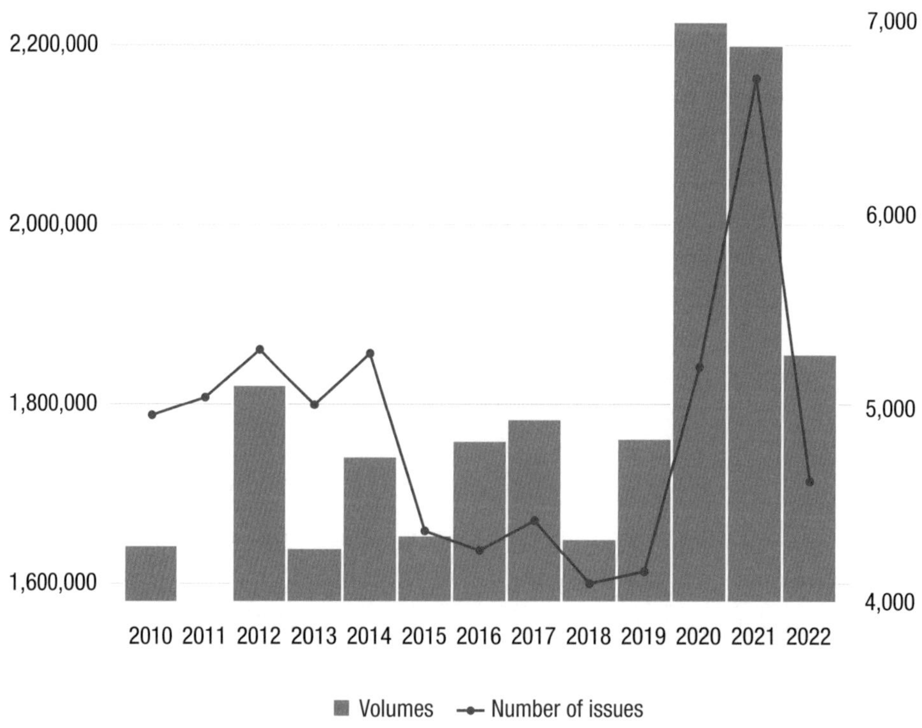

Source: author's elaboration of Refinitiv data.

Whereas **Figure 1.3** shows the bond deals skyrocketed in 2020 and 2021 because of the COVID-19 pandemic, **Figure 1.4** offers a different picture. Indeed, loans are consistently stable after 2013, both in terms of number of deals and volumes. The reason why this is interesting is related to a change in preferences of issuers in terms of the composition of their mix of debt instruments that has happened during the past two years. The reason why it is important is twofold. On one hand, the novelty of this variation represents a major change in the landscape of European DCM, and, for such a reason, it will be further analyzed later in this subsection. On the other hand, it points to the fact that firms have decided to issue a different set of instruments to meet new challenges, for instance, coping with

Figure 1.4 **Loans: volumes (left-hand scale) vs. number of issues (right-hand scale)**

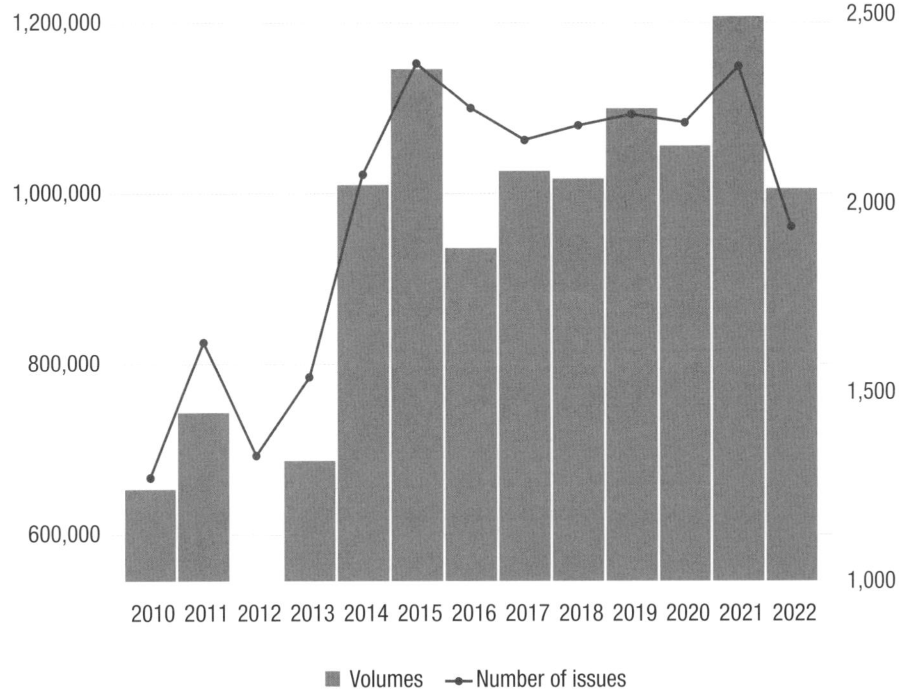

Source: author's elaboration of Refinitiv data.

the pandemic, rising inflation and costs, or following investors' preferences for ESG instruments.

Lastly, another major trend that arises from these figures is how 2022 registered a slowdown of deals. The reasons for that are multiple, in particular the impact of a stricter monetary policy and rising interest rates, which have increased the cost of debt financing for companies. Also, inflationary pressures made companies unwilling to issue new financial instruments, as the markets were shut down and they were not able to find favorable investing conditions.

Figure 1.3 shows that the bond market has been hit the most in 2022 as the change in both number and volumes is way higher than the respective changes for loans, as observed in **Figure 1.4**.

High Yield issues differ in their behaviors between bonds and loans, as shown by **Table 1.2**. Whereas the former have a somehow constant behavior, with High Yield bonds representing only a marginal share of

Table 1.2 Share of High Yield and Investment Grade issues

Year	Bonds		Loans	
	High Yield (%)	Investment Grade (%)	High Yield (%)	Investment Grade (%)
2010	2.8	97.2	17.5	82.5
2011	2.7	97.3	23.3	76.7
2012	3.3	96.7	25.3	74.7
2013	6.4	93.6	30.4	69.6
2014	6.0	94.0	35.4	64.6
2015	5.9	94.1	32.4	67.6
2016	5.7	94.3	30.4	69.6
2017	8.6	91.4	32.7	67.3
2018	7.3	92.7	27.5	72.5
2019	8.9	91.1	27.0	73.0
2020	6.7	93.3	24.7	75.3
2021	7.6	92.4	28.7	71.3
2022	4.7	95.3	22.1	77.9

Source: author's elaboration of Refinitiv data.

total issue, the latter have an inverted-U-like behavior over the years. It can indeed be noticed how they go over 30% of total issues between 2013 and 2016. Surprisingly, these values were not reached even after the COV-ID-19 pandemic. The situation in the High Yield space has been dramatic in 2022, when the level of new issues has dropped to unprecedented levels. Recently, very few leveraged loans were underwritten by investments banks and even fewer were priced in the market. This happened because banks were unable to sell the loans they had previously underwritten to investors and thus were forbidden by their internal Credit Committees to take on any additional deal as that would have meant additional capital requirements. A consequent phenomenon to be experienced also in the future is the rise of financing alternatives, such as private credit.

Before moving to the analysis of the rankings and the League Table, it is worth mentioning what is the target market for the bonds issued in Europe, meaning the geographic location where the security is offered. In general, a polarization of the market can be acknowledged, as deals targeting the Euro Area currently represent at least 10 times the number of deals targeting all European countries.

League Table Analysis and the role played by European banks

Moving away from an analysis of the structure of European DCM markets, another dimension that needs to be discussed is the size of the players. The average market share of the different banks involved either in loans or in bonds deals was considered, dividing them into US-based and European ones. **Figures 1.5** and **Figure 1.6** offer a comparison over time of the average market shares of US versus European banks and show an interesting behavior. When considering bond deals, a sizeable divergence is indeed present between the average market share of EU and US investment banks, with a gap that diverges continuously over time. A similar behavior is instead not present when considering loans deals. Apart from 2021, US and European banks have always had a similar average market share.

In these two figures, another fact can also be noticed, which is how the average market size for banks involved in loans deals is lower than

Figure 1.5 Bonds: average market share of a US or European IB

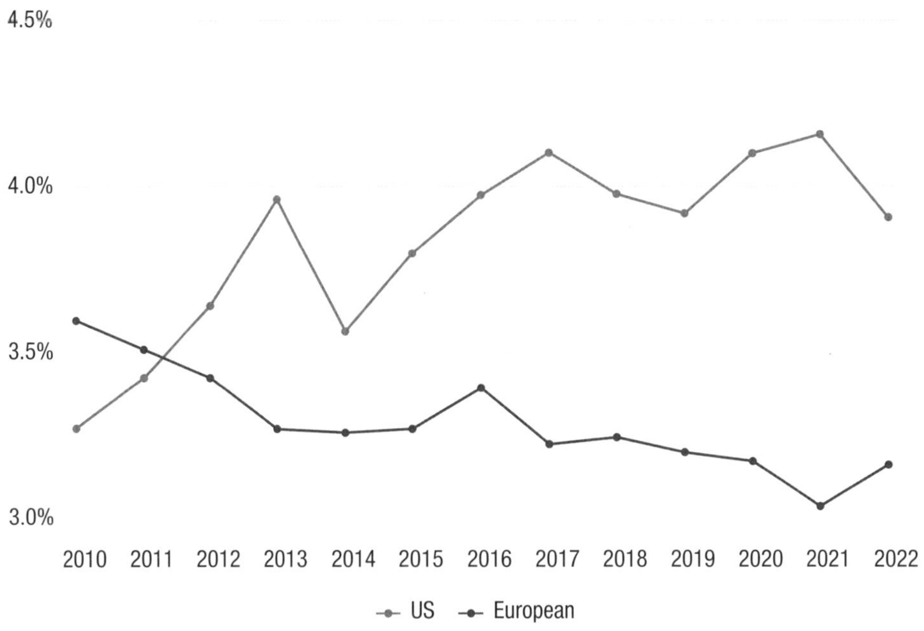

Source: author's elaboration of Refinitiv data.

that for bonds deals. Whereas the former is never below 3%, peaking also at levels around 4% when it is the case of US banks, the latter is always around 2%.

In **Tables 1.3** and **1.4**, it can be observed how many times the following banks ranked among the top 25 managing underwriters separately for loans and bond deals. The picture they provide – at least for what concerns bonds – is partly at odds with what was shown by **Figure 1.5**. Indeed, whereas the latter shows that Europe-based investment banks have a consistently lower market share, they dominate the scene as to number of times they have been among the top 25 scorers. In both cases, for loans and bonds, European banks are by far more present, and Boutique and Middle Market European banks also have a large presence in this list. Bulge Bracket banks show a market share of around 70% of total bond

Figure 1.6 Loans: average market share of a US or European IB

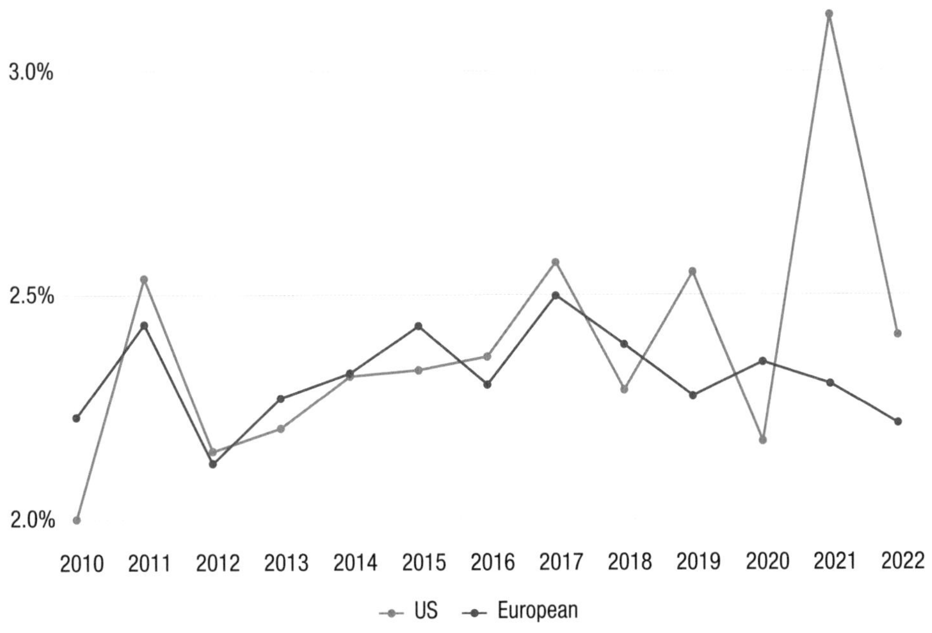

Source: author's elaboration of Refinitiv data.

issues, with the remaining left for Middle Market banks. A different pattern is seen for loans, where, in general, Bulge Brackets banks and Middle Market banks share on average 50% of the total volume. Middle Market banks are more active in the non-leveraged deals, while Bulge Brackets banks play the advisory role mostly in High Yield loans, mainly because, given their greater size, they can take on more risk.

The stable presence of Middle Market banks in the loan segment might well be explained by network and connection factors, especially with regard to small companies. In such category, moreover, there is a predominance of EU banks over US banks, which account for less than 10% of the total loan volume. However, as the size of the issuing company increases, the percentage of deals covered by US banks also does: For larger deals, they account for around 40%. For bonds, the picture is

Table 1.3 Top 10 banks for bond deals

Managing underwriters	Number of times in top 25	Country	Type
NatWest Markets	13	Europe	Boutique and Middle Market
Nomura	13	Others	Boutique and Middle Market
Deutsche Bank	13	Europe	Bulge Bracket
Société Generale	13	Europe	Boutique and Middle Market
Barclays	13	Europe	Bulge Bracket
HSBC Holdings PLC	13	Europe	Boutique and Middle Market
UBS	13	Europe	Bulge Bracket
BNP Paribas SA	13	Europe	Boutique and Middle Market
Goldman Sachs & Co	13	US	Bulge Bracket
Santander Corp & Invest Banking	13	Europe	Boutique and Middle Market

Source: author's elaboration of Refinitiv data.

Table 1.4 Top 10 banks for loan deals

Managing underwriters	Number of times in top 25	Country	Type
Citi	13	US	Bulge Bracket
Barclays	13	Europe	Bulge Bracket
Santander Corp & Invest Banking	13	Europe	Boutique and Middle Market
Mitsubishi UFJ Financial Group	13	Others	Boutique and Middle Market
Deutsche Bank	13	Europe	Bulge Bracket
Société Generale	13	Europe	Boutique and Middle Market
Commerzbank AG	13	Europe	Boutique and Middle Market
BofA Securities Inc	13	US	Bulge Bracket
UniCredit	13	Europe	Boutique and Middle Market
JP Morgan	13	US	Bulge Bracket

Source: author's elaboration of Refinitiv data.

slightly different: For small issuers, the market seems to be equally split between Bulge Brackets and Middle Market banks, while for larger deals, the predominance of Bulge Bracket banks is evident. In this respect, the size of the bond deal, which is typically greater than loans, plays a key role in explaining the divergences between these financing instruments.

However, the change in names between these two figures is per se an interesting fact that hints at national preferences over bonds and loans. It is indeed noticeable how French banks are more present among the top bond issuers, whereas German ones among the top loans' issuers. As mentioned earlier, this peculiarity of European DCM will be further analyzed in this subsection.

Bond versus Loans: What has changed over the years

As hinted at before, a peculiar aspect of European DCM that should be pointed out are the preferences over the mix of bonds and loans that are issued in some countries. May it be for causes related to the 2013 sovereign debt crisis or for measures enacted to cope with the pandemic, a quite different landscape is observed in **Figure 1.7**. In this map, the amount of deals, both loans and bonds, are compared between 2010 and 2021. Countries depicted in orange are the ones with a predominance of loans, while countries in blue show a preference for bond instruments. The more orange the country, the higher the mean amount of loans; the bluer the country, the higher the mean amount of bonds; the browner the country, the higher the mean amount of both, with all the various shades in between.

Two interesting phenomena can be noticed from this map. On the one hand, France, Italy, and Spain seem to have changed their preferences towards more bonds than loans. On the other hand, northern countries seem to always prefer loans over bonds. Along with the previous graphs, this points to some interesting and novel evidence on DCMs in Europe. Borrowers have changed their preferences in some countries, demanding more bonds over loans. If this piece of evidence is combined with **Figures 1.3** and **1.4** on the yearly volumes of DCM deals, it might be inferred that the COVID-19 pandemic period was associated with a greater need of

Figure 1.7 Change in the mix of loans and bonds over the years

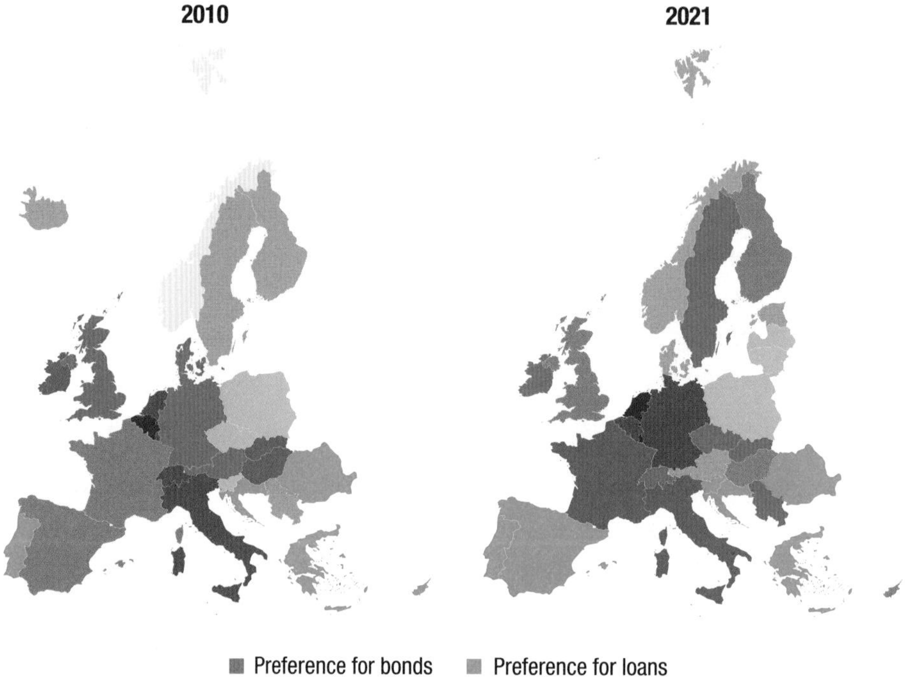

Source: author's elaboration of Refinitiv data.

bonds in some countries, possibly to better cope with its adverse effects. However, we cannot talk of any causal relationship here as there might have been some pre-trends that actually caused it or some hidden and contemporaneous shocks, such as a surge in green bonds issuing, that were at the core of this phenomenon. As will be highlighted further on in Section 4 of Chapter 4, in fact, COVID-19 has accelerated the focus on sustainability in response both to the effects of climate change and the need for a more inclusive society.

As another possible channel through which the surge in bonds can be explained, it ought to be discussed the increasing importance of sustainable finance. Whether it is ESG investing or other provision, it has been on the rise for the past few years, as summarized in the Climate Bonds

Initiative's 2021 report (Harrison et al., 2022). As per the report, Europe has played a key role in achieving such numbers and a vast majority of the most prominent players – particularly in terms of issues – of green bonds are represented by European institutions and firms. To this extent, the role of development banks and sovereign institutions has been of paramount importance in making this shift towards this type of instrument. It could also be argued that the shifts in the bonds–loans mix of **Figure 1.7** could in part be explained by this change in preferences, as most of the green debt instruments are only marginally constituted by loans, whereas bonds represent the vast majority.

As a further note, another major development in this respect is due to the change in investment mix of many funds and institutional investors which have pledged to become carbon neutral in the near future.[5] Although the outcome of these decisions has not happened yet in most of the cases – as it is a slow process that might require some years – it is worth underlying that DCMs will see a shift in the composition of the mix of issuer as bond-holder institutions have changed (and will change) their preferences, demanding an always growing number of sustainable finance options. To highlight some notable cases in which this has already happened, the European Investment Bank – one of the largest bond-issuers and financing institution in Europe – has ceased to finance projects that involve fossil fuel.[6]

Table 1.5 shows how this shift has already occurred between 2010 and 2022 once financial sector firms are excluded.

To sum up and conclude on this section, DCMs have changed twice over the timespan of this analysis. The first is after 2013 and the second is in the aftermath of the COVID-19 pandemic. This has undoubtedly caused a necessary adaptation from banks which have found themselves in the need to innovate and keep up with their markets and clients. What has however been the most disruptive change is for sure the rise in interest rates and inflation that has occurred over 2022. Its effect on the

---

[5] As an example, please refer to the Glasgow Financial Alliance for Net Zero (GFANZ): gfanzero.com.

[6] See the European Investment Bank website: eib.org.

Table 1.5 Economic sectors of bond issuers

Sector	2010		2022	
	Number of deals	Share (%)	Number of deals	Share (%)
Academic and educational services	–	–	3	0.05
Basic materials	62	1.12	49	0.82
Consumer cyclicals	71	1.28	63	1.05
Consumer non-cyclicals	68	1.22	51	0.85
Energy	28	0.50	25	0.42
Government activity	710	12.78	610	10.16
Healthcare	22	0.40	35	0.58
Industrials	172	3.10	209	3.48
Institutions	60	1.08	76	1.27
Real estate	29	0.52	198	3.30
Technology	61	1.10	50	0.83
Utilities	77	1.39	121	2.01

Source: author's elaboration of Refinitiv data.

number of deals was already discussed in these paragraphs; what will be also greatly affected are banks earnings and balance sheets, as bad loans might have a harsh comeback into Europe (and Italy in particular).

1.1.3 M&A

M&A is where investment banks offer financial and advisory services dedicated to supporting firms on strategic issues, corporate governance, or optimization of the financial structure. In general, M&A activity is a cyclical business, strongly influenced by the competitive dynamics of the single sectors and by the macroeconomic trends of the market; moreover, it is defined by the type of operations, inter alia: mergers, acquisitions, carve-outs, joint ventures, break-ups, and spin-offs.

Before turning into the analysis of the recent market trends, it is worth mentioning the peculiarities of the M&A operations, which gather under their umbrella a vast number of peculiar transactions. First, investment banks involved in an M&A transaction are usually split between sell-side advisors, who advise the target, and buy-side advisors, which offer their brokerage services to potential buyers. In terms of process, an M&A deal can be pursued through a public auction, a targeted sale, or a private negotiation, with the latter having increased levels of confidentiality, flexibility, and a greater length of the operation. In terms of consideration paid, a distinction can be made between share deals, cash offers, or mixed offers, depending on how the buyer decides to structure the acquisition.

Investment banks are deeply involved both in the origination phase and in the execution one. Their main tasks consist in managing the negotiation between the two parties, conducting the proper financial due diligence, and coming up with a fair valuation for the merged entity. Finally, an often neglected but very crucial job is played by both sell-side and buy-side investment banks once the deal has been closed, when they have to coordinate the post-merger integration. From this brief introduction, it should now be clear how fundamental is the role of these intermediaries in order to guarantee the success of the M&A transaction. Now, let's turn to the analysis of the deal volumes.

M&A trends and volumes: A European outlook

Earlier in the chapter, it was mentioned that M&A is a cyclical activity, meaning that it follows, in its trends, the business cycle. **Figure 1.8** shows that this is indeed the case in Europe, at least for what concerns the number of deals. Their number (the line in the figure) has been consistently increasing after 2013, and their volumes have shown a roughly similar behavior. A peak is observed in 2016 with respect to the number of deals, while for volumes 2018 represented a record level after two years of apparent slowdown. In general, the number of M&A deals has shown some stability over the period, reflecting the intense reorganization activity that has characterized European companies, especially the smaller ones.

Figure 1.8 M&A: volumes (left-hand scale) vs. number of deals (right-hand scale)

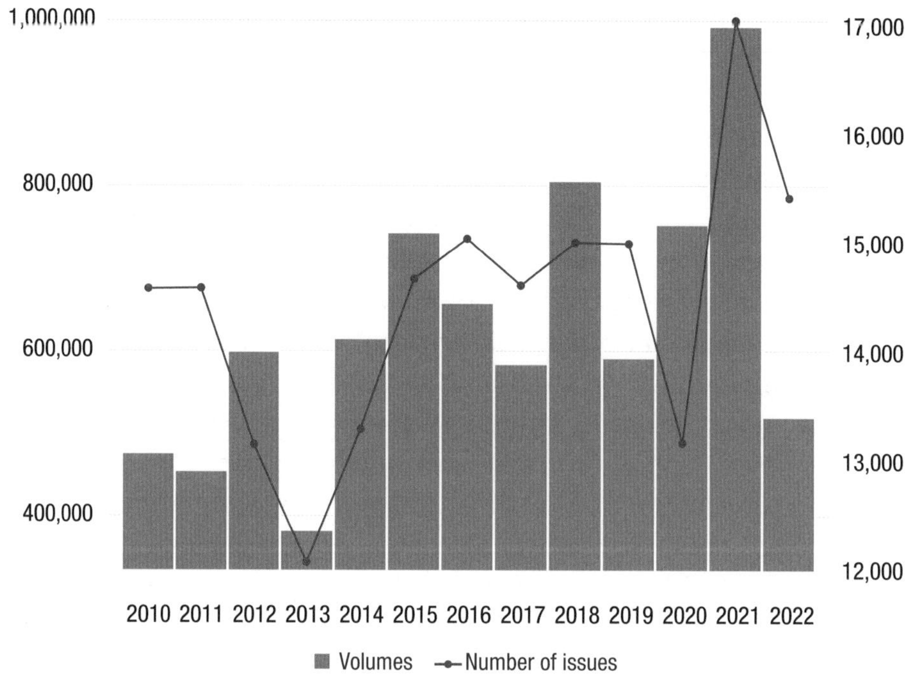

Source: author's elaboration of Refinitiv data.

However, there is a major outlier that needs to be explained. 2020 was a particular year from this graph as it had similar volumes to 2021, despite having a lower number of deals. This might well be explained by firms deciding to embark on a deal or to wait for the situation to become better: In such a case, only those deals that were deemed to be good enough were executed in 2020, whereas all the others were postponed. In fact, there was a significant increase in the M&A activity in Europe already in the second half of 2020, which, according to Dealogic, registered the second highest level over the past decade. A possible explanation for this surge is the strong recovery in strategic M&A dialogue, that was put on hold when COVID started, as strategic buyers were willing again to reposition their portfolio. In addition to that, activity from financial sponsors registered a significant uptick in volumes and deal sizes towards the end of 2020.

Being cyclical has its drawbacks and 2022 is emblematic in this. Lower liquidity due to a stricter monetary policy, international tensions, and inflation are only some of the causes of this slowdown. In addition to that, the increased volatility in the market not only has negatively impacted the number of new equity issues, as seen before, but also the number of M&A transactions that were closed in 2022 (especially also considering cross-border deals with the United States).

In order to better understand M&A trends in Europe, it is necessary to discover which countries rank first in terms of overall size of the markets and, most importantly, where these flows of money go. **Figure 1.9** shows the flows of M&A transactions across countries in terms of rank value. On the right, there is the Acquiror company's nation, whereas on the left, there is the Target company's nation. The thicker the line between a pair of countries, the greater the total rank value of M&A transactions that has flowed from one to the other.

Unsurprisingly, UK, France, and Germany dominate the scene as greatest nations of origin of the acquiring companies involved in the deals. On top of this, domestic transactions generate the greatest share of investments, as the figure shows. What strikes the most is represented by the direction of some flows that are in the chart. On the one hand, the influx from France to Italy points towards a close relationship between Italian and French firms, at least from the ownership side, as it has come to the news with some notable deals over the past few years, such as EssilorLuxottica or Stellantis. On the other hand, it is interesting to see how some small countries such as Belgium or the Netherlands can originate such noticeable flows, either as influxes or effluxes. Clearly, the reason behind some of these anomalies might well be due to the fact that some countries have business environments – including more lenient taxation and better regulation and incentives scheme – that enhance the presence of financial firms. In this respect, it will be interesting to see in the next years how the situation related to the UK will evolve, so as to better grasp the overall effect of Brexit on financial markets and investment banking in Europe.

Figure 1.9 Flows M&A transactions from Acquiror (left) to Target (right) countries

Source: author's elaboration of Refinitiv data.

The polarization of the intermediation services

After having analyzed the M&A segment in terms of size and number of deals, it is important to focus on the banks which play a major role in this market. US banks have a consistently higher market share vis-à-vis European banks, as shown in **Figure 1.10**. This pattern is clearly evident throughout the years and the behavior of the two trends has clearly diverged in two years, namely, in 2015 and in 2022. In this segment of IB activity, the size and ability to manage complex operations are at the core of most of the deals. And this is well remarked by **Table 1.6** that shows the top 10 banks by the time they have appeared in the list of top 25 deal makers. The predominance of US banks is especially marked for cross-border deals, both within and outside the EU. It seems as if the presence of an overseas bank was a requisite for a company wishing to undertake an internationalization strategy, even when neither the target nor the acquirer has US nationality.

Additionally, the M&A market appears, like the ECM, dominated by Bulge Bracket banks which are able to secure the largest and most highly remunerated deals. 2021, although being characterized by a record number of deals, is followed by a decrease in the average market share of IBs. This informs us of two distinct behaviors of the market. The first is competition among banks and financial advisors, which drives down the average market share. The second, instead, points out how in 2020 only a few big deals were executed, thus confirming previous results (**Figure 1.10**).

Table 1.6 provides another useful piece of information, which is the presence of some banks that are not classified as Bulge Bracket. This fact represents an interesting phenomenon and peculiarity of this market, which is the presence of highly specialized players that can achieve important goals within the industry and directly compete with other major global players. In general, over the years, the market share of specialists, mainly M&A boutiques, has increased, especially for small domestic deals. In fact, when looking only at domestic transactions, the role of Bulge Bracket banks is far less dominant, with a share of around 25% registered in the last three years.

Figure 1.10 M&A: average market share of a US or European IB

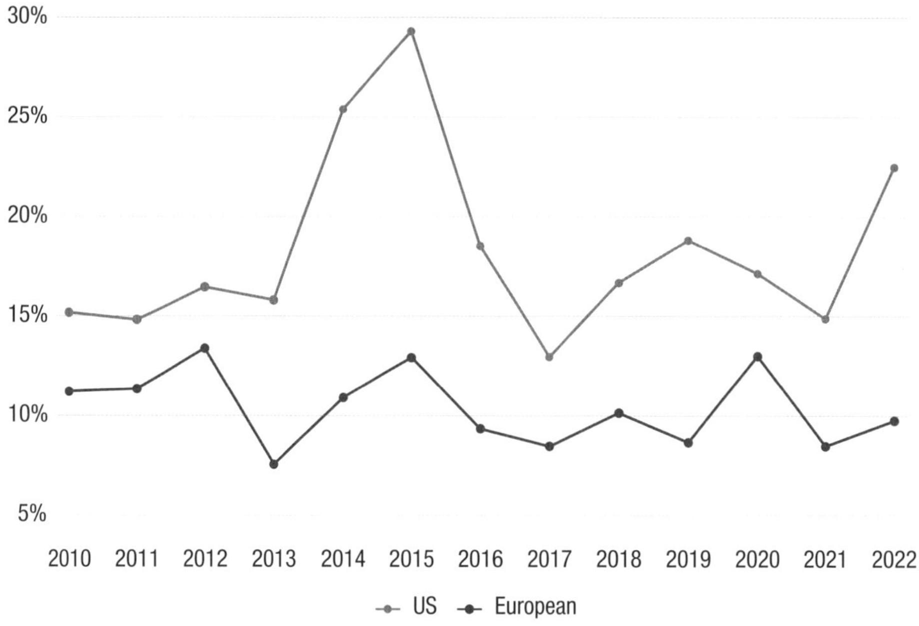

Source: author's elaboration of Refinitiv data.

Table 1.6 Top 10 banks by M&A activity

Name	Number of times in top 25	Country	Type
BofA Securities	13	US	Bulge Bracket
Lazard	13	US	Boutique and Middle Market
Citi	13	US	Bulge Bracket
BNP Paribas SA	13	Europe	Boutique and Middle Market
Morgan Stanley	13	US	Bulge Bracket
JP Morgan	13	US	Bulge Bracket
Goldman Sachs	13	US	Bulge Bracket
Soc. Generale	13	Europe	Boutique and Middle Market
Deutsche Bank	13	Europe	Bulge Bracket
Credit Suisse	13	Europe	Bulge Bracket

Source: author's elaboration of Refinitiv data.

The predominance of US banks in the European investment banking system

To conclude this section about investment banking in Europe, a key take-away of the analysis of the market is that the bigger the size, the higher is the tendency for a firm to look for a US bank as its advisor. This trend, which is especially marked in the ECM and the M&A markets, seems to be on the rise overall.

A consequence of that is the wide gap in the fees obtained by US banks compared to their European counterparties. As **Figure 1.11** shows, excluding 2020, which has been an exception for European banks due to the COVID-19 pandemic, the amount of fees received on average by US banks is almost double the value of the fees received by European banks. This result comes to no surprise considering that US banks covered the mandates for the largest transactions, as they are appointed Global

Figure 1.11 Average amount of fees of US and European IBs (€ million)

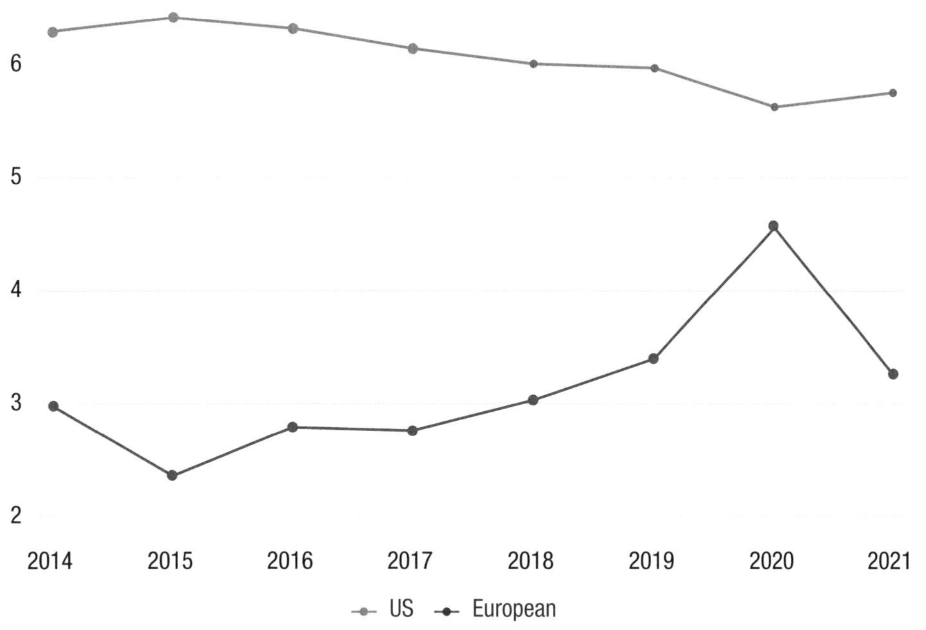

Source: author's elaboration of Refinitiv data.

Coordinators of major IPOs and they took part in the biggest cross-border deals, and the amount of fees paid by corporate clients is usually computed as a percentage of the overall deal value. For the sake of clarity, the overall transaction fees which compose the remuneration of investment banks are a comprehensive package that include different types of fees, such as retainer fees, success fees, drop-dead fees, and fairness opinion fees. The first two are the most common: Retainer fees are automatically given to the bank when it gets the mandate, while the success fees depend on the final outcome of the transaction.

The differences that have been observed point to US IBs having competitive advantages compared with their European peers. Among these factors, the diversity of their domestic markets, dissimilar macroeconomic conditions, and different regulatory requirements are only some of the reasons that are the core of these trends.

First, US banks are characterized by a higher level of concentration, and they can leverage on a larger domestic market compared to Europe. Just as an example, the largest market in the Old Continent, that is the UK market, is almost half as deep as the US capital market. The situation is even worse in continental Europe, where the depth is, on average, one-third of that of the US market. The main reason for that is the lack of harmonization between European regulations, that hammer the circulation of capital, the extension of credit, and new investments in general.

What needs to be considered, in addition, is the different regulatory environment faced by banks in the United States and in Europe. Indeed, whereas all the financial institutions need to comply with European regulations in Europe, US banks can have a better time in their home country. As an example, MiFID II's more disruptive impact is on secondary markets, where it bans investment banks from bundling research with trade execution. This has driven a change in the industry, whereby the buy side started to prefer the cheapest trades with the best execution, often in block sizes. Consequently, sell-side revenues were affected, especially for smaller companies. As trading, research and investing in small-caps have become uneconomical, the market for research has started to concentrate and shrink. The headcount for equity research is down by 12% in the three years from 2018, according to a survey by research consultancy Substantive Research.[7]

Finally, a different macroeconomic outlook seems to characterize Europe and the United States: The latter has experienced, during the last ten years, a period of sustained economic growth, fulfilled by rising short-term interest rates. This had the effect of boosting investment banks' revenues and size, at the expense of their European counterparties. In Europe, the zero-interest rates environment, coupled with the Euro Sovereign debt crisis in 2012, have put an increasing pressure on financial intermediaries, whose profitability has shrunk. In addition to that, the stringent capital requirements imposed by Basel guidelines have determined a slowdown in banks' new borrowings, with a negative impact on the growth of the overall ecosystem. The situation has started to recover after COVID, but the surge in inflation and the geopolitical tensions due to the Russian conflict have put the European banking system once again in a precarious position.

1.2 Investment Banking in Italy

This paragraph is devoted to the analysis of the investment banking environment in Italy, which represent a peculiar ecosystem characterized by the predominance of SMEs. Such companies have historically relied on bank loans as their major source of financing, with some implications that will be further expanded in the next section. A distinction between the segments of ECM, DCM, and M&A is conducted, similarly to what was done previously for the case of Europe.

Italy has been during renaissance the epitome of finance, with its financial companies being thought to be the creator of a (rather) modern system of banking. Yet, the situation has deteriorated over the years. May it be for a weaker industrial sector, Italian banks are now smaller among their international peers and often fail to be the innovator within the

---

[7] Source: Survey from Substantive Research, August 2022. Press release available at: substantiveresearch.com/press-archive/substantive-research-publishes-buy-side-reaction-to-sec-mifid-ii-no-action-letter-expiry/.

sector. On top of this, the presence of bad debt in their portfolio in the wake of the public debt crisis of the Eurozone has affected the sector in recent years by leaving it weaker and in need of a major change.

The presence of a resilient banking sector is of extreme importance especially in Italy, where the banking system plays a predominant role in financing businesses. If a closer look is taken at the financing structure of most Italian companies, in fact, we can recognize two patterns: First, the size of the average Italian firm is quite small, and they are often undercapitalized, and second, the main source of financing is represented by bank loans. This is in contrast to what happens in the rest of Europe, where capital markets seem to be more efficient and evolved. For instance, while bank loans account for around 60% of financial debt for Italian firms, in UK, this percentage is only 30%. Italian firms are reluctant to address the capital markets as source of funding mainly because of the underdevelopment of the Italian financial market and only few large players decide to issue their shares publicly. For instance, the market capitalization of Italian companies on Borsa Italiana is the lowest among all the major European Stock Exchanges and since the privatization of Borsa Italiana in 1998, the number of new listings has been the same of the delisting, thus hammering the growth potential of the market. In addition to that, most Italian companies are reluctant to access the market, they are risk-averse towards complex financial instruments, and they prefer to rely on safest options such as bank loans and credit lines.

Therefore, it comes to no surprise that those companies were most hit by the credit crunch that characterized the Eurozone in the aftermath of the 2012 Sovereign debt crisis. Many banks experienced a widespread deterioration of the creditworthiness of their customers, thus increasing the percentage of non-performing loans kept in their portfolios. In 2012, in fact, non-performing loans (NPLs) in Italy reached an unprecedented level, totaling almost 20% of overall bank loans volume. In addition to that, Quantitative Easing had a beneficial effect only for big loans, showing a narrowing gap between the cost of debt financing for smaller and bigger firms. Most banks, constrained by the severe capital requirements imposed by regulators, reduced the amount of credit devoted to SMEs, and many bank loans applications were rejected given they were deemed unprofitable or too risky.

In light of this situation, it clearly emerges the necessity to develop strong and efficient capital markets which will enable SMEs to diversify their funding sources and thus rebalance their capital structure. Some interventions have been made along the years by the Italian Government, first with the Decreto Sviluppo in 2012 (Decree for Development) and the project Destinazione Italia. In 2013, Borsa Italiana had also launched "ExtraMOT Pro," a new segment dedicated to debt instruments for SMEs, the so-called minibonds. Now, the total issuance volume of minibonds has reached a level well above €5 billion. Moreover, in 2017, a new type of financial instrument was introduced, the so-called PIRs (in Italian, "Piani Individuali di Risparmio"), which enabled retail investors to invest in SMEs through mutual funds, without paying a tax on capital gain. The list of concrete initiatives aiming to support the growth of capital markets in Italy is not exhaustive, still it remains necessary to simplify the regulatory frameworks in order to facilitate firms' access to the Italian capital market and make it more appealing to investors. In light of this, an important initiative led by the Italian Minister for Economy and Finance was the publication of the *MEF Green Book and the Proposal of the EU Listing Act*. As discussed in the introduction to this book, the European Union, and Italy in particular, have now understood how crucial it is for the relaunch of the Eurozone and for the growth of SMEs to have strong and competitive capital markets.

Finally, critical is the role played by intermediaries, as investment banks are the link between firms and investors and thus should be able to assist the former in obtaining the financial resources on capital markets. The problem is, however, that Italy experiences very few national players that operate in the sector. Another aspect worth mentioning is which clients are addressed by investment banks, that seem to concentrate mainly on big corporates, leaving small companies, the pillar of the Italian ecosystem, unserved. Looking at the demand side, also the number of foreign and institutional investors in the Italian market is quite small, as investors have been concerned about the unstable political context and the fragile public finances that characterize Italy. Despite this, bond issues by SMEs are an appetible asset class in terms of risk-return profile, and they offer a good alternative for investors willing to diversify their portfolios. However, the illiquidity of those instruments, together with their low unit volume, often make them less attractive both for investors and for companies themselves. In light of this, domestic investments banks, which have a deeper knowledge of the market and of the companies operating in it, can play a crucial role in helping to assess the financial profile of small businesses and guide investors towards the most attractive opportunities.

After this brief introduction on the overall investment banking sector in Italy, it is thus important to have a broad picture of its different segments to shed some light on the current situation of Italian banking and capital markets. This section thus tries to provide as much information as possible by conducting an analysis of the sector by dividing it into its three usual components: equity, debt, and M&A advisory. The focus will be on how big the synergies from being in the EU are and whether there is some evidence of Italy trying to gain a broader international stance over time. In doing this, it will also try to show what are the main trends of the industry in relation to their international counterparts.

1.2.1 ECM

This first subsection will analyze the trends that are shaping the Italian Stock Market and who are the main players operating in it. Milan Stock Exchange has come to the news over the last years mostly for some notable delisting that have occurred over 2022. However, the importance of the exchange needs to be analyzed with other measures as well so that it can be better put in comparison with other European exchanges. As it was outlined above, the Italian Stock Market is less developed if compared to the other European counterparties, mainly UK and France. In fact, according to Borsa Italiana (2022a), the market capitalization in the country represent today around 34% of Italian GDP, while in France, the percentage is around 150% and in UK even 170%. These numbers reflect a general market aversion to capital markets by Italian SMEs, which is due to several factors, mainly volatility of share prices and the reluctance to open the company's ownership to outside investors. Another penalizing aspect is the burden of compliance and regulatory requirements, which represent a huge fixed cost for listed firms. In this context, it is undoubtedly that companies prefer to remain unlisted: According to Borsa Italiana (2022b), in fact, in Italy there are currently over a thousand of non-listed firms that theoretically could go public, as they already fulfil all the requirements for public trading with regard to minimum capitalization and earnings.

Before delving into the analysis of numbers, a focus has to be made on the composition of the Italian Stock Market, which goes under the name of Milan Stock Exchange. In fact, the breakdown into its different segments enables a more careful analysis of the Italian ECMs. The Milan Stock Exchange is composed of the following three segments: Euronext Milan, Euronext STAR, and Euronext Growth (also called AIM Italia). The first comprises medium and big enterprises, while the latter is made out of promising SMEs listed on the Italian market. Finally, the STAR segment includes SMEs that adhere to stricter requirements: For instance, a minimum of €40 million of market capitalization is required, as well as the mandatory presence of an Independent Board of Director, an Internal Audit Committee, and a Remuneration Committee.

Different trends in the Italian Stock Exchange

The relevance and the importance of a stock exchange are directly related to its attractiveness in terms of new IPOs that are hosted by such exchange. **Table 1.7** lists for each year the number and the share of IPOs whose first stock exchange was either Milan or other European exchanges. The data do not show a consistent trend as the number of IPOs moves from peaks of 10% of overall IPOs in 2019, to much lower values right after, namely, less than 5% in 2020. 2021 was a record year in terms of IPOs, which doubled the level of 2019 showing a sign of recovery from the COVID-19 pandemic. These numbers were driven by the Euronext Growth segment, in which there were 38 IPOs, while the STAR segment continues its downward trend, confirmed by an increased number of delisting.

Table 1.7 **IPOs: numbers on Milan and other European exchanges**

	Others		Milan	
Year	Number of deals	Share (%)	Number of deals	Share (%)
2010	298	99.33	2	0.67
2011	208	98.58	3	1.42
2012	152	98.06	3	1.94
2013	194	97.49	5	2.51
2014	296	98.01	6	1.99
2015	263	94.27	16	5.73
2016	195	95.12	10	4.88
2017	264	92.96	20	7.04
2018	236	94.40	14	5.60
2019	144	90.00	16	10.00
2020	202	95.28	10	4.72
2021	646	94.44	38	5.56
2022	190	90.91	19	9.09

Source: author's elaboration of Refinitiv data.

However, when looking at the mean proceeds of each deal, as in **Figure 1.12**, it can be seen that Milan exchanges are in line with the European average. In general, there is a tendency of a reduction in the size of quotations, that went from €240 million in 2017 to just €38 million in 2021. Over the years, apart from the aftermath of the sovereign debt crisis, Milanese IPOs were similar to other European ones. The two lines do indeed follow a similar trend and, on top of this, their values remain rather stable over time. Interestingly, a little decrease can be seen in 2022.

By analyzing listed companies in both markets, there are two divergent trends: starting from 2018, due to a constant presence of the delisting phenomenon because of extraordinary transactions (M&A), bankruptcies, and privatizations, listed companies in the STAR market have decreased

Figure 1.12 **IPOs: mean proceeds (€ million) of deals in Milan vs. other primary stock exchanges**

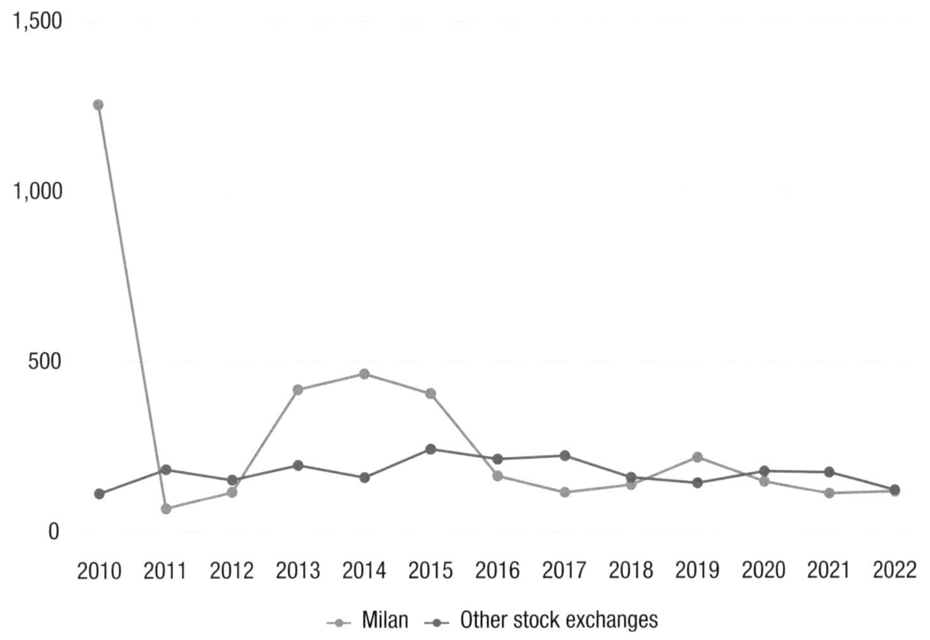

Source: author's elaboration of Refinitiv data.

from 339 to 317, while the Euronext Growth market has shown a growing trend from 113 to 175 listed companies.[8]

The picture that emerges from **Table 1.8** gives the complete picture of what just said, namely, that in recent years, mostly smaller firms are willing to go public. A pessimist would say that the business landscape in Italy has deteriorated to the point that there no more large companies that are willing to go public, although it would only be a partially complete picture. It is indeed necessary to put this table in comparison with two major facts. The first is that, as the table itself shows, many smaller firms

[8] An updated list of listed companies can be found on the website of the Italian Financial Markets Authority CONSOB. Available at: consob.it.

Table 1.8 Number of new IPOs by segment of Milan Stock Exchange

Year	Numbers in AIM	Numbers in Milan	Numbers in STAR
2010	–	2	–
2011	–	3	–
2012	–	3	–
2013	–	4	1
2014	–	6	–
2015	–	11	5
2016	2	8	–
2017	1	16	3
2018	1	12	1
2019	10	4	2
2020	8	2	V
2021	34	3	1
2022	16	3	V

Source: author's elaboration of Refinitiv data.

are willing to go public, meaning that the supply side is active. The other is that this has to be put in relationship with the overall capital markets landscape, in particular with M&A. Their increase has represented a major threat to IPOs, although it should be interpreted only as move towards other forms of financing and investments, rather as a complete immobility of the Italian business landscape.

However, the past year has been accompanied by some notable delistings, and the difference between the size of IPOs and delistings is notable (Dal Maso, 2022). According to prominent studies (You, 2008; You et al., 2012), there are two main determinants for companies to go private:

- ECMs inefficiencies: Periods of high volatility tend to decrease investor confidence and affect firms' equity trading volume and undervaluation.

- Legislation: The increasing importance and interdependence of capital markets have led to the introduction of stricter regulations and, consequently, higher costs.

The main factors that drive companies' decision to privatize (Geranio, 2004) are information disclosure requirements, ongoing costs due to the implementation of mandatory organizational structures, fees required by the Italian Stock Exchange itself, and above all, companies' exposure to negative economic cycles and market volatility. It is not uncommon to find healthy companies with excellent business results that see their share price fall due to turbulence within the market, the exposure to which is priced in by reducing the company's capitalization. In addition, a company's risk of remaining public might also be due to the possibility of a spillover of relevant corporate information that could reduce or eliminate any competitive advantages to competitors (Maksimovic & Pichler, 2001). As a last remark, it must be noted that some companies delisted because of their decision to change primary exchange to better meet their organizational structure.

To conclude this first part on ECM volumes, it is worth noting how the trends in 2023 might look different from 2022. The actual picture will depend on whether the actual situation will be evolving or not, but the market has already been rumoring about some possible IPOs that will make it possible to completely disrupt these trends.

The role of intermediation in the ECM world

The analysis of the Italian Equity Market has to be completed by looking at the structure of the IPO-related service offerings from financial intermediaries. These players can be split into basically three segments: foreign players, national champions, and other local banks and advisory boutiques. Taking a closer look at the League Tables in the last decade, Mediobanca, Banca IMI (Intesa Sanpaolo), and UniCredit were the only three Italian banks which were ranked in the top 10 for IPOs. Together with most well-known US banks, they tend to cover mostly big companies that go public, acting either as bookrunners or global coordinators. On the other hand, small deals are left for domestic intermediaries, even though they do not act, usually, as global coordinators in such operations.

A peculiar aspect of the Italian Equity market is the conspicuous presence of commercial banks, which usually act as bookrunners. This happens because such banks can leverage on a well-established relationship with their customers. In addition to that, local boutiques have started following deals of discrete size, for instance, Capitalia and Equita SIM. The reason they are preferred by Italian firms over national and international players is their deep knowledge about domestic institutional investors interested in buying into Italian equity.

In conclusion, the Italian market still remains fragmented in terms of players operating the market, and the decision whether to address a local intermediary or a well-established Bulge Bracket bank is mainly linked to the size of the firm wishing to go public. Now that the ECM has been analyzed in depth, it is time to turn the attention to the DCM world.

1.2.2 DCM

The focus of this section will be on the peculiarities of the Italian DCM, with a distinction based on the type of issue, loans, or bonds and the credit worthiness of the issuer, that is, Investment Grade or High Yield.

Italy's relationship with DCMs has always been a difficult one. Whereas banks have suffered (and are suffering) for the presence of NPLs among their portfolio, Italians firms have always been fascinated by these instruments. Thus, the trends of Italian DCMs might well be informative of the health status of Italian economy. In this study, only Italian issuers were considered, and deals from 2010 until today were analyzed.

The Italian debt mix

A major trend that was analyzed in previous sections of this chapter was the shift that occurred in Europe between the issuance of loans and bonds over the years. Italy is in line with the overall European trend, that is, a major growth in the number of issuers and the value of bond issues, both for public and private placements. In particular, a big jump in the level of bond issues has characterized the years immediately following the credit crunch, as Italian firms were struggling to find alternative sources of financing. **Table 1.9** provides evidence on this topic by comparing issues and overall proceeds by year of bonds and loans deals. Interestingly, what was observed before can be found in the overall proceeds of bonds deals that have experienced a peak in 2020. This is further evidence of the twofold reason why there has been such an increase, namely, shift in preferences (green bonds) and funding requirements during COVID. Unsurprisingly, in 2022, bonds have decreased to pre-2019 levels.

Eurobonds are indeed the most preferred instrument by Italian companies to access the market. In terms of deal size, Eurobonds are also the highest issue in terms of value, on average around €800 million, with more than 40% of issues worth over €1 billion. In terms of maturities,

Table 1.9 **Loans and bonds issues in Europe: proceeds and numbers**

	Loans		Bonds	
Year	Issues	Overall proceeds	Issues	Overall proceeds
2010	112	37,253.89	143	87,567.12
2011	84	21,481.24	146	82,871.64
2012	55	26,881.41	129	116,147.62
2013	95	36,674.82	157	134,954.94
2014	118	34,443.52	147	112,277.92
2015	168	68,183.60	109	84,916.34
2016	154	39,614.12	103	88,888.06
2017	166	65,550.01	140	103,022.08
2018	186	69,512.78	99	83,839.42
2019	174	40,801.01	146	115,135.02
2020	211	60,830.74	124	162,590.47
2021	180	66,047.42	130	138,985.10
2022	201	88,125.82	81	87,679.37

Source: author's elaboration of Refinitiv data.

most instruments range between 5 and 10 years, and an early redemption option is present only in a few cases.

The High Yield segment in Italy is not well established, mainly because of the more stringent regulatory requirements associated with such instruments, given they bear a higher risk. However, in recent years, more issuers have decided to tap the High Yield market, in part because some Investment Grade companies were downgraded by Rating Agencies after the crisis, in part due to the fiscal incentives put ahead by the Italian Government for non-listed firms. In fact, with the Decreto Sviluppo of 2012, all statutory limits which prevented non-listed firms from issuing notes in excess of twice their equity were eliminated. This resulted in an increase in the bond issues by all businesses, with the level that almost doubled compared to 2011, as more and more companies were taking advantage of this accommodative regulatory framework. Despite this, a closer look at the issuers reveals that they are still confined to medium to big enterprises. It is necessary to wait until 2013 to see more small businesses tapering the market, with the official debut of minibonds. As the name suggests, they are characterized by very small size and short maturity, thus representing a useful and flexible form of financing for most SMEs.

Who are the issuers

As a general pattern, the firms who access DCM are either listed or characterized by Investment Grade creditworthiness. For this reason, the categories of new issuers are usually restricted to big, large organizations. According to S&P Global Ratings (2021), just around 50 firms which are not part of the financial sector have a public rating, and the only way for an unrated company to tap the public market is to convince investors of its high profile and investment class, as well as having a consolidated reputation in the industry. As a first glimpse of the landscape of Italian issuers, **Figure 1.13** shows the progression of the number of deals by financial and non-financial firms between 2010 and 2022. The formers clearly dominate the Italian market as to this dimension. When looking more into the details of how each sector fares in these respects, the predominance of the financial sector is even more accentuated. **Table 1.10** shows indeed that

Figure 1.13 Number of bond deals by financial and non-financial issuers

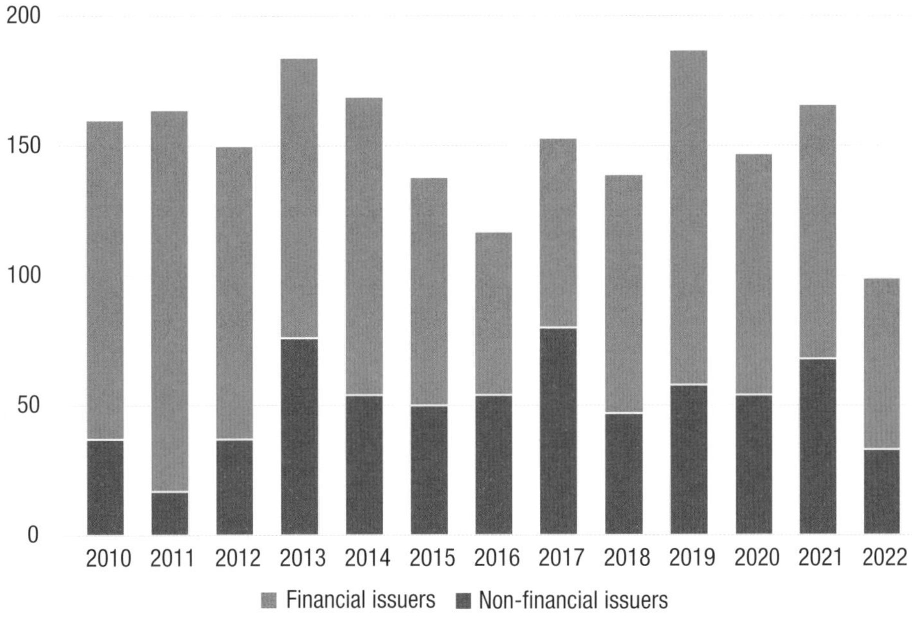

Source: author's elaboration of Refinitiv data.

both in 2010 and in 2022, the financial sector has been by far the greatest issuer of bonds in Italy.

The number of bond deals seems to have a counter cyclical behavior: It expands during recessions. Indeed, it can be seen how the share of bonds issued by financial firms peaked in 2011, to revert to lower levels in the following years, to then increase once again with the COVID-19 pandemic. This phenomenon is driven by other concurring factors as well, which are mostly related to sustainable finance.

Table 1.10 shows that among the sectors there is a massive decrease in the number of bonds issues by the financial sector between 2010 and 2022, while utilities and industrials have increased their issues.

Looking at volumes, the picture is rather different. Companies in the financial sector still represent, among the bond issuers, one of the groups that has the greatest share of new issues in terms of total proceeds.

Table 1.10 Number of bond deals by sector

Sector	2010 Number of deals	2010 Share (%)	2022 Number of deals	2022 Share (%)
Basic materials	2	1.25		
Consumer cyclicals	4	2.50	1	1.01
Energy	5	3.13	1	1.01
Financials	123	76.88	66	66.67
Government activity	11	6.88	9	9.09
Healthcare	3	1.88	1	1.01
Industrials	4	2.50	9	9.09
Technology	2	1.25	1	1.01
Utilities	6	3.75	11	11.11

Source: author's elaboration of Refinitiv data.

However, it must be acknowledged that other sectors do play a major role in the bonds market. In the wake of COVID-19 pandemic, the public sector is not a lightweight issuer, as **Table 1.11** shows. On top of this, an overall change in the sectors that issue bonds can be noticed. In particular, financial companies had a sharp and sizeable decline in the overall volumes of bonds issues, as it is also depicted in **Figure 1.14**. In particular, this shows how exceptional 2011 is in terms of the share of volumes by the financial sector.

Who are the major intermediaries in the Debt Capital Market

To conclude the analysis of the DCM in Italy, attention should be devoted on the main players operating in this segment and the service offerings they proposed. As done for ECM, it is useful to split such intermediaries into three categories: foreign banks, national champions, and other Italian banks, SIMs, and advisory boutiques. A first point to highlight is that the Italian bond market pertains almost exclusively to foreign US banks and national champions like Mediobanca, UniCredit, and Banca IMI, which

Table 1.11 Volumes by sector

Sector	2010 Total proceeds (€ million)	2010 Share (%)	2022 Total proceeds (€ million)	2022 Share (%)
Basic materials	294.53	0.27	–	–
Consumer cyclicals	1,512.35	1.39	350.00	0.32
Energy	3,441.29	3.16	100.00	0.09
Financials	67,852.21	62.40	42,102.33	39.04
Government activity	21,920.17	20.16	49,929.92	46.30
Healthcare	735.79	0.68	350.00	0.32
Industrials	3,877.18	3.57	7,951.48	7.37
Technology	1,348.90	1.24	63.00	0.06
Utilities	7,751.37	7.13	6,988.54	6.48

Source: author's elaboration of Refinitiv data.

Figure 1.14 Volume of deals by financial and non-financial institutions

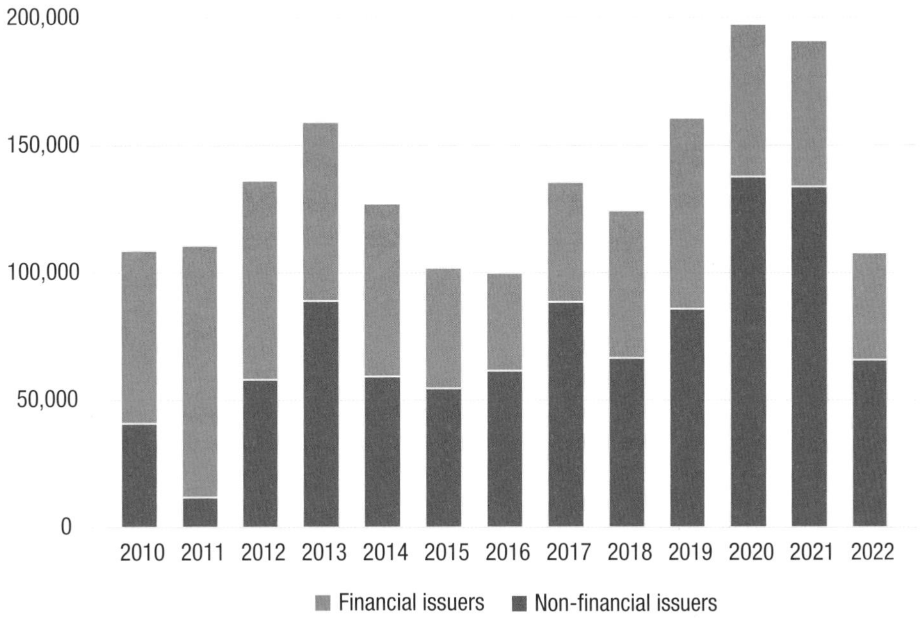

Source: author's elaboration of Refinitiv data.

were the only three banks that appeared in the League Table rankings for bond Issues in the last decade. This result is due to the fact that other national and local players have a limited space in such an environment, where the size of the deal is often very large. In addition to that, US banks have privileged access to international investors, and this aspect often plays a key role in the decisions of companies to address a Bulge Bracket bank specifically.

In conclusion, as outlined also in the introduction to this section on investment banking in Italy, the Italian DCM is still underdeveloped, and most SMEs continue to rely too much on bank capital as their main source of financing. However, as the market grows in size and competitiveness and a more attractive framework is established by regulators, there are more opportunities arising for Italian businesses to address the DCM.

The following section is devoted to the analysis of the M&A activity in Italy: whereas the DCM seems to be – at least partly – following dynamics that are common to other European markets as well, the M&A market is way more national, as will be described in the following subsection.

1.2.3 M&A

In this section, we focus on the main dynamics characterizing the Italian M&A market. Although M&A activity in Italy seems to have followed similar trends of European markets, the surge observed in 2021 in the latter has not happened with the same magnitude in Italy. This is probably due to the peculiarities characterizing the Italian market, mainly the presence of a small number of big national players, the prevalence of foreign banks covering largest cross-border deals, and the remaining local intermediaries serving the bulk of small companies that populate the Italian economic system.

Given the relatively small size of Italian companies, M&A play a pivotal role in helping those businesses to grow and reach the necessary size requirements that will enable them to access capital markets. For the purpose of this analysis, all M&A deals involving European targets and acquirers that occur in Italy between 2010 and 2022 were studied. In general, the Italian M&A market can be described as highly concentrated, with the top 10 deals that, on average, represent more than 60% of the overall deal value. The predominance of large deals is also a consequence of the adoption of the NRRP by the Italian government, which has led to an increase of large transactions in the transportation, energy, and telecommunication sector, often backed by Private Equity sponsors, as was highlighted in the Introduction to the book.

Domestic vs. foreign deals

Italian dealmaking is mostly a national phenomenon, as shown by **Figure 1.15** and by the last column of **Table 1.12**. It can indeed be observed that the vast majority of deals are represented by domestic acquisitions and mergers. Moreover, such share of deals is rather constant over the years, as shown by **Figure 1.15**.

Figure 1.15 Number of cross-border and domestic deals

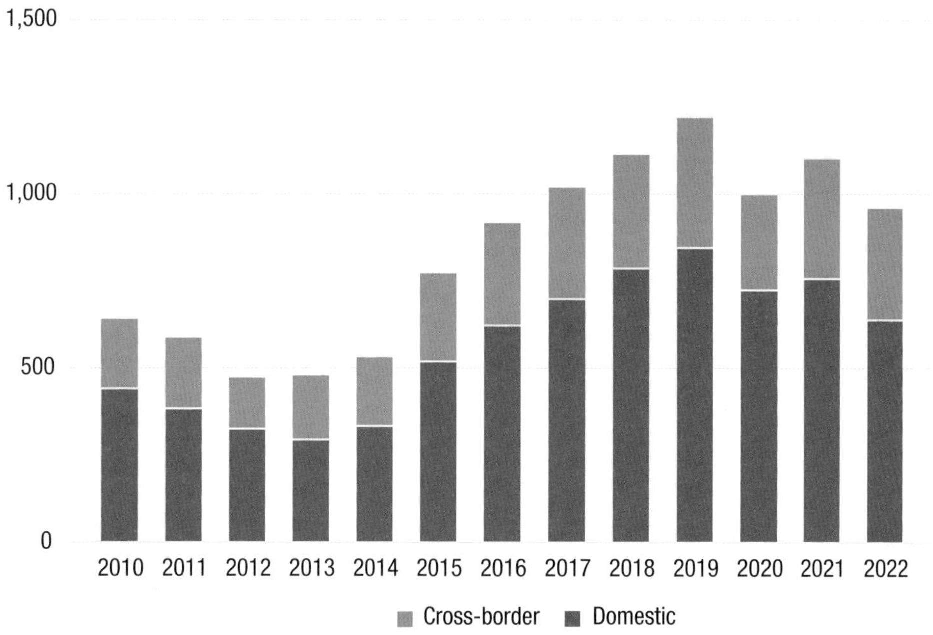

Source: author's elaboration of Refinitiv data.

Table 1.12 M&A: how international the market in Italy is

Year	Italy on foreign (%)	Foreign on Italy (%)	Domestic (%)
2010	35	65	68
2011	33	67	65
2012	38	62	69
2013	33	67	61
2014	32	68	63
2015	28	72	67
2016	33	67	68
2017	22	78	68
2018	35	65	71
2019	35	65	69
2020	32	68	73
2021	34	66	69
2022	32	68	66

Source: author's elaboration of Refinitiv data.

When looking at the internationalization of Italian deals, it is important to look at three different measures. The first is the share of deals that are domestic, reported in the last column of **Table 1.12**. The other two measures are the share – among all the deals that, in spite of not being domestic, involve Italian firms – of Italian targets and of Italian acquirors, respectively, in the first and second columns of **Table 1.12**. In all the cases, a stagnating internationalization of deals is seen: The share of domestic deals does increase over the years, from a low of 61% in 2013 to a high of 73% in 2020. A decline in cross-border deals was experienced in 2012, due to several factors among which the most relevant one was the Italian political instability in that moment, that made foreign investors less willing to enter the market.

Although the very last years are not emblematic of the actual situation, as they were biased by the pandemic, it is still interesting to notice how Italian firms have difficulties in "shopping abroad." The first column of the table is crystal clear in this respect, as it shows unequivocally that vis-à-vis foreign acquisitions, Italian acquisitions abroad represent a rarer phenomenon. This is probably due to the relatively small size of Italian firms, which makes them less inclined towards large-scale deals, preferring instead medium sized deals that are more aligned with the entrepreneurial spirit characterizing the Italian country.

Who are the buyers and the targets

M&A is a two-sided market as it consists, for each deal, of a target and of an acquirer. It is thus important to distinguish what are the trends that characterize the former and the latter, as each group might be having a different behavior due to a multiplicity of factors. Among these factors, differential trends within-sector innovation are for sure a major driver of this, although it should not be neglected that the attractiveness of some particular sectors of the Italian business landscape is another major force at the basis of M&A trends.

An evolution has occurred in the sectoral composition of the targets, although **Figure 1.16** shows that the relative share of deals in related and non-related sectors has remained roughly stable over the years. Indeed, in spite of this rather constant behavior, when looking in the detail at the target's sector the situation is completely different. **Table 1.13** shows how the situation has changed over the years by comparing together 2010 and 2022 sectoral compositions of all the deals in which an Italian target was involved, both in cross-border and in domestic deals. What comes to sight is the rise in deals involving Technology or Consumer Products companies, with a fall in the deals related to Energy. Financials have experienced a decline while Healthcare has risen, mostly due to a greater attention towards this sector after the pandemic.

Moving now to the other side of the market, a distinction must be done between Italian and foreign acquirers to better understand what the key trends of this industry are. But before going into this sectoral analysis, **Table 1.14** shows which are the most important buyers of Italian firms in terms of overall number of deals done over the years under analysis, excluding financial sector targets and considering only deals greater than

Figure 1.16 Number of related and unrelated deals

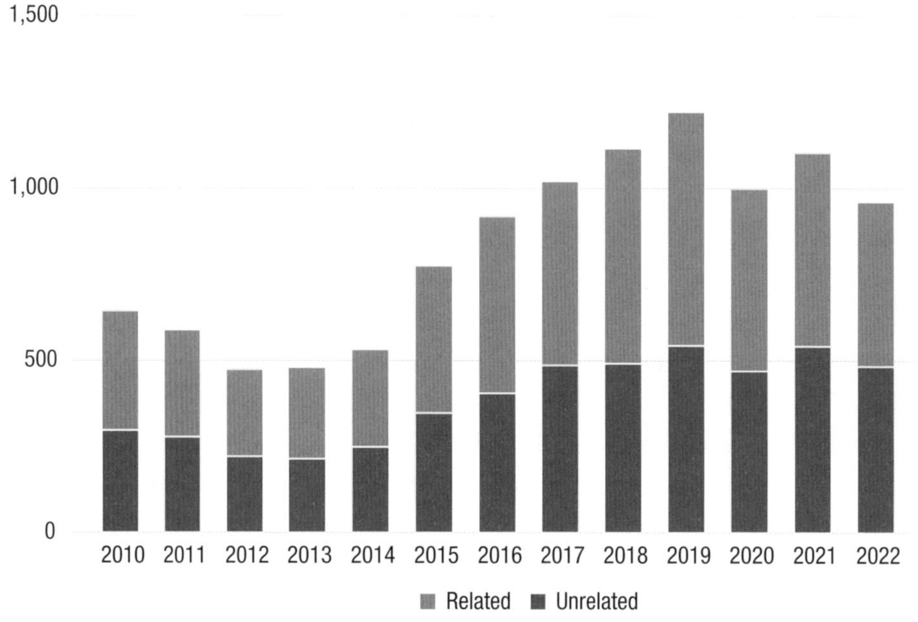

Source: author's elaboration of Refinitiv data.

€10 million. Some notable names appear in this list due to their extensive PE activity. However, when looking at the mean rank value, the situation is different.

The picture in terms of mean value is given by **Table 1.15**. Here, the list puts in evidence different companies. It is important to realize that the deal-making dimension is related also to the purpose of the deal itself and this ranking is a more accurate depiction of this. Should companies focus more on fewer, yet better, and bigger deals?

For what concerns the sectors of the acquirers, **Table 1.16** provides some figures on the sectoral composition of acquirers while comparing Italian to foreign ones in 2010, whereas **Table 1.17** shows how it has changed in 2022. In 2010, financials dominated the scene both in terms of Italian and foreign acquirors with an overall share greater than a third of the total

Table 1.13 Economic sectors of Italian targets

	2010		2022	
Target sector	Number of deals	Share (%)	Number of deals	Share (%)
Consumer products and services	49	8.55	112	13.02
Consumer staples	34	5.93	98	11.40
Energy and power	81	14.14	67	7.79
Financials	68	11.87	66	7.67
Government and agencies	1	0.17	1	0.12
Healthcare	20	3.49	49	5.70
High technology	47	8.20	142	16.51
Industrials	110	19.20	156	18.14
Materials	52	9.08	37	4.30
Media and entertainment	46	8.03	62	7.21
Real estate	23	4.01	32	3.72
Retail	31	5.41	36	4.19
Telecommunications	11	1.92	2	0.23

Source: author's elaboration of Refinitiv data.

Table 1.14 Top 10 acquirors by number of deals, excluding financial targets

Acquiror	Number of deals
Fondo Italiano d'Investimento SGR SpA	14
Italmobiliare SpA	10
Italgas SpA	8
F2i Fondi Italiani per le Infrastrutture SGR SpA	7
BNP Paribas REIM SGR SpA	7
Ascopiave SpA	7
Immobiliare Grande Distribuzione SIIQ SpA	6
IMA Industria Macchine Automatiche SpA	6
Coima Res SpA SIIQ	5
Fondo Strategico Italiano SpA	5

Source: author's elaboration of Refinitiv data.

Table 1.15 Top 10 acquirors by mean rank value, excluding financial targets

Acquiror	Rank value (€ million)
Schemaquarantatre SpA	47,824.12
VimpelCom Ltd (NOW 3F8982)	15,452.74
Essilor International SA	11,871.15
Marco Polo Industrial Holding SpA	4,104.42
Wind Telecomunicazioni SpA	4,056.50
Amundi SA	35,45.00
Atlantia SpA	3,154.57
Sky Italian Holdings SpA	3,093.32
Cassa Depositi e Prestiti SpA	3,073.66
Rossini Investimenti SpA	3,050.00

Source: author's elaboration of Refinitiv data.

number of deals. Interestingly, industrial acquirors are relatively more common among Italians rather than among foreigners.

The situation is unsurprisingly different in 2022. **Table 1.17** does indeed show that the relative predominance of each sector has evolved in line with what is observed all over Europe. The share of financial acquirors has indeed decreased, leaving room for High Technology and, to a lower extent, Healthcare. Consumers products are on the rise as well, having doubled their share from 2010 to 2022. We can therefore see a thriving, although mostly national, M&A market in Italy. Behind this fact a series of factors related to the Italian business landscape itself have to be considered. Indeed, whereas some sectors are attractive – for instance, the luxury industry – many businesses fail to achieve a big enough international presence. Despite this, the so-called "Made in Italy" has experienced a continuous draw in the last decade, which has been signed by many cross-border deals involving foreign buyers and Italian targets. Famous well-known brands such as Valentino, Lamborghini, and Ferretti are examples of it.

Table 1.16 **Sectors of acquirors of Italian targets divided by origin in 2010**

	Foreign acquiror		Italian acquiror	
Sector	**Number of deals**	**Share (%)**	**Number of deals**	**Share (%)**
Consumer products	3	0.47	27	4.19
Consumer staples	3	0.47	16	2.48
Energy and power	11	1.71	44	6.83
Financials	52	8.07	172	26.71
Government and agencies	3	0.47	4	0.62
Healthcare	5	0.78	10	1.55
High technology	8	1.24	17	2.64
Industrials	17	2.64	53	8.23
Materials	17	2.64	26	4.04
Media and entertainment	3	0.47	27	4.19
Real estate	3	0.47	6	0.93
Retail	1	0.16	33	5.12
Telecommunications	6	0.93	6	0.93

Source: author's elaboration of Refinitiv data.

Table 1.17 **Sectors of acquirors of Italian targets divided by origin in 2022**

	Foreign acquiror		Italian acquiror	
Sector	**Number of deals**	**Share (%)**	**Number of deals**	**Share (%)**
Consumer products	18	1.87	82	8.52
Consumer staples	14	1.46	56	5.82
Energy and power	5	0.52	54	5.61
Financials	79	8.21	194	20.17
Government and agencies			2	0.21
Healthcare	7	0.73	21	2.18
High technology	23	2.39	92	9.56
Industrials	36	3.74	62	6.44
Materials	14	1.46	24	2.49
Media and entertainment	9	0.94	26	2.70
Real estate	9	0.94	13	1.35
Retail	5	0.52	11	1.14
Telecommunications	2	0.21	2	0.21

Source: author's elaboration of Refinitiv data.

The predominance of US banks in the Italian M&A market

Before concluding this section on M&A, it is of foremost importance to analyze in depth the composition of the advisory side, given their prominent role in guaranteeing the success of M&A operations. Looking at the Italian advisory market, it is interesting to notice that a small number of national players together with foreign US banks occupy a crucial position both in the buy-side and in the sell-side. In particular, almost two-thirds of the advisory mandates are obtained by top 10 advisors. A predominant role is played by US Bulge Bracket banks, especially for what concerns cross-border deals. In light of this, domestic banks and small advisory boutiques are only able to secure fewer mandates, usually involving small to medium companies. Most well-known Italian boutiques are Equita SIM, Tamburi Investment Partners, and Vitale e Associati. Another pattern commonly observed is the tendency for foreign buyers to rely on domestic advisors when approaching the Italian M&A market, and for Italian buyers to ask for the support of foreign US banks when trying to acquire a foreign target.

In conclusion to this section on M&A, the main takeaways are summarized here: First, the relatively small size of Italian domestic intermediaries leave Italian firms without efficient financing, hammering the possibility for them to pursue very large acquisitions. For this reason, there is a predominance of foreign buyers, attracted by the Made in Italy luxury, whereas the number of Italian acquirers targeting the foreign M&A market is still limited. An immediate consequence of that is also the polarization of the intermediation system, with US Bulge Bracket banks securing almost the totality of large deals.

1.3 Conclusions

As seen in multiple occasions in this first chapter, the role of investment banks is of paramount importance in the financial system, given their ability to efficiently allocate resources between subjects who are in surplus of capital, that is, investors and subjects who are in deficit of it, that are companies. Intermediaries were born in the past to facilitate firms' access to resources, as the latter are fundamental to fulfil companies' future business growth. However, the macroeconomic outlook inevitably affects financial markets and the banking sector as well. In light of this, the effect of the GFC and the sovereign debt crisis before, and of COVID-19 pandemic and the conflict in Ukraine after, are still visible on the European capital markets, impacting the number of deals concluded and the overall size of the transactions.

To conclude the chapter, it is worth stressing the duality of European Capital Markets. Indeed, the predominance of US banks is mostly seen in the ECM and M&A segments, whereas the chapter has highlighted how DCM are peculiar, especially in the aftermath of the COVID-19 pandemic. In particular, a change in preferences of debt instruments has happened over time among issuers, with a special focus due to the COVID-19 pandemic. In general, 2021 was an exceptional year in all the segments, as the volume and number of deals show. The situation has however deteriorated in 2022 for a series of factors, notably a rise in interest rates and energy prices, on top of an unstable international political situation. It has to be seen whether this will map into banks' profitability, although announced mass layoffs and decrease in deals could signal a probable slowdown in the banking industry.

The IB landscape has evolved over the years and the sectoral composition of targets in the M&A market is emblematic of this. In particular, the scope of investors and the supply of investment opportunities has changed together with the underlying economic situation. In addition to technology, the healthcare sector has reported an increase in the number of deals which was not expected before the pandemic. Moreover, deals by financial firms have decreased relatively.

Lastly, Italy seems to be a market with its own peculiar characteristics: Most of its M&A deals are still domestic and Milan Stock Exchange has faced some notable delistings. The next few months will say whether the situation will get better. However, many structural problems are at the core of the actual situation and they span from a restrictive regulatory framework, to low levels of trust, to a stagnating country. Comparing Italy to the other financial system, a clear predominance of bank financing can be observed, while capital markets are growing in size but offer still very few attractive opportunities both for investors and for companies. SMEs, the bulk of the Italian economic system, are still reluctant to address public capital, mainly because of historical legacy, burdensome requirements in terms of disclosure, and high costs associated with being public. Without recurring to the public financing to support growth, inevitably Italian companies mature a disadvantage compared to their foreign peers, thus hammering the overall development of the system.

This makes it urgent to develop a series of measures and policies that will promote the role of financial intermediaries on one side and the overall investment banking sector on the other. The question on whether Italy will be able to tackle these problems is a one-billion dollars bet. For the moment, the remainder of the book will try to shed light on the situation of capital markets by also analyzing the role of investors, on top of performing a more detailed analysis of issuers.

References

Anadu, K., Kruttli, M., McCabe, P., Osambela, E., & Shin, C.H. (2018). *The shift from active to passive investing: Potential risks to financial stability?*. Finance and Economics Discussion Series 2018-060. Washington: Board of Governors of the Federal Reserve System. https://doi.org/10.17016/FEDS.2018.060

Assogestioni (2013). *L'industria del risparmio gestito e il finanziamento delle PMI*. Position Paper. Available at: assogestioni.it

Assolombarda (2018). *Credito e finanza per la crescita delle imprese*. White Paper. Available at: assolombarda.it

Banca d'Italia (2013). *Supplements to the statistical bulletin: Monetary and financial indicators*. Vol. XXIII, No. 45. Available at: bancaditalia.it

Beck, T. & Casu, B. (eds.) (2016). *The Palgrave handbook of European banking*. London: Palgrave Macmillan.

Bloom, D.E., Canning, D., & Fink, G. (2010). Implications of population ageing for economic growth. *Oxford Review of Economic Policy*, 26(4), 583–612. https://doi.org/10.1093/oxrep/grq038

Borsa Italiana (2022a). *Monthly update*. December. Available at: borsaitaliana.it

Borsa Italiana (2022b, December). *Borsa Italiana per le PMI*. Primary Markets Italy. Available at: borsaitaliana.it

Caselli, S. & Sironi, A. (2015). L'Unione Bancaria: ambizioni, certezze, rischi. *Economia & Management*, 3, 7–12.

Caselli, S., Gigante, G., & Tortoroglio, A. (2021). *Corporate and investment banking: A hands-on approach*. Milan: Bocconi University Press.

CONSOB (2013a). *Ammissione alla quotazione delle piccole e medie imprese: Interventi di incentivazione, ruolo dei mercati e degli operatori*. Documento tecnico programmatico.

CONSOB (2013b). *Statistical bulletin*. Studies and Analyses, No. 2.

Dal Maso, E. (2022, November 12). Piazza Affari: 4,7 miliardi di ipo, 43 miliardi di delisting. Il rischio Cnh e Tim. Come frenare la fuga?. *Milano Finanza*.

Diamond, D.W. & Dyvbig, P.H. (1983). Bank runs, deposit insurance, and liquidity. *Journal of Political Economy*, 91(3), 401–419. https://doi.org/10.1086/261155

ECB (2013). *Corporate finance and economic activity in the euro area: Structural issues report 2013*. ECB Occasional Paper No. 151. Available at: ecb.europa.eu

ECB (2013). *Survey on the access to finance of small and medium-sized enterprises in the euro area*. Available at: ecb.europa.eu

Fitch (2013). *Europe's unrated bond issuers: 2013 update*. Available at: fitchratings.com

Franzoni, D. & Moussawi, R. (2019). Do ETFs increase volatility?. *Journal of Finance*, 73(6), 2471–2535. https://doi.org/10.1111/jofi.12727

Geranio, M. (2004). Funding processes. In Caselli, S. & Gatti, S. (eds.), *Venture Capital* (pp. 53–80). Berlin, Heidelberg: Springer. https://doi.org/10.1007/978-3-540-24829-3_3

Goodhart, C. & Schoenmaker, D. (2016). *The United States dominates global investment banking: Does it matter for Europe?*. Bruegel Policy Contribution, No. 2016/06. Available at: bruegel.org

Guagliano, C., Linciano, N., & Magistro Contento, C. (2013). *The impact of financial analyst reports on small caps prices in Italy*. Quaderni di Finanza, No. 73. Available at: consob.it

Harrison, C., MacGeoch, M., & Michetti, C. (2022). *Sustainable debt, global state of the market 2021*. Climate Bonds Initiative. Available at: climatebonds.net

IMF (2019, October). *Global financial stability report: Lower for longer*. Available at: imf.org

Kaya, O. & Meyer, T. (2013). *Corporate bond issuance in Europe: Where do we stand and where are we heading?*. EU Monitor Global Financial Markets, Deutsche Bank. Available at: dbresearch.com

Maksimovic, V. & Pichler, P. (2001). Technological innovation and initial public offerings. *The Review of Financial Studies*, 14(2), 459–494. https://doi.org/10.1093/rfs/14.2.459

McKinsey (2019). *Private markets come of age*. McKinsey Global Private Markets Review. Available at: mckinsey.com

Morningstar (2019, August). *Morningstar's active/passive barometer.*

Reuters (2019, June 26). Illiquid investment funds 'built on a lie', BoE's Carney says.

S&P (2013). *Italian companies are turning to the capital markets amid weak credit conditions*. Standard & Poor's Ratings Services.

S&P Global (2021, December). *Italian corporate outlook 2022: Recovery widens, with new risks*. Available at: spglobal.com

Societé Generale (2019, September 10). *Global investment banks: Can European investment banks be saved?*. Cross Asset Research.

Sushko, V. & Turner, G. (2018, March). *The implications of passive investing for securities markets*. BIS Quarterly Review. Available at: bis.org

UNCTAD (2019). *World investment report 2019: Special economic zones*. Available at: unctad.org

Willis Towers Watson (2021). *Institutional allocation to private equity: A maturing industry calls for a differentiated approach*. Available at: wtwco.com

Wright, W. & Asimakopoulos, P. (2018, March). *Report: The size, depth & growth opportunity in EU capital markets*. New Financial. Available at: newfinancial.org

You, L. (2008). *Listing and delisting over time and around the globe*. Working Paper.

You, L., Parhizgari, A.M., & Srivastava, S. (2012). Cross listing and subsequent delisting in foreign markets. *Journal of Empirical Finance*, 19(2), 200–216. https://doi.org/10.1016/j.jempfin.2011.11.005

2 Capital Markets Investors

by *Marta Zava*
Bocconi University and Goethe University

In this chapter, we outline the investor base in the Italian capital market, taking into consideration its structure and its offer, and comparing it with the most relevant and analogous markets in Europe, namely France and Germany. It emerges that the Italian IPO market's investor base is mainly dominated by funds headquartered abroad, while only the 9% of funds are in Italy. The percentage of shares allotted to Italian investors only increases when deals are small in size. When comparing institutional investors to retail investors in newly issued stock, as well as domestic investors to foreign investors, it appears that the lack of a strong institutional pillar is the main constraint on the domestic investment base. Our analysis also confirms that Italy does not currently have a sizable private pension investment pillar, which would otherwise contribute significantly to institutional demand. As a result, a significant amount of untapped potential is present: a great opportunity that currently hinders the full development of the domestic equity market. The network analysis of Italian IPOs in 2020 and 2021 also revealed that the most connected investors were not those who made the largest investments, but rather those who made numerous smaller investments in a variety of companies. By contrast, the businesses that attracted the most investors also raised the most money through their IPO. Additionally, investors who use growth and blended strategies dominate the market; however, during the time frame under consideration (2006–2021), their importance reversed, resulting in the former's dominance. The increased number of growth investors suggests that investors believe stock market companies are high risk but have great potential. Analogously, the limits of domestic investment demand are also reflected in the Italian debt market, where the average share of investors in Italian debt is only 4%, while capital from the US and Luxembourg accounts for 50% of the investor base. And finally, high-yield issues have been growing consistently since 2015, reaching a peak in 2021 when they made up about one-third of the issues. The pattern is widespread in Europe. Additionally, between 2011 and 2020, the difference between investment grade and high-yield issues in Italy and throughout Europe decreased steadily; it was only after 2020 that it began to diverge once more: The reasons are outlined through the chapter.

The chapter is structured as follows. Section 2.1 focuses on the structure of capital markets and how to access them, while Section 2.2 provides an indirect assessment of the supply of equity capital by studying the ownership structure of publicly. Section 2.3 outlines the attractiveness of Italian issuers to investors. Consequently, Section 2.4 quantifies how much it pays to invest in Italian capital markets, considering first equity securities and then debt securities. Lastly, some final observations are collected in Section 2.5.

2.1 Access to the Capital Market and Its Structure

How do cross-country differences impact access to the markets and their structure? To answer this question, we provide a comparative analysis of recent IPOs in Italy, France, and Germany. We aim at linking market development to post-IPO performances and shedding light on some procedural differences that may affect market structures.

In our analysis, we consider all IPOs reported by Dealogic–ECM Analytics in Italy, France, and Germany from 2014 to the end of the third quarter of 2021. Overall, our sample comprises 467 IPOs for an aggregate total value of approximately €87 trillion. Note that with regard to Germany, we focused on the Deutsche Börse, since IPOs across the German stock exchanges are hardly comparable due to the differences in their intrinsic nature. Moreover, the Frankfurt Stock Exchange is the biggest and most important in the country. The contribution of Italian capital markets to total deal flow in the three countries is paradoxical: IPOs in Italy represent 50% of the total number of IPOs realized in the period, but only account for approximately 26% of aggregate IPO volume. We split our analysis between main markets and alternative investment markets (AIMs). While in Italy, the alternative market (since 2021 officially Euronext Growth Milan) accounts for 82% of transactions and approximately 19% of IPO volume, in France, it represents 30% of IPO flow and 3% of IPO volume, and in Germany, it collects, respectively, the 12% of the newly listed companies and the 4% of the IPO volume. In this respect, the three capital markets are structurally different, especially when considering AIMs. The different listing type (main market vs. AIM) resembles the typical industrial structure of the countries: Italy is characterized by SMEs, while France and Germany headquarter bigger firms. **Figures 2.1a** and **2.1b** compare IPO deals flow in Italy, France, and Germany since 2014, respectively, in the main markets and in AIMs. We could not interpret these differences in IPO flows across countries without considering the portion of firms deciding to go public in a foreign market. Indeed, 17% German companies decided to get listed abroad, picking NASDAQ and NYSE as favorite markets, compared to the 3% of Italian and French companies. **Figure 2.2** displays an overview of Italian, French, and German firms which got listed in exchanges other than their domestic exchanges (i.e., the Italian Stock Exchange, the Paris Stock Exchange, and the Frankfurt Stock Exchange).

The private industrial sector has provided by far the largest contribution to IPO flow across all markets. Furthermore, in Italy, the financial sector and the public industrial sector has played a more substantial role in Italy than abroad, both in the main market and the AIM, while the public utility sector accounted for a greater number of IPOs in France. Results are in line with the structural characteristics of the two countries. **Figure 2.3** shows the sectoral breakdown of IPO deal flow. However, the peculiarities of the European markets do not seem to have played a role in the attraction of foreign companies. Indeed, mostly domestic companies access the three capital markets under analysis (above 90% in each of the three countries). Thus, the markets do not diverge in terms of attractiveness – the costs of issuing equity in the considered country from abroad

Figure 2.1 IPO deal flow (2014–2021), Italy vs. France vs. Germany: volume (left-hand scale) and count (right-hand scale)

(a) Main markets

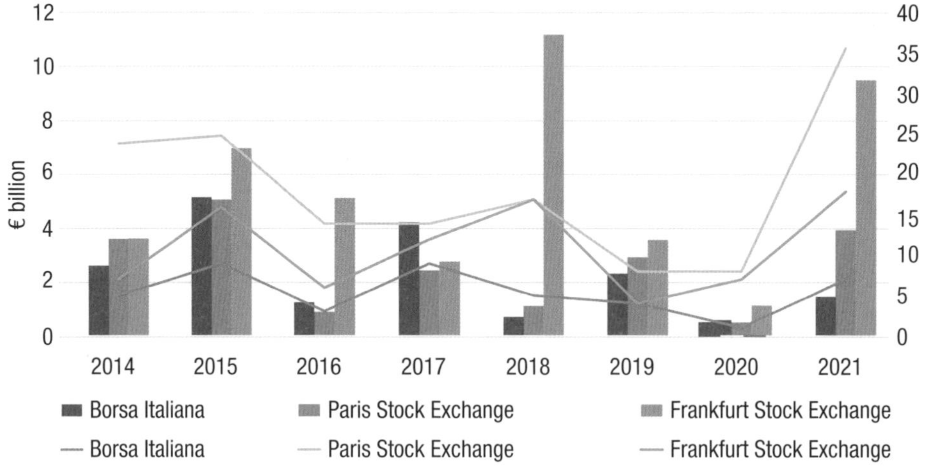

(b) AIMs

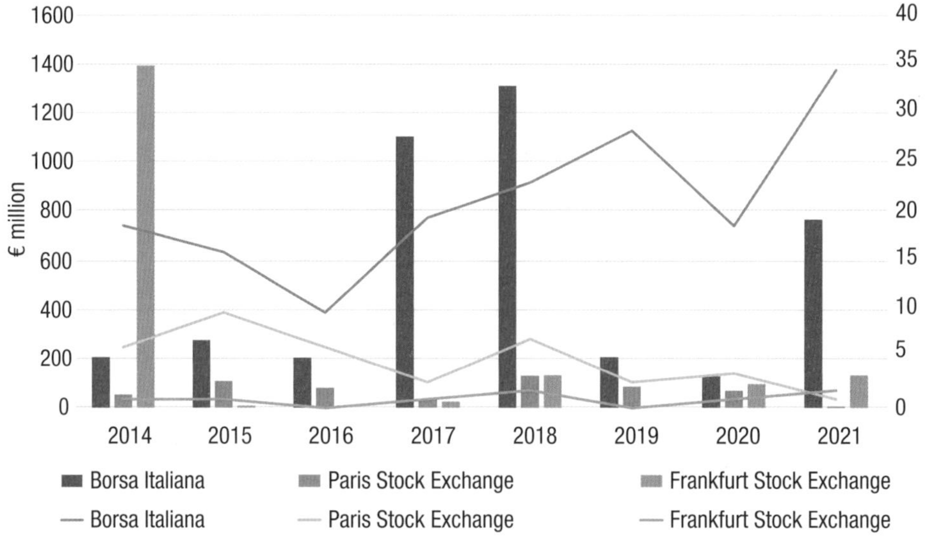

Source: authors' elaboration of Dealogic data.

Figure 2.2 **IPO deals (2014–2021), Italy vs. France vs. Germany: domestic firms listed in the foreign stock exchange**

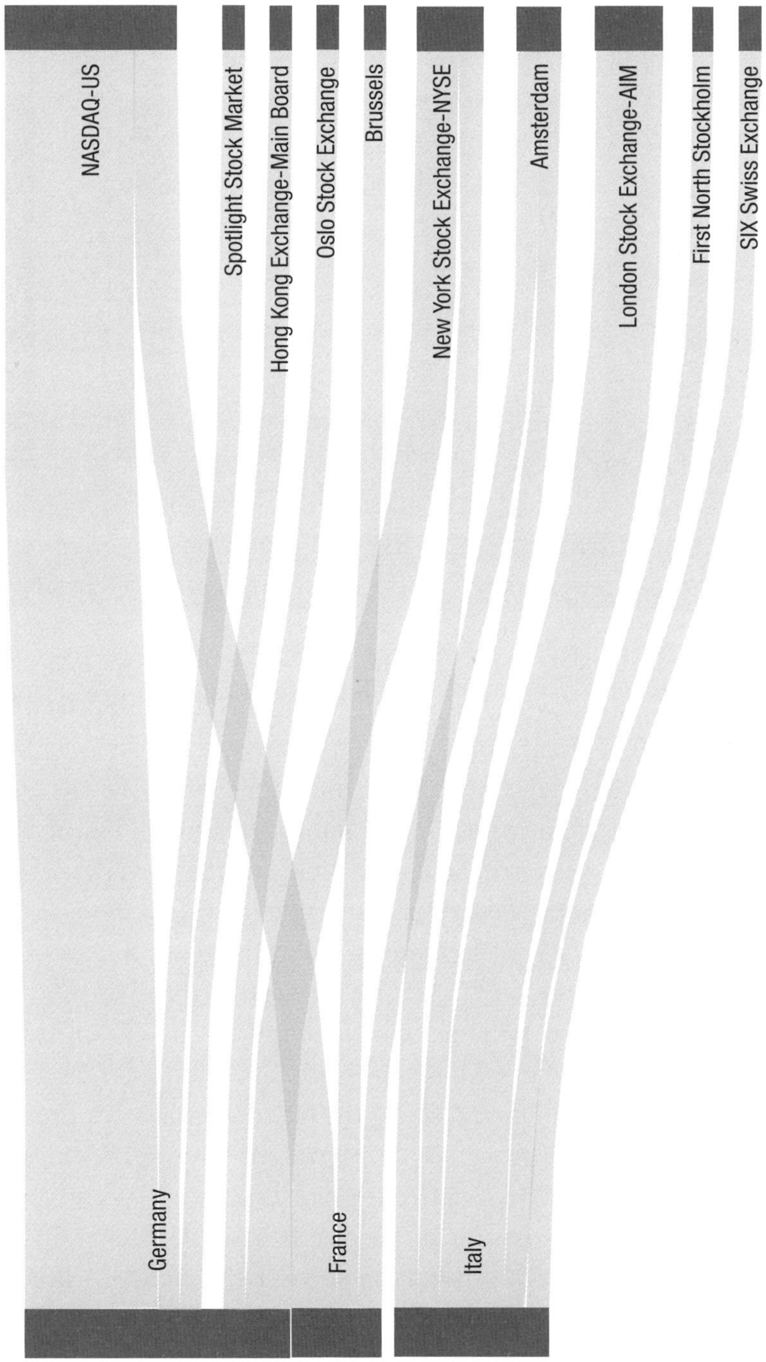

Source: authors' elaboration of Dealogic data.

Figure 2.3 Sectorial breakdown of the IPO deal flow (2014–2021), Italy vs. France vs. Germany: main markets (left) and AIMs (right)

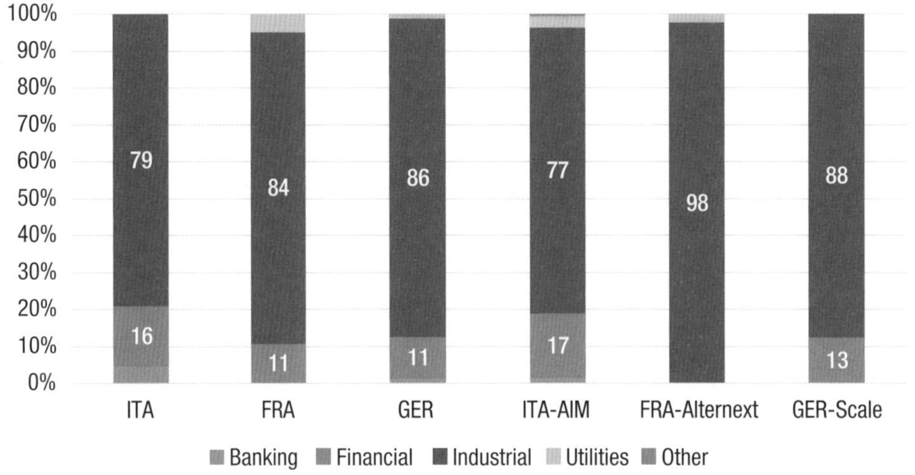

Source: authors' elaboration of Dealogic data.

are not offset by the benefits of gaining access to deeper pools of capital and a more efficient stock market.

The similarities between the Italian, the French, and the German market are explained by the common regulatory framework aimed at ensuring homogeneous approach across Europe, which nevertheless grants national authorities some degree of discretion in their approaches. In Italy, the Italian Companies and Exchange Commission (Consiglio Nazionale per le Società e la Borsa, or CONSOB) is the government agency responsible for regulating the Italian securities market. In France, the role is covered by the Autorité des Marchés Financiers (AMF), while in Germany, the supervision is undertaken by the Bundesanstalt für Finanzdienstleistungsaufsicht (BaFin).

The national authorities control formal compliance with regulations and procedures, and verify, for instance, that the risk factors in the prospectus are compatible with the status of a listed company. Furthermore, they verify in detail the substance of the disclosure offered to investors, since they bear legal responsibility. Consistently, the temporal framework in which the supervisors act is the same, as regulated by European laws (see Art. 94-bis comma 2 of TUF and for the process of authorization, see Art. 8 of Regolamento Emittenti). However, for instance, CONSOB also tends to request additional disclosure and information more frequently, thus exploiting in full the maximum 60 days allocated for the process (as per Art. 8 Regolamento Emittenti). As a consequence, the prospectus in Italy is longer and more complex, even without considering the fact that it has to be drafted in two different versions: one in Italian, the Prospetto Informativo (approved by CONSOB), and one in English, the Offering Circular (not subject to CONSOB approval), a document needed to market the issue to institutional investors during the roadshow and offer period. Similar practices are in act in Germany and France. On top of that, while the financial regulatory authorities oversee the prospectus, the stock exchanges set the listing requirements, which may include minimum share capital and liquidity requirements, as well as requirements for the company's financial condition and governance structure. Germany offers several stock exchanges, the most important being Frankfurt Stock Exchange (Deutsche Börse) and Stuttgart Stock Exchange (Börse Stuttgart). To sum up, the three institutions cover a very similar role and work to ensure that the IPO process is fair, transparent, and efficient and that investors are protected from financial misconduct. The IPO processes are considered time-consuming and costly across the three countries, as companies must prepare and file a prospectus and other required documents with the financial regulatory agency. Both at Italian and European levels, several initiatives have been undertaken in the effort to strengthen capital markets circuits, as the MEF Green Book (MEF, 2022) and the proposal of the EU Listing Act. The latter is another step toward simplifying information requirements and lowering listing costs for IPOs and experienced equity offerings, even though the proposal does not envision a perfectly integrated capital market infrastructure with a single supervisory authority and a European Prospectus automatically recognized by each member state, at least in the short term.

Another structural difference across markets emerges in terms of deal size. As expected, IPOs on the main markets are larger on average than IPOs on AIMs, as displayed in **Figure 2.4**. The median IPO deal value on

Figure 2.4 IPO median deal value (2014–2021), Italy vs. France vs. Germany: main markets (left) and AIMs (right)

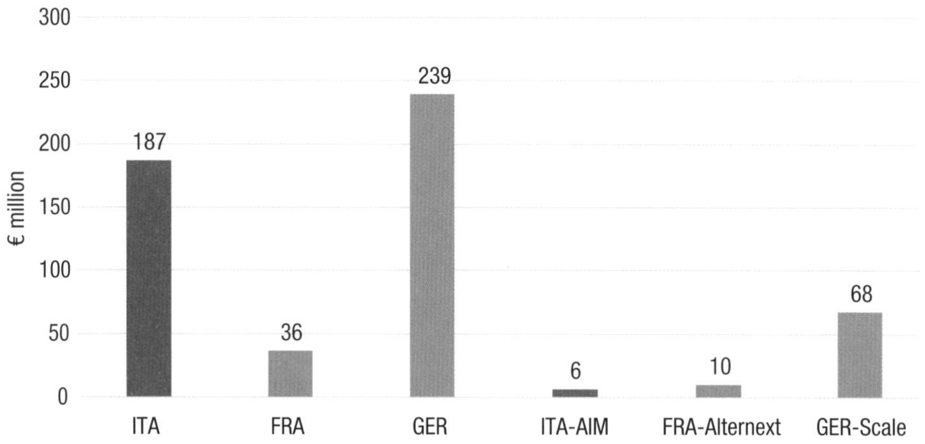

Source: authors' elaboration of Dealogic data.

the main market in France is the smallest, accounting for approximately €36 million, while values abruptly spike in the Italian Stock Exchange (approximately €190 million) and further increase in the Deutsche Börse (approximately €240 million). The difference in the IPO median values is partially reversed in the AIM market: Italian values are at the tail end, showing a median value of €6 million, while French values are around €10 million and German values are out of league at approximately €68 million. It must be noted that the Deutsche Börse Scale segment, regardless it being a formally registered SME Growth Market according to EU standards, offers access to German SMEs, which are substantially bigger than Italian companies, in line with the industrial structure of the respective countries. Having a smaller median IPO value in the AIM is an asset for small companies, which can have access to the advantages of being listed while being smaller in size and in capital requirements – resilience and quality over dimension.

Figure 2.5 compares across markets the proportion of existing shares sold by shareholders to newly issued stock. As expected, IPOs on the

Figure 2.5 **Breakdown of IPO shares (2014–2021), Italy vs. France vs. Germany: main markets (left) and AIMs (right)**

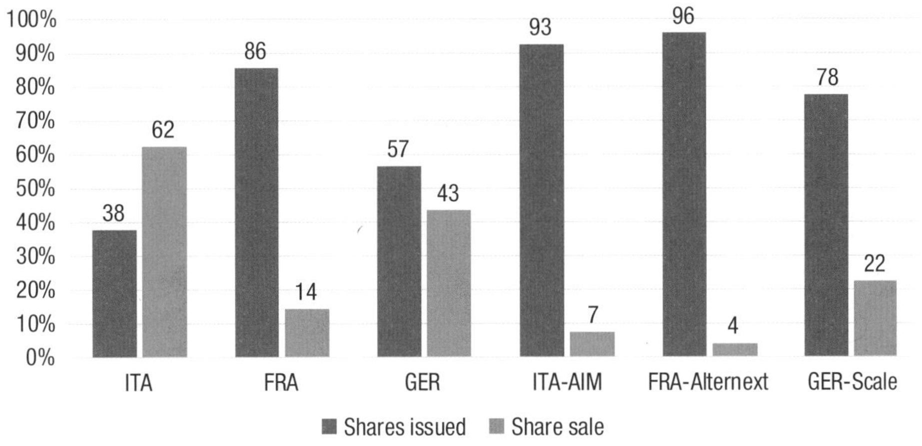

Source: authors' elaboration of Dealogic data.

main markets involve a larger proportion of existing shares sold by shareholders than IPOs on AIMs, where companies mostly issue new shares. Differences are striking across the three main markets. The French main market is mostly populated by newly issued shares (86%), the German main market is more balanced (57% newly issued vs. 43% sale), while the Italian main market is mostly allocating existing shares (only 38% newly issued shares). Further details and analysis on deal sizes is available at Chapter 1, but however we focus on how the fundraising function of equity capital markets is more relevant in France than in Italy, where the main market serves the function of ownership transferring to a greater extent. Differently, the AIMs are dominated by newly issued shares, in line with the intrinsic nature of the listed companies. Being smaller, their reason to approach public listing often relies on gaining access to fresh capital. Indeed, in Italy, France, ad Germany, the newly issued shares account for 93%, 96%, and 78%, respectively. As expected, the Scale segment (German AIM) foresees a lower number of newly issues shares, in line with the dimension of the underlying firms.

As outlined in Chapter 1, the role of intermediaries in IPOs does not differ across main markets. On the main markets, however, a greater number of global coordinators and bookrunners collaborate, compared to secondary markets of the same countries. **Figure 2.6a** displays the average number of global coordinators (left) and bookrunners (center) per IPO in the three main markets. In Italy, it emerges that 84% of IPOs are organized by more than one global coordinator, and 93% are tracked by more than one bookrunner. In France, the figures are, respectively, 75% and 70%, and in Germany 68% and 82%. Syndication is more common in Italy, but it is high in all the three countries' main markets. It could be explained by the fact that in Europe banks that act as lenders to a company usually gain a role as part in its IPO. **Figure 2.6b** shows the corresponding values for the AIMs. A flashing difference is the decreased figures: Cooperation among global coordinators and bookrunners, as syndication, plays a role but to a much lower extent. Indeed, smaller companies do not have that many actors involved in their financial structure. Moreover, being the deals' size more contained, the need for capital and paperwork is less burdensome and can be dealt with by one intermediary.

More global coordinators might play a positive role in responding to the challenges faced when pricing an issue. Indeed, **Figure 2.7** compares the pricing range at filing across markets, computed as the difference between the upper and the lower bound over the lower bound. The pricing range at filing is on average the widest in France, followed by Germany and Italy, both in the main markets and the AIMs. It could be helped by the fact that, in Italy, when a company files an application with CONSOB and Borsa Italiana, a press release is issued. Thus, investors have the information well in advance with respect to the issue date. Surprisingly, the Italian AIM market displays, on average, a much smaller range, indicating strictness in pricing. The widest range is displayed by the French AIM market, but the results could be influenced by the small number of deals.

How do structural differences across countries influence market performance? We compute underpricing as the percentage difference between the close price at the end of the first day of trading with respect to the offering price.

Figure 2.6 **Collaboration between intermediaries (2014–2021), Italy vs. France vs. Germany: frequency of multiple global coordinators (left), of multiple bookrunners (center), and of syndication (right)**

(a) Main markets

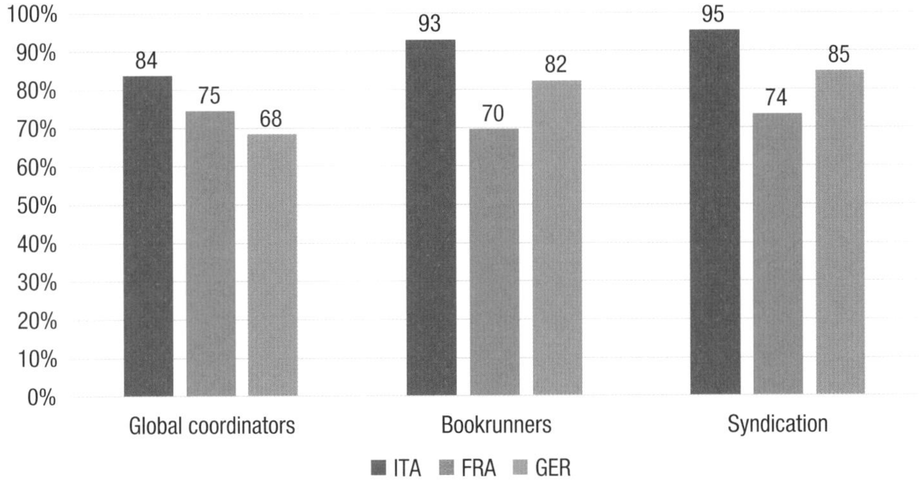

Source: authors' elaboration of Dealogic data.

(b) AIMs

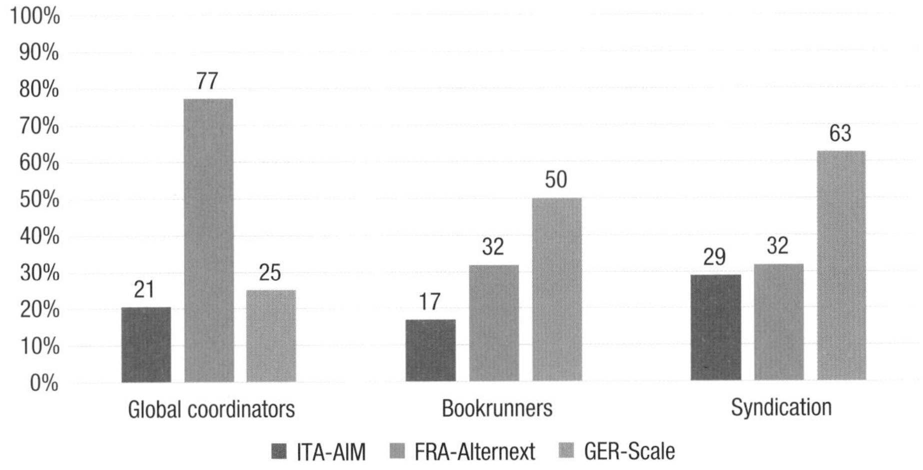

Source: authors' elaboration of Dealogic data.

Figure 2.7 **Price range at filing (2014–2021), Italy vs. France vs. Germany: main markets (left) and AIMs (right)**

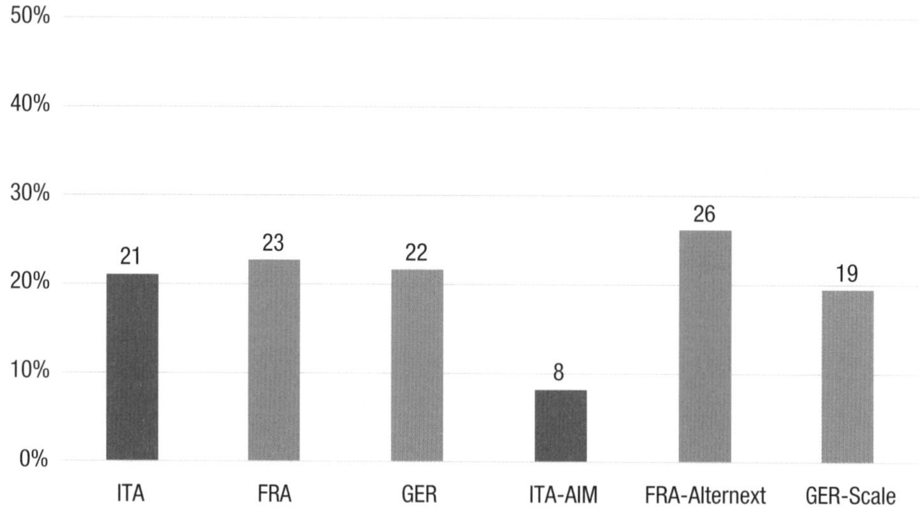

Source: authors' elaboration of Dealogic data.

Figure 2.8 compares IPO underpricing across the markets considered. As the main markets are considered, underpricing is on average higher in Germany than in Italy and France. But as comes to the AIMs, the Italian market results to be the most underpriced. However, the latter is also the most volatile among AIMs while, in the main markets, underpricing is the most volatile in Germany. Indeed, strong cross-country discrepancies are observed in terms of standard deviations.

It is common to assume that AIMs are subject to a higher level of underpricing, since stock is offered at a substantial discount due to the more severe informational problems, and in some cases also due to the lack of liquidity. However, this underpricing is often not so visible in actual market prices, due to low trade volumes in the post-IPO period resulting in only minor price movements in a daily horizon. Low post-IPO trade volumes on the AIMs are mainly due to the absence of a strong domestic investor base, the small size of the issues, and the scarce liquidity of the

Figure 2.8 **IPO underpricing (2014–2021), Italy vs. France vs. Germany: main markets (left) and AIMs (right)**

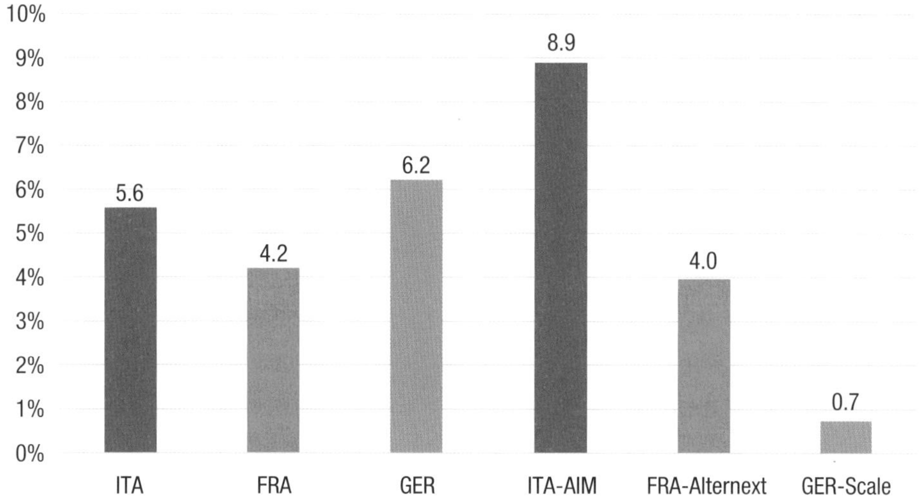

Source: authors' elaboration of Dealogic data.

stocks which discourages foreign investors. Those investors interested in one issue would be able to get the shares in the IPO and would then find it hard to liquidate their holdings in the short term, dying up liquidity in the immediate post-IPO trading phase. To support the argument, we further investigate first-day abnormal underpricing for IPOs. We dig into the frequency with which IPOs realize, respectively, a first-day negative underpricing or an underpricing in excess of 10%, to highlight structural differences across countries and markets in mispricing.

Table 2.1 shows that overpricing in the main market is twice as common in Germany than in France, while the difference is even more marked in Italy. Excessive underpricing occurs evenly often in the three main markets. However, overpricing is more frequent in the French AIM, as is excessive underpricing. Thus, deals in the French AIM are the most mispriced. Nevertheless, deals in the Italian and German AIMs are mispriced more often than in the respective main markets too.

Table 2.1 Mispricing in IPOs (2014–2021), Italy vs. France vs. Germany

	IPO first-day abnormal underpricing	
	Negative (frequency, %)	In excess of 10% (frequency, %)
Borsa Italiana	27.91	27.91
Paris	10.48	30.65
Frankfurt Stock Exchange	22.08	29.87
Borsa Italiana–AIM Italia	33.68	30.53
Paris–Alternext	36.36	59.09
Frankfurt Stock Exchange Scale	20.00	40.00

Source: authors' elaboration of Dealogic data.

Figure 2.9 displays long-term IPO performance, computing post-IPO long-run performance as the one-year return on stock and comparing it across different markets. Performance is better in Italy than in the other two comparable markets. Overall, the performance is on average higher in the

Figure 2.9 One-year IPO performance (2014–2021), Italy vs. France vs. Germany: main markets (left) and AIMs (right)

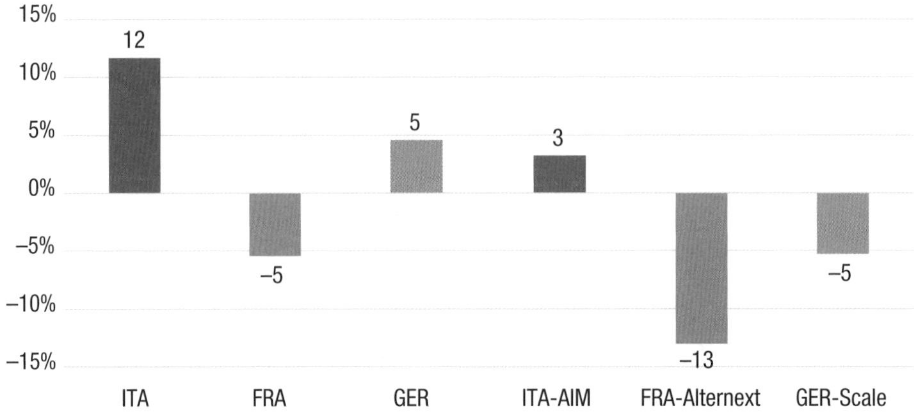

Source: authors' elaboration of Dealogic data.

main market than in the AIM, as expected due to the smaller size and the higher risk of the companies listed here, which are penalized in more precarious economic conditions as the ones we are currently living. Said conditions are responsible also for the negative long-term performances of half of the considered markets.

2.2 The Investors' Offer in the Italian Market

In this section, we provide an indirect assessment of the supply of equity capital by studying the ownership structure of publicly listed companies in Italy, straight after the IPO.

In **Figure 2.10**, we show two sets of data. First, the triangle indicates the percentage of share free float in the all-share markets in Italy. Second, columns indicate the percentage of float owned by each category of investor. In Italy, float is limited, accounting for the 22% of total ownership.

Figure 2.10 Breakdown by investor type at IPO (2006–2021)

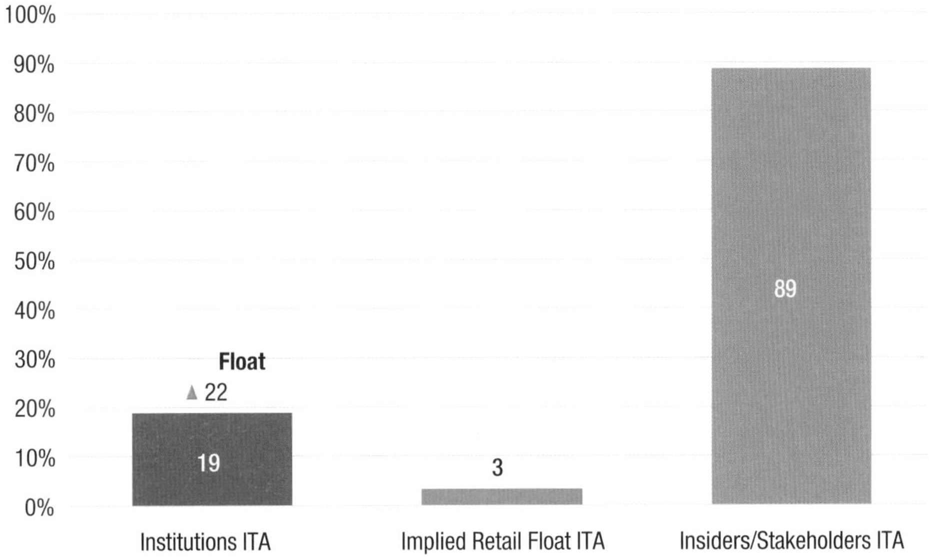

Source: data collected on Bloomberg.

Insiders/stakeholders are dominant in the Italian market, accounting for 89%, while institutional investors hold 3% of total ownership and implied retail float is around 18%. By considering uniquely float, the institutional investors own 17% of float shares, while 83% is implied retail float.

By hand-collecting information on each institutional investor which invested in at least one of the IPO deals, we were able to trace geographical information on almost €6 billion in capital across the 15 years considered. Some interesting insights about the Italian equity market emerged. As shown in **Figure 2.11** and **Table 2.2**, the Italian IPO market is mainly dominated by funds headquartered abroad, while only the 9% of funds are in Italy. Foreign funds are mostly located in Luxembourg (39%), the United States (29%), and the UK (9%). It should be pointed out that several Italian, French, and German institutions place some of their investment vehicles in Luxembourg due to fiscal reasons. European countries (Italy, Luxembourg, and Switzerland excluded) covered the 12% of invested funds, while Asian countries played a very marginal but still interesting role, making up for the 0.5% of funds. There are several factors that can contribute to the cost of investing in firms in different countries. One factor is the location of the company itself, as investing in closer companies may be less expensive than investing in a distant company due to lower fees, exchange rates, costs of visiting the firm, etc. Another factor is that geographically and culturally closer countries may be more familiar to investors and may have regulatory environments that are more similar to those in the investors' home countries. This can make it easier and less costly for investors to research and evaluate investment opportunities. Nevertheless, it is important to note that the cost of investing in firms can vary significantly depending on the specific circumstances of the investment, the firm, the fund, and the specific industry market. Considering the top 15 countries in our analysis, all these factors have had a role in the average size of the investment committed by funds located in jurisdictions other than the one of the IPO.

Consequently, we collected information on the strategic and geographical focus of institutional investors, as a way for us to indirectly test the strategic drivers behind the evidence detailed in the previous paragraph. The investment styles that best characterize investor activity in the Italian financial markets are grouped in the following nine distinct categories:

Figure 2.11 Breakdown by geographic origin: investors in IPO deals in Borsa Italiana

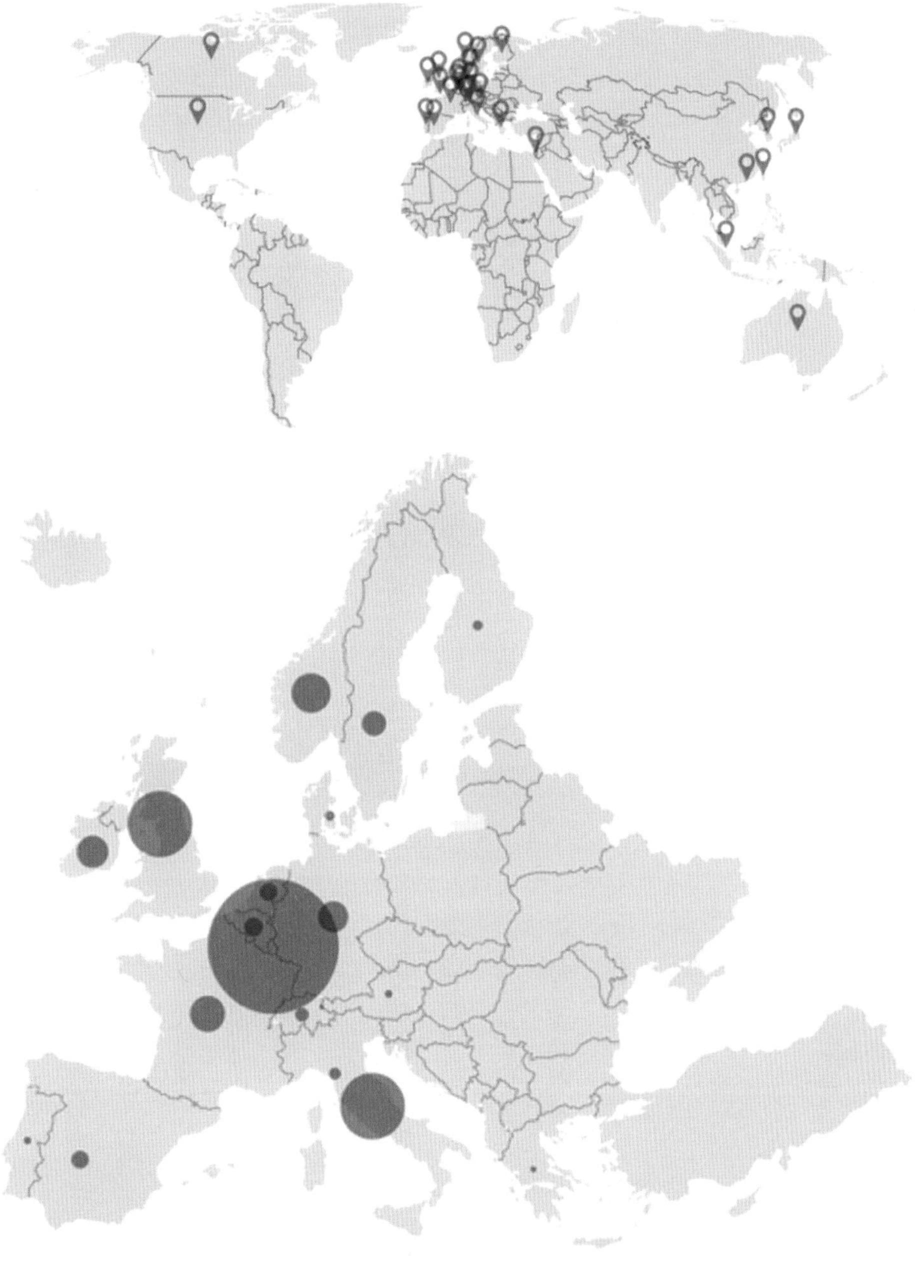

Source: data collected on Bloomberg.

Table 2.2 **Breakdown by geographic origin: investors in IPO deals in Borsa Italiana**

Country	Investment (€ million)	Investment (%)	Average investment size (€ million)	Number of firms
Luxembourg	2,302.42	39.41	1.27	1812
United States	1,671.77	28.61	3.42	489
Italy	534.24	9.14	0.56	956
United Kingdom	527.06	9.02	3.42	154
Norway	178.47	3.05	9.92	18
France	142.96	2.45	1.09	131
Ireland	110.84	1.90	0.92	121
Germany	102.27	1.75	1.46	70
Sweden	60.74	1.04	1.96	31
Canada	56.61	0.97	0.99	57
Belgium	34.09	0.58	1.48	23
Netherlands	29.20	0.50	1.46	20
Spain	27.73	0.47	0.77	36
South Korea	16.56	0.28	2.76	6
Switzerland	15.04	0.26	0.36	42
Japan	10.54	0.18	1.32	8
Denmark	6.81	0.12	2.27	3
Finland	6.12	0.10	1.02	6
Austria	2.40	0.04	0.24	10
Portugal	2.36	0.04	0.24	10
Hong Kong	1.35	0.02	1.35	1
Greece	1.04	0.02	0.52	2
Guernsey	0.80	0.01	0.80	1
Taiwan	0.64	0.01	0.32	2
Liechtenstein	0.20	0.00	0.10	2
Singapore	0.10	0.00	0.10	1
Australia	0.02	0.00	0.02	1
Israel	0.00	0.00	0.00	1

Source: data collected on Bloomberg.

- *Blend*: A blend investment strategy involves combining different asset classes, such as stocks, bonds, and cash, in a single portfolio. The goal of a blend strategy is to balance risk and return by diversifying the portfolio across different asset classes.
- *Growth*: A growth investment strategy focuses on investing in companies with the potential for strong earnings and revenue growth. Growth investors are typically willing to accept higher levels of risk in exchange for the potential for higher returns.
- *Equity Hedge*: An equity hedge is a type of investment strategy that aims to reduce the risk of losses in a portfolio by using financial instruments such as options and futures contracts to hedge against declines in the value of the portfolio's underlying stocks.
- *Value*: A value investment strategy involves buying securities that are believed to be undervalued by the market. Value investors seek to identify companies that are trading at a discount to their intrinsic value and have the potential to generate strong returns over the long term.
- *Dynamic Allocation*: Dynamic allocation is a type of investment strategy that involves actively adjusting the allocation of assets in a portfolio based on market conditions. The goal of dynamic allocation is to take advantage of market opportunities and maximize returns while minimizing risk.
- *Global Allocation*: A global allocation investment strategy involves investing in a diversified portfolio of assets across different regions, countries, and asset classes. The goal of global allocation is to achieve diversification and reduce risk through investments in a broad range of markets.
- *Conservative Allocation*: A conservative allocation investment strategy involves investing a larger portion of the portfolio in low-risk assets such as cash and fixed income securities, with a smaller portion invested in high-risk assets such as stocks. The goal of a conservative allocation is to minimize risk and preserve capital.
- *Moderate Allocation*: A moderate allocation investment strategy involves investing a balanced portion of the portfolio in both low-risk and high-risk assets. The goal of a moderate allocation is to achieve a balance between risk and return by investing in a mix of asset classes.

- *Aggregate*: In the context of investing, the term "aggregate" typically refers to the total market value of a portfolio or a group of securities. For example, an investor might refer to the aggregate value of their portfolio, which is the total market value of all the securities they own.

We also set a category denominated "Other," in which various investment strategies followed by smaller numbers of institutional investors in our database are collected, as aggressive allocation, event driven, market neutral, and multi-strategy allocations.

Findings are displayed in **Figure 2.12**. The most common investment style is the blend strategy (54% of invested capital), mainly used to diversify the portfolio among asset classes, followed by the growth strategy (25%), a good proxy indicating that companies in the stock exchange face high risk but are rich in potential. The equity hedge strategy is the third most common one among institutional investors in Italian IPOs, account-

Figure 2.12 Breakdown of investment amounts by investment style: investors in IPO deals in Borsa Italiana

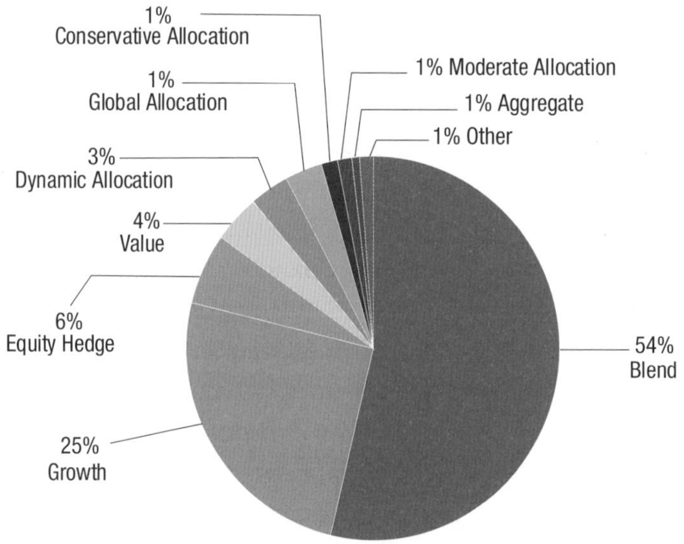

Source: data collected on Bloomberg.

ing for 6% of invested capital, indicating a developed market. Lastly, we considered the value investment strategy (4%), which suggests that some investors are turning to the Italian market when looking for mispriced assets, or in Layman's terms, to buy on sale.

2.3 The Attractiveness of Italian Issuers to Investors

2.3.1 Investors in newly listed companies

Is the disconnection between Italian companies and capital markets due to a lack of interest among investors in equity securities issued by Italian companies? Or are companies unable to tap into these pools of capital?

The aim of our empirical analysis is to disentangle these two potential drivers of the communication breakdown between Italian companies and capital markets. We do so by studying in more detail the attitudes of investors toward equity securities issued by Italian companies to assess the potential demand for this investment class. Ultimately, we seek to understand the possible role of capital markets in financing Italian companies.

To obtain direct evidence on the structure and evolution of investor demand for Italian securities, we take a closer look at new equity and debt issues. In particular, we collect data on demand for equity securities issued by Italian companies during the book building phase; we then break down this demand by different types of investors. The ultimate goal is to clarify the contribution of various categories of investors to aggregate demand.

Our sample includes the 330 IPOs on the Borsa Italiana main market and AIM market dating from 2006 to 2021. Our analysis of investor demand for newly issued equity securities of Italian companies focuses on the proportions of shares allocated to different groups of investors, classified on the basis of their nationality and their institutional or retail profile. We built the sample by collecting data directly from Bloomberg.

Figure 2.13 shows the relative allocations to domestic and foreign investors. Overall, the share of Italian investors is clearly much smaller than the contribution of foreign investors. Only when deals are limited and

Figure 2.13 Allocation to different investors: domestic vs. foreign (2006–2021)

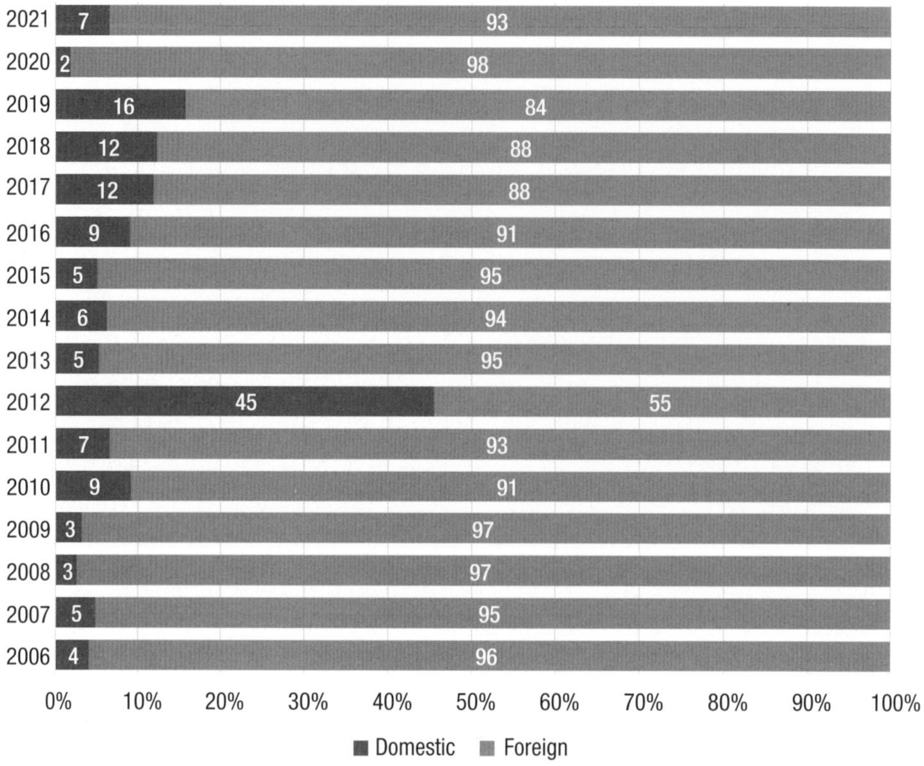

Source: data collected on Bloomberg.

their size is small, the proportion of shares allocated to Italian investors grows. This is striking evidence of the limits of the domestic investment base. As a consequence, when IPO volume and deal size picks up, foreign investors take the lead. Indeed, in the last few years, as IPO activity has started to regain momentum, we observe that the allocations to domestic investors have diminished.

Figure 2.14 shows that the allocation to foreign investors is predominant, regardless of the size of the deal. Blue Chips are larger companies, with market capitalization greater than €1 billion, while those companies with a market capitalization below €1 billion are labeled SMEs. The presence of

Figure 2.14 Allocation to different investors according to the size of the company: Blue Chips vs. SMEs (2006–2021)

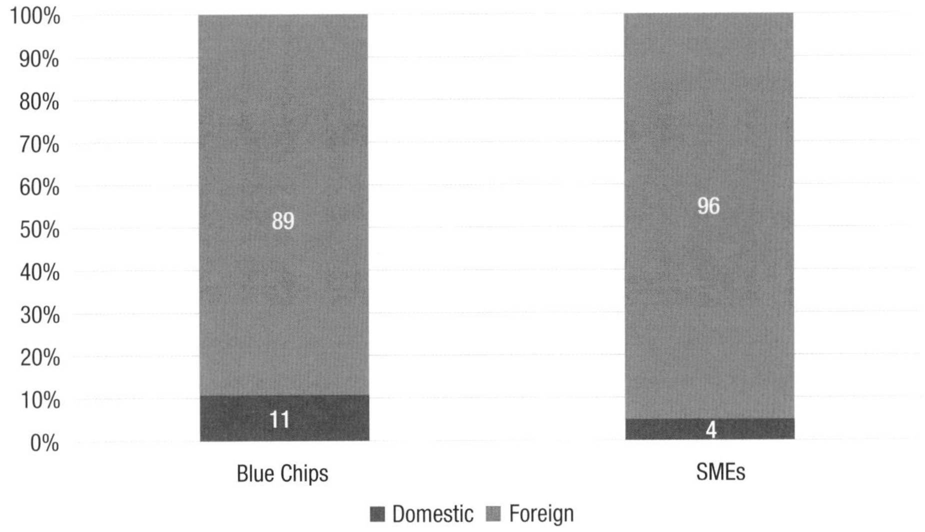

Source: data collected on Bloomberg.

foreign investors compared to Italian investors is more significant in deals supporting smaller companies (96%) compared to larger companies (89%).

An additional insight into investor demand for newly issued equity is provided in **Figure 2.15**, which shows the relative allocations to retail and institutional investors shortly after the IPO. The data refers to the shares' allocation three months after the IPO date. Overall, the share of retail investors is bigger than the contribution of institutional investors. Taking into account also the evidence highlighted in **Figures 2.13** and **2.14**, the dominance of retail investors in the allocation of newly issued equity securities seems to indicate that the major limit to the domestic investment base can be found in the lack of a solid institutional pillar.

Figure 2.16 shows the proportion of retail and institutional investors in IPOs undertaken by Blue Chips and SMEs. For SMEs, a more significant role for institutional investors emerges, with them accounting for 29% of the investment base, compared to the 20% of the investment base for Blue

Figure 2.15 Allocation to different investors: retail vs. institutional (2006–2021)

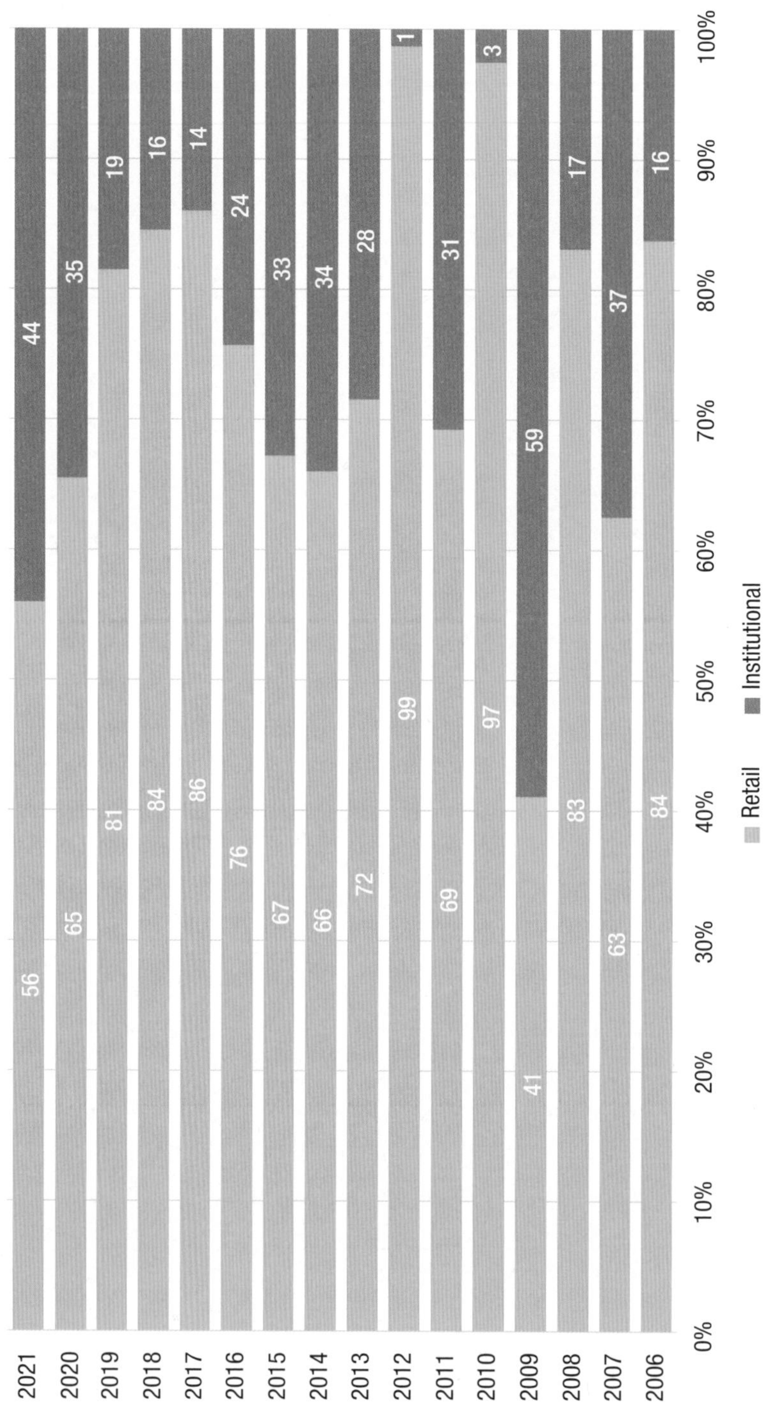

Source: data collected on Bloomberg.

Figure 2.16 Allocation to different investors: Blue Chips vs. SMEs (2006–2021)

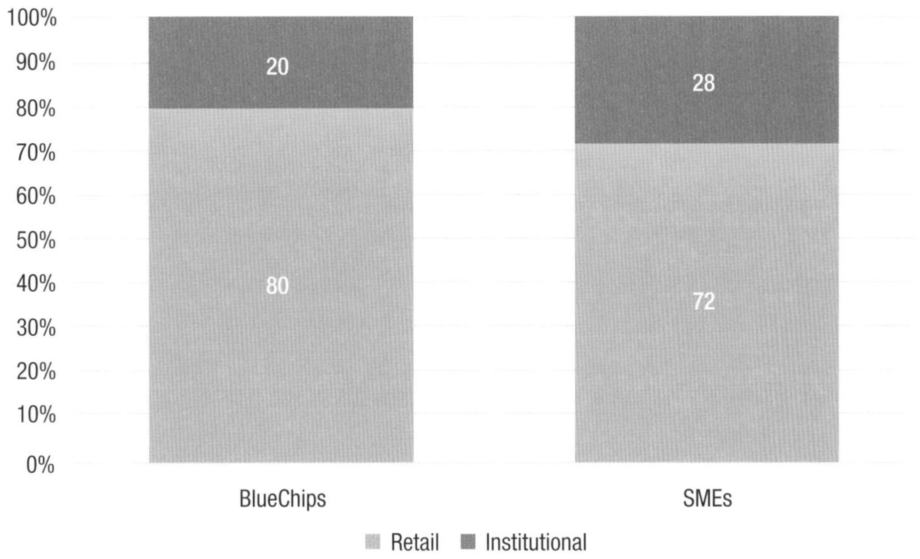

Source: data collected on Bloomberg.

Chips. Therefore, it is clear that institutional investors are more concerned about SME risk, and at the same time, they are more attracted by larger (and safer) companies for which they can easily make informed investment decisions. On the other hand, retail investors look proactively at SMEs, trying to cash in on higher expected returns.

In any case, the final allocation to any particular class of investors is simply an indirect proxy of actual demand. This means that analyzing demand exclusively on the basis of allocated shares is prone to potential biases to the extent that strategic and commercial considerations concur to determine whether and how any investor demand is satisfied, either fully or partially. Therefore, we need to confirm our findings with direct observations of demand, which also allows us to further break institutional demand down across different classes of investors according to their relative contribution. **Figure 2.17** shows the geographic breakdown of demand across domestic and foreign investors, considering the books.

Figure 2.17 Book breakdown by investor nationality: foreign vs. domestic (2006–2021)

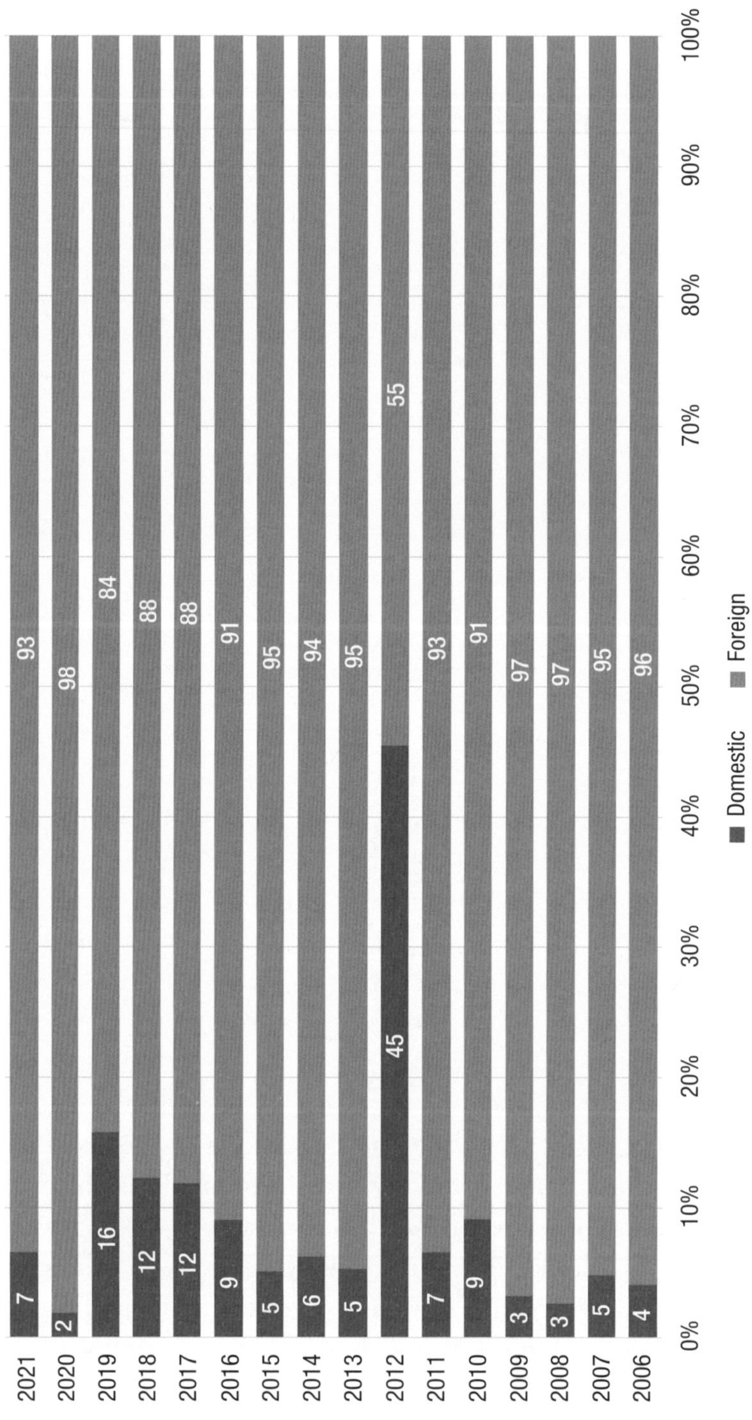

Source: data collected on Bloomberg.

Also in this case, the contribution to overall demand by Italian investors is much smaller than that of foreign investors, confirming the limits of the domestic investment base. As a consequence, especially in the last two years when deal volumes and size have picked up, foreign investors have stepped in to fill the gap in domestic demand.

Figure 2.18 breaks down institutional demand across different investment styles. A broad variety of investment styles contribute to the demand for this instrument, but most of the capital provided is linked either to the blended or the growth investment strategies. However, our analysis also confirms the lack of a large private pension investment pillar in Italy, which currently contributes only residually to institutional demand. As such, this represents a huge unexploited potential as well as a drag on the full development of the domestic equity market.

A confirmation of the challenging environment for equity investment in Italy emerges also by looking at the AIM, where demand by investors is sluggish.

Table 2.3 provides the list of new issues on AIM Italia in 2021. Even if the volume of deals hit a record high during the year, in more than 55% of the IPOs the offer price of the issue had been closer to the lower bound of the filing range rather than the higher bound, due to the lack of demand by investors.

We took a final look on the investors in IPO by focusing on the deals which took place between 2020 and 2021, acknowledging the extraordinary circumstances of the period considered.

As displayed in **Figure 2.19**, we focused on the bipartite network created among investors and companies. In the period under examination, a total of 95 different investors played a role in 64 IPOs, often by means of distinct funds. The most connected investors are Azimut, Natam, and Lemanik: They invested in the highest number of different companies. Moreover, investors also often in the same companies through the means of different entities. On the other side, Ariston and Intercos are the companies that raised capital from the amplest investor base. It is important to distinguish between the number of investments and value of the investments. Indeed, the investors that devoted the largest amount of capital are Norges Bank (€129 million), if we consider overall invested cap-

Figure 2.18 Book breakdown by investors' investment strategy (2006–2021)

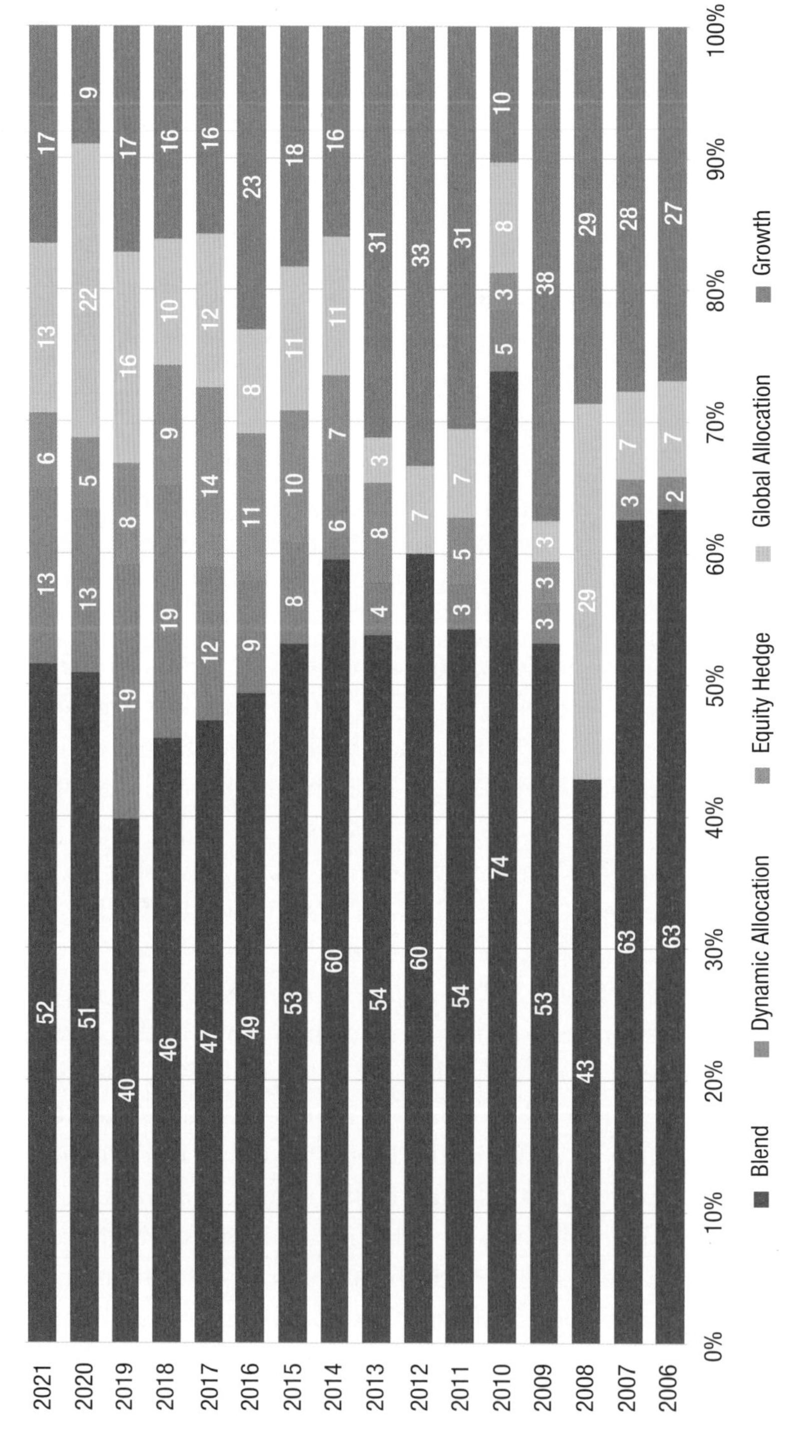

Source: data collected on Bloomberg.

Table 2.3 IPOs on AIM Italia, 2021

Date	Company	Total value (€ million)	Filing range low	Filing range high	Offer price
25/01/2021	Vantea Smart SpA	4.40			2.20
09/03/2021	Almawave SpA	27.30			4.25
16/03/2021	Casasold SpA	2.67	3.33	4.00	3.33
31/03/2021	Reevo SpA	5.53	7.48	8.00	7.74
22/04/2021	Premia Finance SpA	1.10	3.00	3.00	3.00
30/04/2021	Jonix SpA	6.17	4.80	5.60	4.00
11/05/2021	Acquazzurra SpA	2.04			3.50
21/05/2021	REVO SpA	220.00	10.00	10.00	10.00
24/05/2021	G Rent SpA	3.26			3.00
15/06/2021	ATON Green Storage SpA	10.00			4.00
24/06/2021	MeglioQuesto SpA	15.00			1.40
02/07/2021	Spindox SpA	7.05			7.50
02/07/2021	ID-Entity SpA	2.50			1.70
06/07/2021	Industrial Stars of Italy 4 SpA	138.00			10.00
16/07/2021	ALA SpA – Advanced Logistics for Aerospace	22.50	10.00	11.00	10.00
26/07/2021	Compagnia dei Caraibi SpA	12.00			3.45
30/07/2021	OMER SpA	22.10	3.40	4.20	3.40
30/07/2021	Ulisse Biomed Spa	4.50		2.00	2.00
02/08/2021	Nusco SpA	4.00			1.20
18/10/2021	Intermonte Partners SIM SpA	36.58	2.60	2.90	2.80
18/10/2021	Destination Italia SpA	3.00			0.95
27/10/2021	Defence Tech Holding SpA	25.00	3.30	4.00	3.50
01/11/2021	Medica SpA	22.89			27.00
03/11/2021	Soluzione Tasse SpA	12.96			2.70
09/11/2021	COFLE SpA	17.25	13.00	17.00	13.00
12/11/2021	Racing Force SpA	28.35			4.50
16/11/2021	Alfonsino SpA	4.00			1.60

(Continued on next page)

(Continued)

Date	Company	Total value (€ million)	Filing range low	Filing range high	Offer price
16/11/2021	Nice Footwear SpA	5.00	9.00	10.00	10.00
23/11/2021	Take Off SpA	12.50	3.92	4.08	4.00
01/12/2021	Datrix Srl	15.00			4.10
14/12/2021	Homizy SpA	10.04			5.40
14/12/2021	SIF Italia	2.75			2.60
15/12/2021	Directa SIM SpA	6.75	2.80	3.20	3.00
15/12/2021	Sababa Security SpA	8.62			3.70
16/12/2021	Biro	15.00	3.50	5.00	3.50
16/12/2021	Lindbergh SpA	4.25			1.70
20/12/2021	Integrated System Credit Consulting Fintech SpA	16.00	4.00	7.00	5.00
21/12/2021	Star7 SpA	15.02			8.25
27/12/2021	Finanza.Tech Spa SB	3.48			1.20

Source: data collected on Bloomberg.

ital, and Capital Research Global Investor (€93 million) if we consider the single investment. As a comparison, Azimut Holdings invested overall €46 million with 26 funds, resulting in a total number of investments (and therefore connections fund-company) equal to 144 and an average investment size of €0.46 million. When it comes to the companies, the situation turns out to be the opposite: Often IPOs able to gather the higher number of investors are also the ones raising the higher amounts of capital. Indeed, Ariston raised €802 million and is the biggest IPO by size in our sample, while Intercos raised €317 million and results to be the third IPO by size in the sample. GVS, the second IPO by size in our sample (€570 million), raised capital by 9 different investors, through 66 funds, confirming our thesis. As anticipated, the degree distribution related to investors is scale-free, indicating that few investors enter in a high number of IPO deals, while the most participated in a very limited part of deals. The same is true in relation to the companies' degree – a few have many investors, while most have few.

Figure 2.19 **Investors in Italian IPO deals in 2020 and 2021: network of investors and companies**

● investors ● companies size = degree

(Continued on next page)

(Continued)

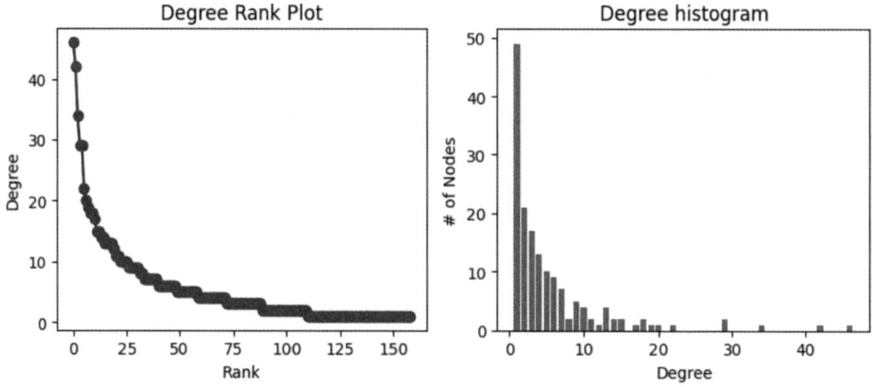

Source: data collected on Bloomberg.

2.3.2 The ownership structure of publicly listed Italian companies

With respect to investor demand for the equity of Italian companies, we complement the direct evidence from the breakdown of investor demand for newly issued securities with an indirect assessment of said demand by studying the ownership structure of publicly listed Italian companies and how it has evolved.

More specifically, we focus our analysis on the comparison between the composition of the shareholders' group in Blue Chips and SMEs. The sample we consider includes all companies whose stocks are listed on Borsa Italiana between 2006 and 2021, classified on the basis of their market capitalization at the relevant date. As mentioned before, Blue Chips are larger companies with market capitalization greater than €1 billion, while those companies with a market capitalization below €1 billion are labeled SMEs.

We first look at differences in the liquidity of stocks across our two groups of companies. **Figure 2.20** shows the floating stocks for both Blue Chips and SMEs. The larger firms are characterized by a higher percentage of outstanding shares available for trading, meaning that their liquidity is higher than that of SMEs.

Figure 2.20 Blue Chips and SMEs float (2006–2021)

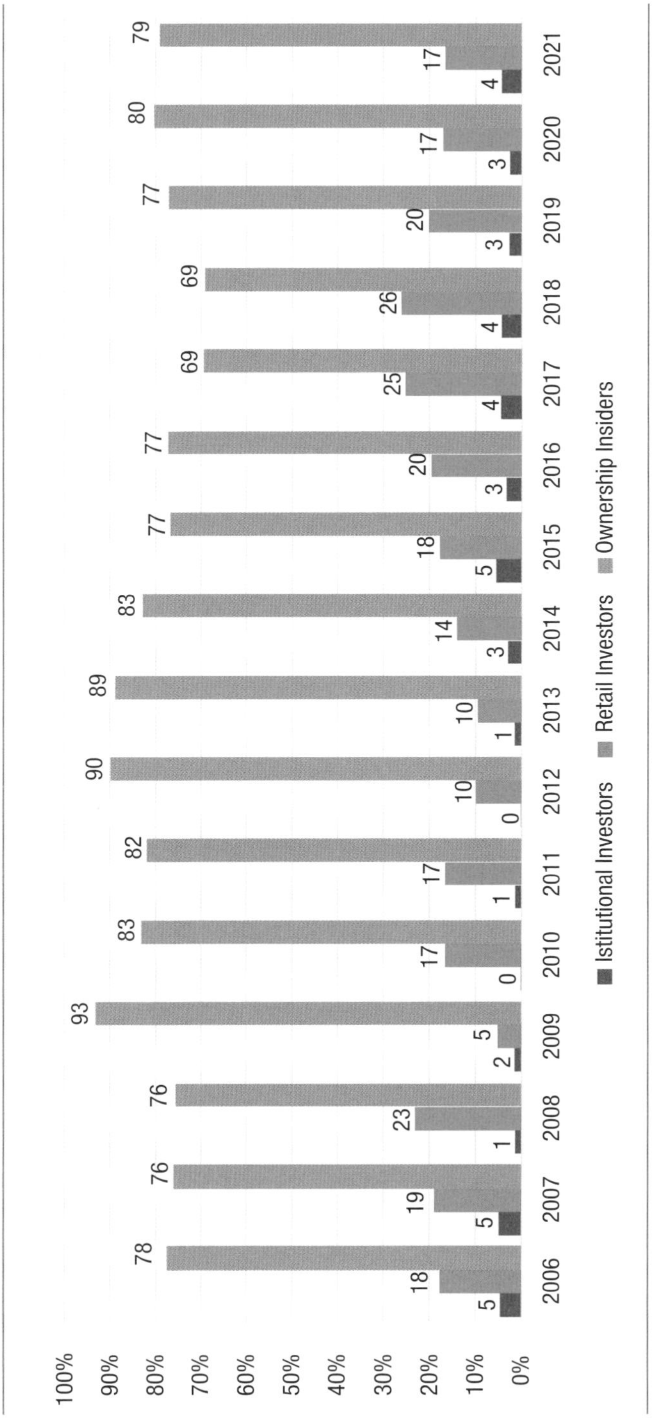

Source: data collected on Bloomberg.

Afterwards, we look at the relative contribution of domestic and foreign institutional investors, retail investors, and insiders/stakeholders to the ownership base across our two groups of companies. **Figure 2.21** shows the proportion of shares held by institutional investors, retail investors, and insiders/stakeholders over time for both Blue Chips and SMEs. Evidence shows that the amounts allocated to each type of investor fluctuate vastly year by year. Although the contribution of insiders and stakeholders to the ownership of Blue Chips and SMEs is fairly stable over time, both Blue Chips and SMEs display the very significant role of insiders in the ownership structure. It follows that both Blue Chips and SMEs are less reluctant to accept outside investors (both foreign and domestic). Institutional investors have a higher presence in the ownership structures of larger companies than of SMEs. On the other hand, SMEs' shares prevalently remain family owned or retailed owned, de facto limiting the number of investors with decision power.

We then examine in more detail institutional holdings. Our aim here is to understand more fully the concentration or dispersion of their stakes in Italian companies, their nationality, and the relative contribution of different categories of institutional investors.

As far as the geographic breakdown of the institutions investing both in Blue Chips and SMEs, **Figure 2.22a** compares the relative contribution of foreign and domestic institutional investors in 2006 and 2021. US investors represented more than 50% of the total institutional holdings, and their share has been abruptly decreasing increasing over time, landing to only 4% in 2021, due to rare and unforeseen market conditions. Interestingly, Italian institutional investors decreased from 13% to 9% over the sample period. The preponderance of foreign institutional investors in the float of Italian companies reflects one of the major fragilities of the system. This calls for a stronger base of domestic investors to step in to reduce the dependence of Italian companies on bank lending and to guarantee the feasibility of strategic operations on equity capital markets such as privatizations.

With regard to the type of institutional investors holding stock in Italian companies in their portfolios over time, **Figure 2.22b** breaks down total holdings across major investors, as classified by Borsa Italiana. Both in 2006 and 2021, the market was dominated by investors following the blended and the growth strategies, but their roles have been

Figure 2.21 **Blue Chips and SMEs ownership: institutional investors, retail investors, and insiders/stakeholders (2006–2021)**

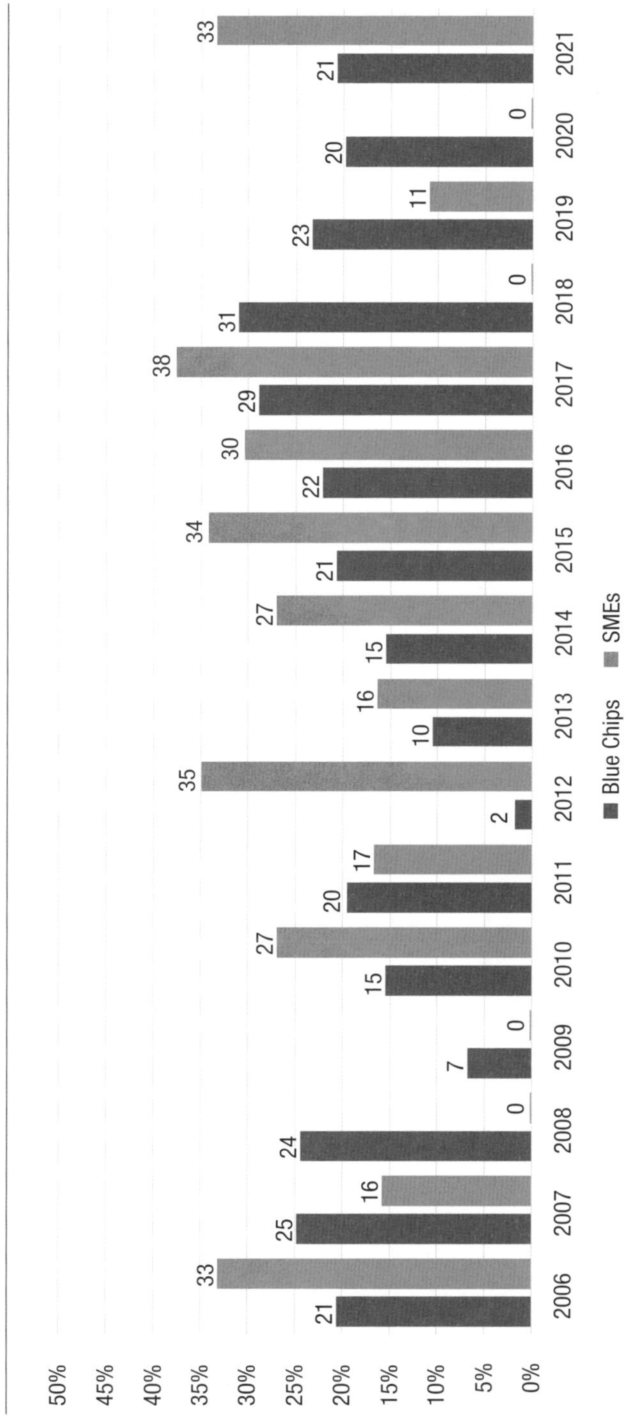

Source: data collected on Bloomberg.

Figure 2.22 Institutional investors in IPO deals, 2006 vs. 2021

(a) Domestic vs. foreign

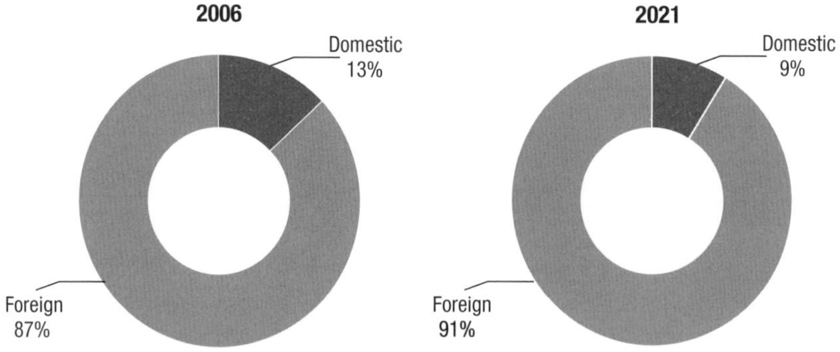

(b) Investment style

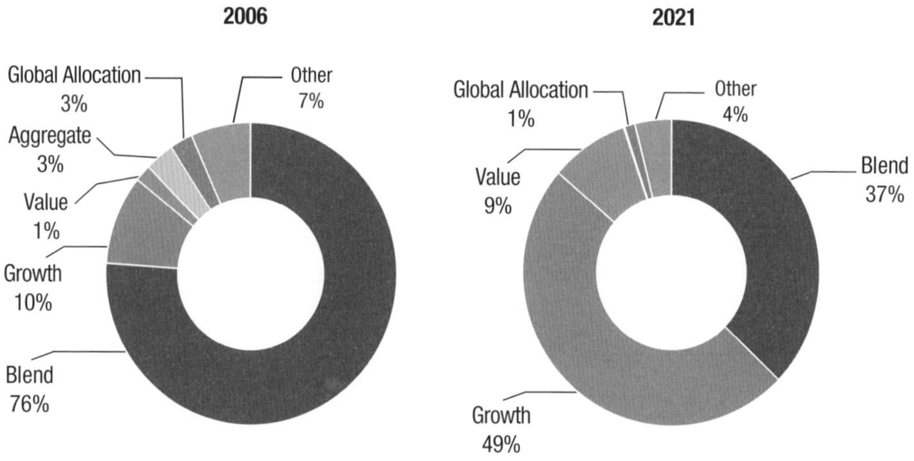

Source: data collected on Bloomberg.

gradually reverted. Indeed, in 2006, investors following the blended strategy accounted for 76% of capital invested and funds operating under the growth strategy covered 10% of the market, while in 2021, they respectively accounted for 37% and 49%. The increased presence of growth investors indicates the belief of investors that companies in the stock exchange face high risk but are rich in potential. Added to this, once more we find striking evidence of the absence of a strong private pension pillar, which limits the Italian institutional investor base.

2.3.3 Investors in debt securities

Analogous inferences can be drawn by looking at newly issued bonds. We consider a sample that includes 565 different bond issues by Italian companies in the period between 2006 and 2018. Our analysis of investor demand for debt securities newly issued by Italian companies focuses on the relative contributions to the book by different groups of investors, classified on the basis of nationality and profile. We retrieved relevant data from Bloomberg.

Figure 2.23 shows the relative contribution to the book building by domestic and foreign investors. Overall, the share of Italian investors is on average just 4% of the investors' base, reflecting the limits of the domestic investment demand and significance. However, a related factor is the inadequacy of the domestic capital market, which has favored the development of foreign markets dominated by large foreign investors. In addition, a closer look at the individual issues shows that access to these markets is restricted only to larger Italian companies. Instead, the majority of medium- and small-sized companies, which are the backbone of the Italian economy, are left out of this form of financing. A significant stream of capital is moved from Luxembourg and the United States, which together represent half of the investment base in Italy. Spain, Ireland, and France combined constitute more than 25% of the demand, stressing the importance of European investors in our country. The UK, Switzerland, Germany, and the Netherlands also cover an important role. Lastly, Asian investors increased their presence in investments in Italian bonds. **Figure 2.24** offers a further insight onto investor demand for new

Figure 2.23 Investors in Italian, French, and German bonds (2006–2018) by investor nationality

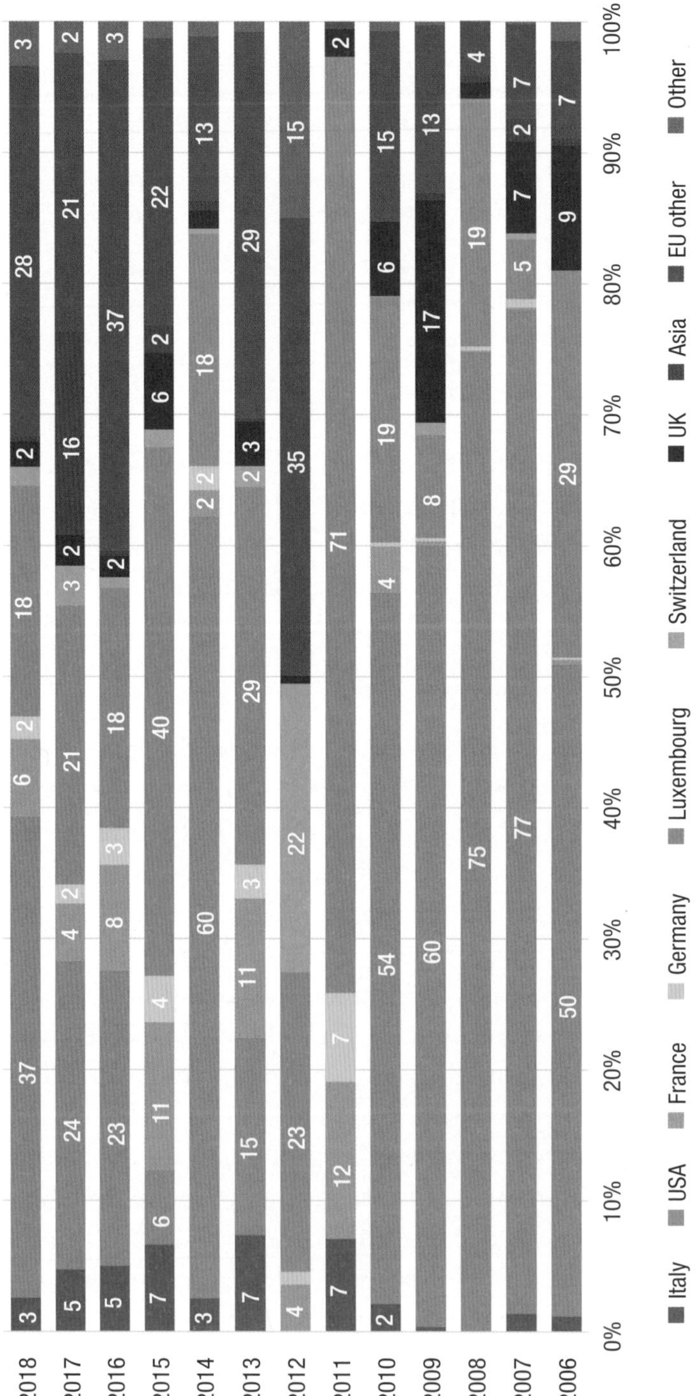

Source: data collected on Bloomberg.

Figure 2.24 Investors in Italian, French, and German bonds (2006–2018) by investor type

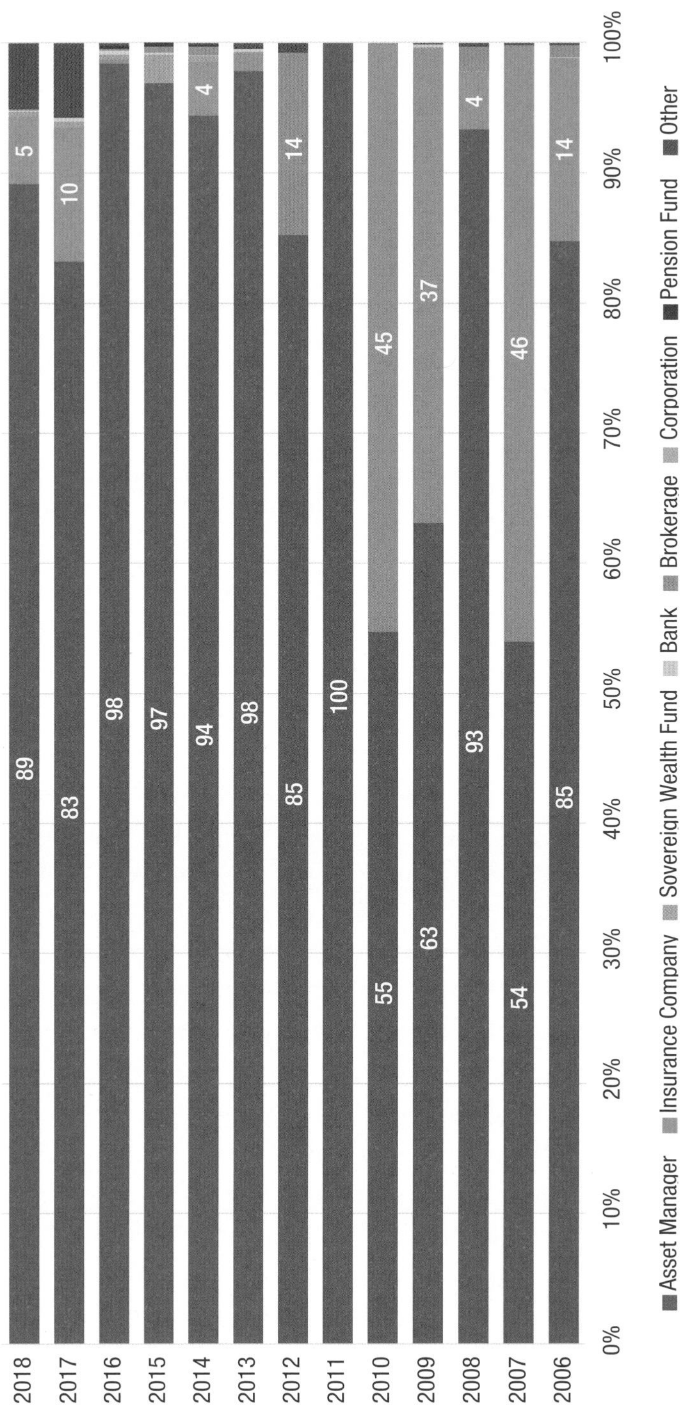

Source: data collected on Bloomberg.

debt securities issued by Italian companies, showing the relative contributions to book building by different types of investors, classified on the basis of their profile. Overall, the breakdown of institutional investors' demand for newly issued debt securities seems to indicate a strong interest in this investment class by asset managers and insurance companies. A loud absence is the one of pension funds, which constitute a tiny percentage of the investor base.

2.4 How Much Does It Pay to Invest in Italian Capital Markets?

2.4.1 Equity securities

In this section, we focus on investments in the stock market. We analyze all firms listed in Borsa Italiana main market and AIM between 2014 and 2021, gathering the financial information on Dealogic. Our sample includes 233 individual firms. As a comparison, we also consider all firms listed in the Deutsche Börse (Frankfurt Stock Exchange) and Paris Euronext, both in the main market and the AIMs. Respectively, we analyze 87 and 146 deals. Approximately, 80% of Italian IPO deals occur on the AIM, compared to 30% of French listings and 10% of German ones. Companies in the field of computers and electronics have been listed all across Europe. Apart from them, in the Italian stock exchange, most underlying companies operate in the field of finance or professional services. Similarly, in Germany, the most targeted industries are finance and automotive. Lastly, French IPO deals often regard companies in healthcare or utilities and energy. Further evidence is displayed in **Figure 2.25a**.

Figure 2.25b reports the breakdown of the stocks we analyzed by size, because of its market capitalization. In Germany, stocks are almost equally divided in small (less than €250 million), lower medium (between €250 and €500 million), upper medium (in the range above €500 million and below €1 billion), and large (more than €1 billion). As a direct consequence of the Italian economic framework, which is based on SMEs and on a more fragmented organization, we see a much higher presence of

Figure 2.25 Stocks listed in Borsa Italiana, Paris Euronext, and Deutsche Börse (2006–2016)

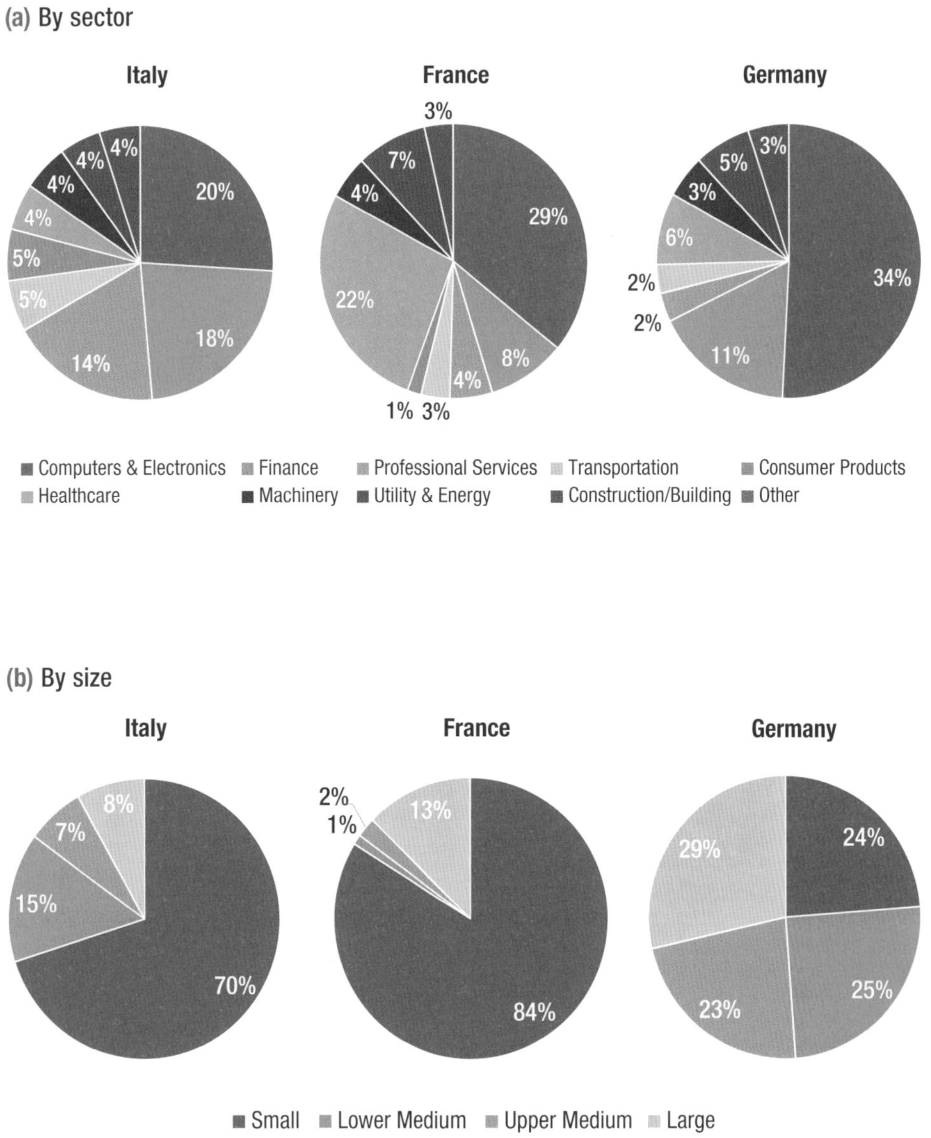

Source: data collected on Bloomberg.

small and lower medium firms in Borsa Italiana. A similar outlook is displayed in the French stock exchange.

Addressing the Italian stock exchange, we are interested in analyzing their performance and, due to the limited size of the sample related to the biggest sizes, upper medium and large, we focus on the differences among industries. We address this question by assigning each stock in our sample to a specific portfolio according to its industry and monitor each portfolio over 2022.

Figures 2.26a and **2.26b** show the absolute and relative performances of the industries that performed better than the overall market, while **Figures 2.27a** and **2.27b** show the absolute and relative performances of the industries that performed worse than the overall market. These performances, however, do not take into account dividend yields, which also varied substantially across industries, whose negative performances would in some cases be mitigated by the dividend yields themselves. Consumer Products, Automotive, and Food & Beverage, the typical excellences of the Italian economy, are among the top performers. The industries in our analysis which displayed the best performance throughout the forecast period exhibit positive growth metrics (CAGR for Sales, EBITDA, and EBIT), persistent deleveraging, and a rising percentage of export sales relative to total sales. However, even for industries with positive returns, profitability measures (EBITDA%, EBIT%, Net Income%, and particularly ROE) have decreased dramatically as a result of the consequences of the economic crisis. At the same time, leisure and recreation, publishing, and machinery showed abrupt negative performances. The extraordinary negative results during the period considered are to be considered relative to the aftermath of the pandemic.

2.4.2 Debt securities

In this section, we focus on investments in corporate debt. We study the yields offered by bonds issued by Italian corporates from 2006 to 2021, as well as the evolution of the credit quality of Italian issuers. Accordingly, we compare them to their French and German counterparts. Then we take a closer look at whether small and medium-sized enterprises (SMEs)

Figure 2.26 Best performing industries with stocks listed in Borsa Italiana, in 2022

(a) Buy and hold returns

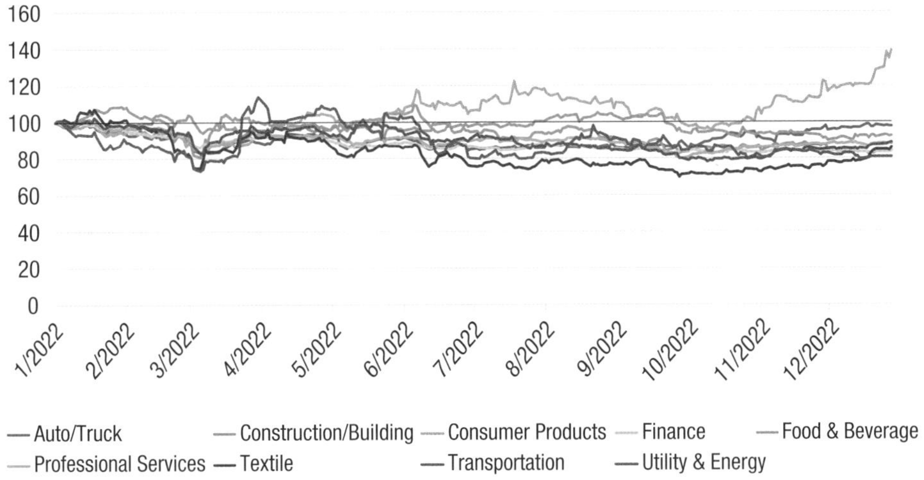

(b) Compound relative returns

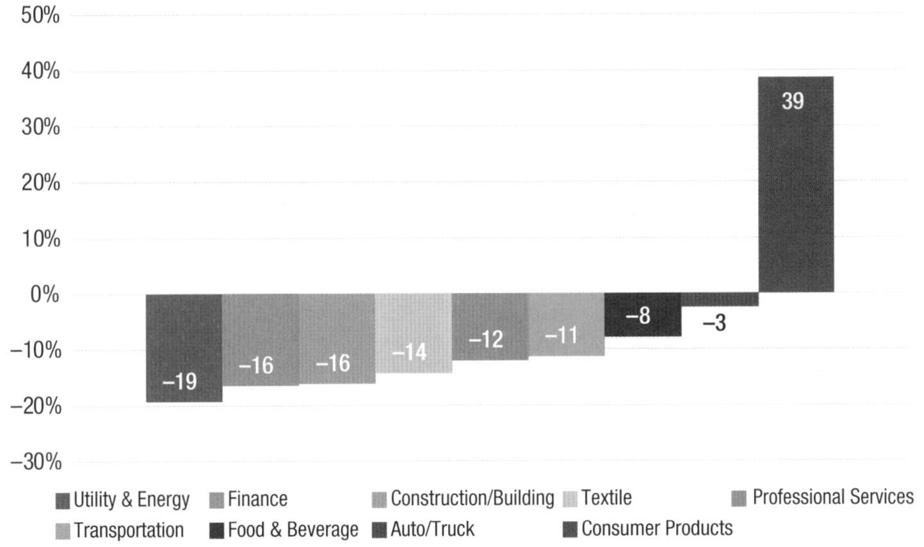

Source: data collected on Refinitiv.

Figure 2.27 Worst performing industries with stocks listed in Borsa Italiana, in 2022

(a) Buy and hold returns

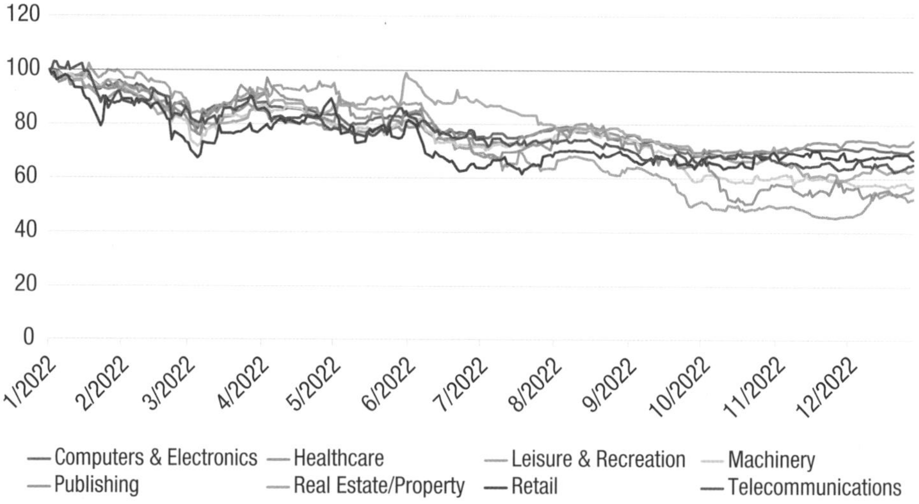

(b) Compound relative returns

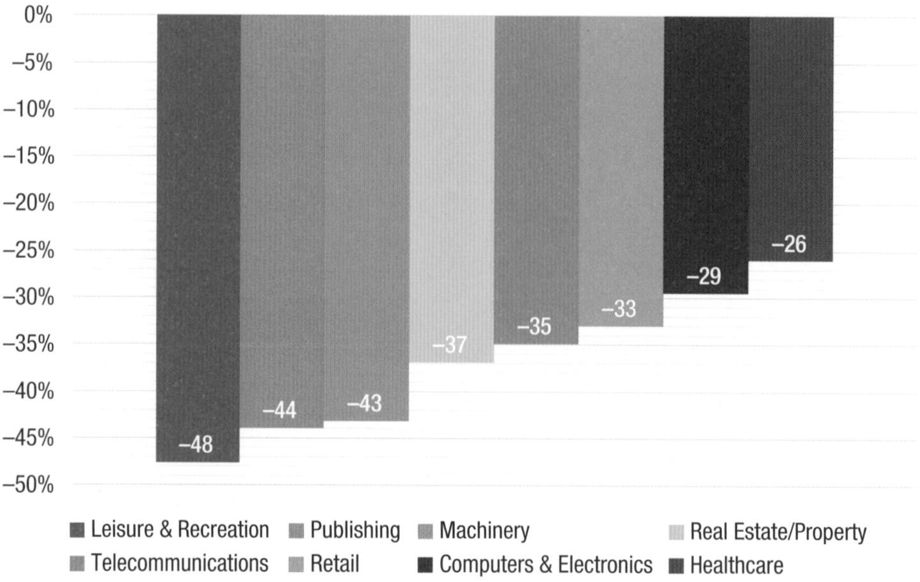

Source: data collected on Refinitiv.

have benefited from improved access to debt capital markets to fill their funding gaps by means of dedicated instruments, such as minibonds.

Since the euro was adopted as the shared currency, the debt financing structure of euro area companies has expanded. While a large portion of corporate debt is still made up of bank loans, euro area businesses are increasingly turning to bond financing, particularly in the wake of the global financial crisis of 2008–2009. As a result, from about 15% in mid-2008, the outstanding volume of bonds in relation to bank borrowing by euro area companies has increased to over 30%. Consequently, during the past 15 years, corporate bond markets have become a more important factor in determining credit conditions in the euro area. While following different drivers, the rise in bond financing has continued during the pandemic (Holm-Hadulla et al., 2022).

Figure 2.28 considers the aggregate of all public issues of debt instruments by Italian companies over the period 2006–2021, with information available on Bloomberg. Our sample includes 4,678 public debt issues by 327 different corporate issuers for a total amount of more than €2,184 billion. Issuers are generally large firms from mature industries. Although the exact proportions vary from year to year, approximately 87% of these bonds are issued by financial companies. The situation differs for France and Germany. In the former, the sample considered includes 5,126 bonds, emitted by 382 different corporate issuers, for a total value of €3,059 billion. As the latter is regarded, 15,683 issues are considered, stemming from 460 corporate issuers, for a total value of €5,668 billion. In France, approximately 65% of bonds are issued by financial companies, while the value reaches 71% in Germany. In Italy, the portion of corporate debt issued by financial companies is higher than both France and Germany.

Figure 2.29 displays the variation in the number of issues per year in Italy, France, and Germany. The range of issues in Italy varies from 493 in 2008 to 148 in 2018, with an average of about 292 issues per year. Typically, the issuers in Italy are large firms from mature industries. In France, the number of issues ranges from 230 in 2008 to 413 in 2020, with an average of about 320 issues per year. On the other hand, in Germany, the range of issues per year fluctuates from 1,608 in 2009 to 752 in 2017, with an average of about 980 issues per year.

Figure 2.28 Corporate bond issuers in Italy, France, Germany (2006–2021): financial vs. non-financial, overall

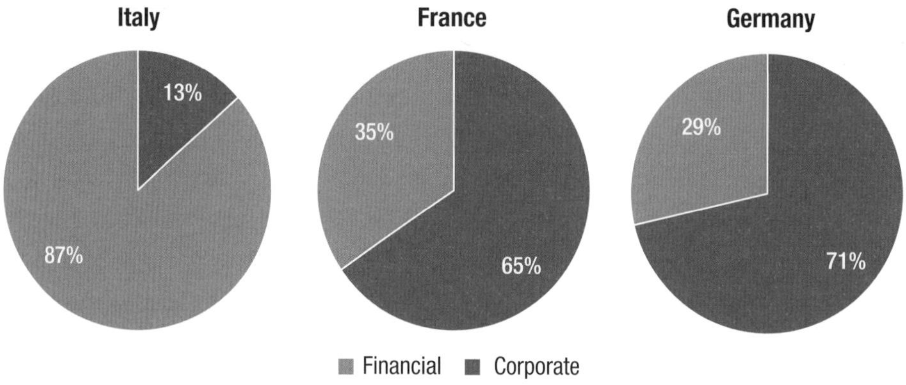

Source: data collected on Bloomberg.

We then focus on the sectorial breakdown of corporate bond issuers in the period between 2006 and 2021. The biggest players operate in the financial industry, while the predominance of sectors other than banking varies from country to country. In Italy, we witness a higher presence of players operating in Utilities and Communications, while in France, the market is dominated by issuers in Consumer Discretionary, Industrials, and Government. Lastly, Germany is similar to France with regard to the high number of issuers in Consumer Discretionary and Industrials, but also sees a higher presence of players operating in Health Care.

Table 2.4 reports the top 10 issuers in terms of total volumes for the period in question. Among them, nine are banks (Intesa Sanpaolo, Unicredit, Banca Monte dei Paschi di Siena, Banca Popolare di Milano, Credit Agricole Italia, UBI Banca, Mediobanca, Banca IMI, and Banca Nazionale del Lavoro). The other issuer is a non-financial firm: Enel, operating in Utilities. The table once again stresses the extraordinary importance of financial issuers in Italy.

With regard to the credit quality of the issues in our sample, **Figures 2.30** and **2.31** show that above 80% are investment grade. It must be noted that the sample sizes to which the following figures refer diminished

Figure 2.29 **Corporate bond issuers in Italy, France, Germany (2006–2021): financial vs. non-financial, by year**

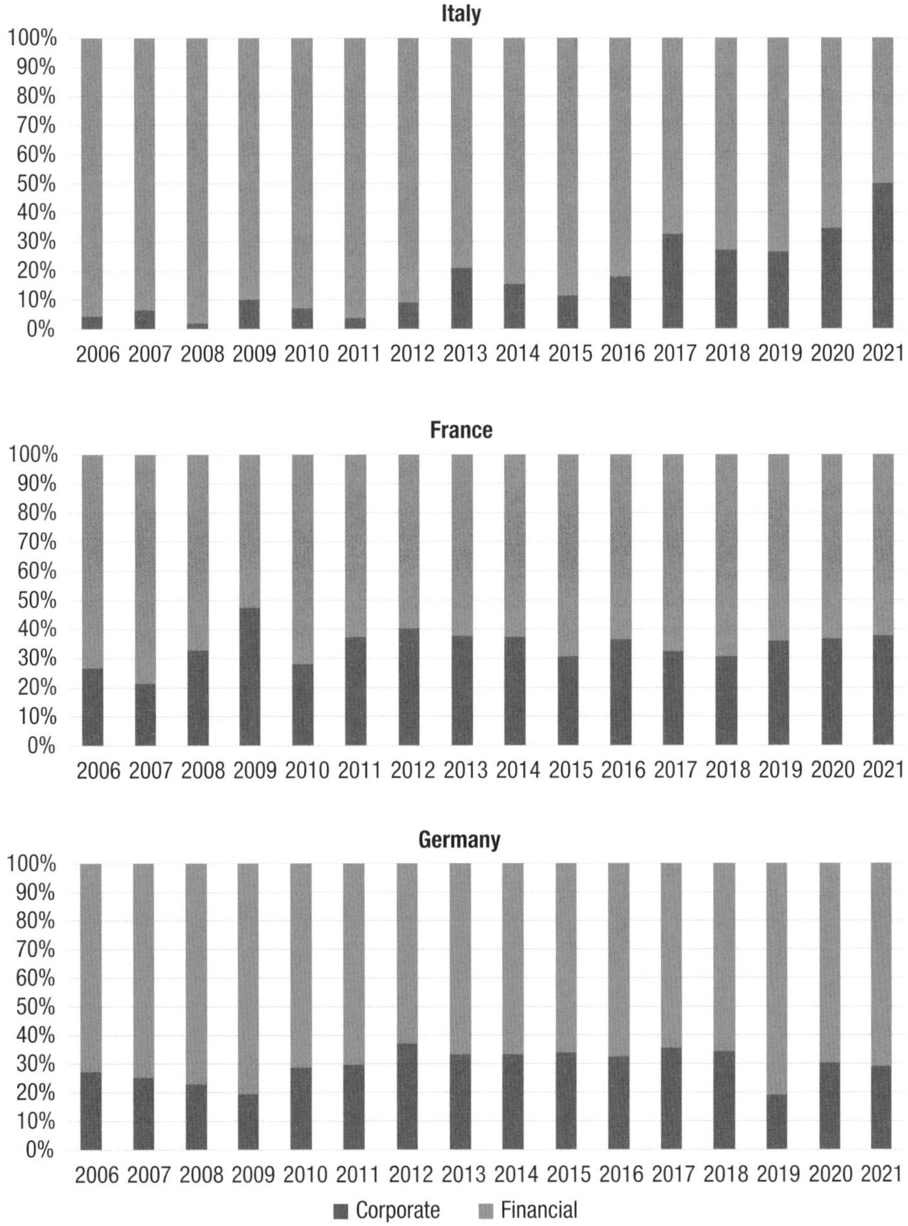

Source: data collected on Bloomberg.

Table 2.4 Italian corporate bond issuers (2006–2021): top 10 issuers by volume

Ranking	Issuer name	Total issue volume (€ billion)
1	Intesa Sanpaolo SpA	448
2	UniCredit SpA	279
3	Banca Monte dei Paschi di Siena SpA	155
4	Banco Popolare SC	86
5	Credit Agricole Italia SpA	81
6	Enel Finance International NV	71
7	Unione di Banche Italiane SpA	68
8	Mediobanca Banca di Credito Finanziario SpA	64
9	Banca IMI SpA	56
10	Banca Nazionale del Lavoro SpA	52

Source: data collected on Bloomberg.

Figure 2.30 Corporate bond issues in Italy, France, and Germany (2006–2021): rating at issue, overall

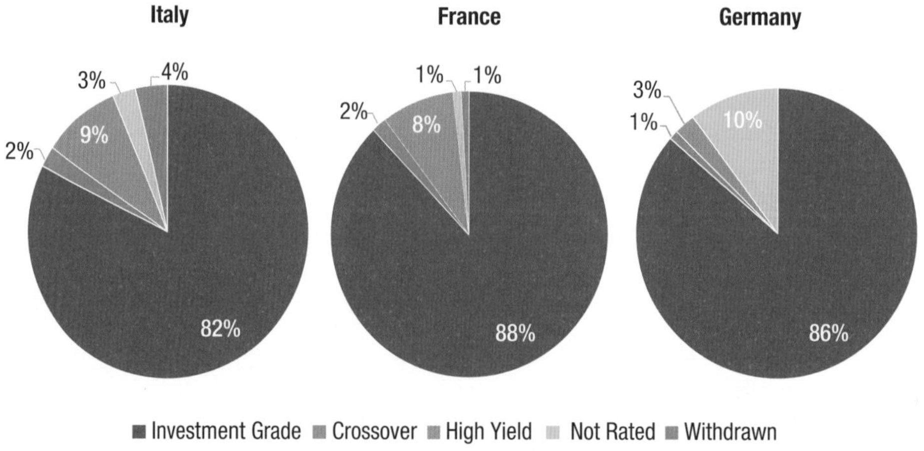

Source: data collected on Bloomberg.

Figure 2.31 Corporate bond issues in Italy, France, and Germany (2006–2021): rating at issue, by year

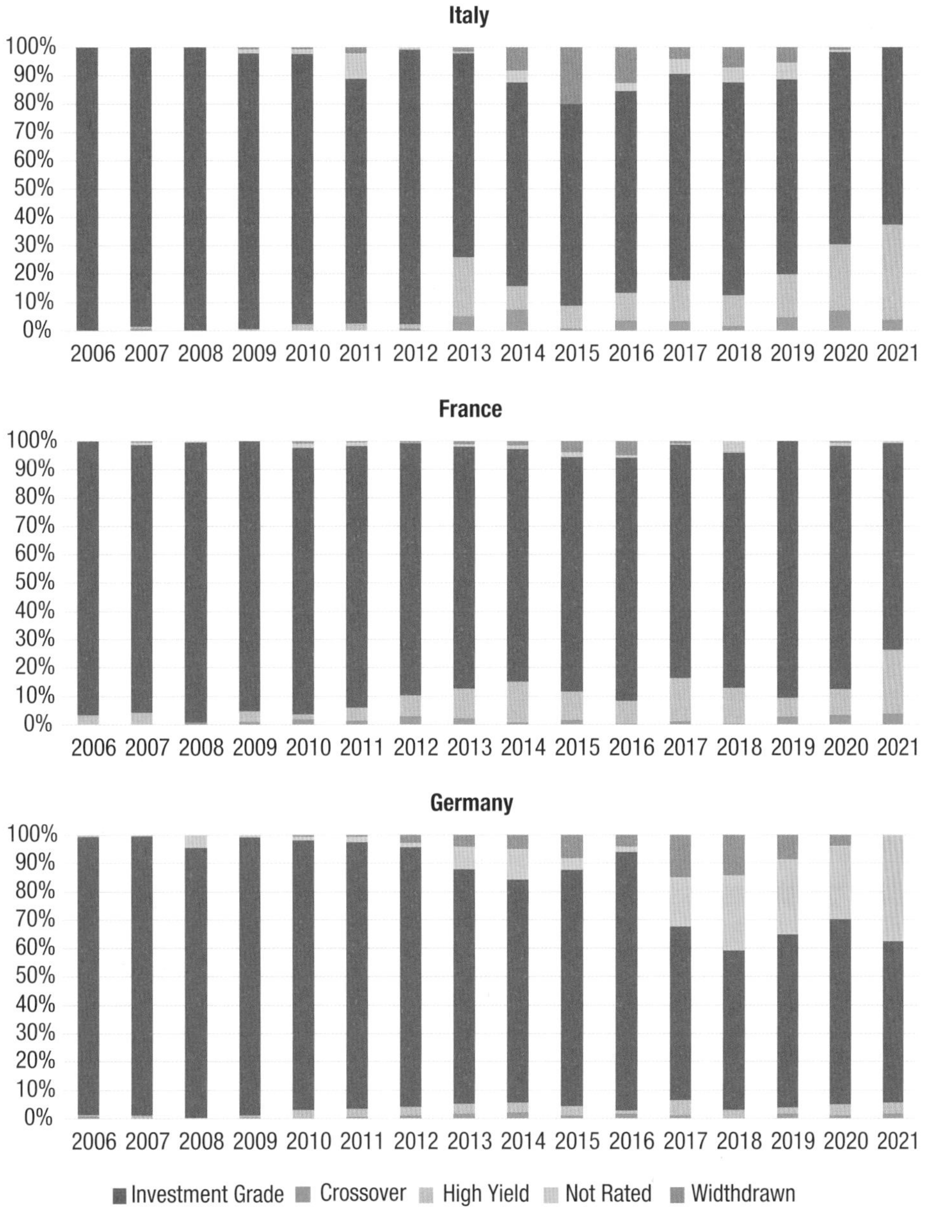

Source: data collected on Bloomberg.

substantially, in accordance with the availability of data regarding the rating at issue. The new sample sizes are 2,298, 4,323, and 12,568 corresponding to Italy, France, and Germany, respectively. In Italy and France, less than 10% have a high-yield rating and their relevance varies significantly over time. Indeed, high-yield issues started raising around 2013, when the sovereign debt crisis took over Europe and quantitative easing was established, and kept their pace, increasing steadily. This trend is common across Europe and is facilitated by the progressive narrowing of the yield spread between high-yield and investment grade issues, which occurred between 2011 and 2020. This is the outcome, on the one hand, of an increased demand of high-yield bonds by yield starving investors. When, on the other hand, sub-investment grade issuers more frequently turned to market-based sources of debt in response to the bank credit crunch following the sovereign debt crisis. In Germany, large bulks of high-yield issues never took place, and their role is substituted by non-rated issues.

Finally, **Table 2.5** reports some comparative statistics on the issues in our sample, classified according to issuer types and classes of rating. The issue average size does not vary significantly among countries or types of issues, apart from the German market, in which the corporate issues are three times the financial issues. On average, corporate issues have longer maturities than financial issues. The French issues display the longest maturities, and generally the three countries display very diverse maturities according to the rating. However, it is interesting to note that high-yield issues have similar time to maturity across countries, averaging around six years.

How has corporate debt performed as an asset class?

In order to answer this question, we assess the performance of corporate debt in light of the initial effective yields provided by the bonds in our sample. Our goal is to achieve the returns experienced by investors who purchased these bonds on the day of issue with the intention of holding them until maturity and reinvesting all of the proceeds. We first evaluate the performance of corporate debt as an asset class before segmenting it based on the different categories of issuers and rating classes.

Table 2.5 **Italian, French, and German corporate bond issues (2006–2021): summary statistics**

Italian corporate bond issues	Total number of issuers	Total issue volume (€ million)	Average issue size (€ million)	Average time to maturity (years)
All samples	2,298	1,349.5	587.2	6.2
Corporate	534	345.5	647.0	8.9
Financial	1,764	1,004.0	569.2	5.3
Investment Grade	1,892	1,194.8	631.5	6.2
High Yield	210	89.7	426.9	6.2
Withdrawn	84	18.9	225.1	3.7
Not Rated	59	16,726.7	283.5	5.7
Crossover	53	29,346.8	553.7	8.9

French corporate bond issues	Total number of issuers	Total issue volume (€ million)	Average issue size (€ million)	Average time to maturity (years)
All samples	4,323	2,805.5	649.0	7.6
Corporate	1,540	940.3	610.6	8.2
Financial	2,783	1,865.1	670.2	7.2
Investment Grade	3,802	2,567.7	675.4	7,.6
High Yield	366	182.1	497.5	6.5
Withdrawn	39	7.1	181.3	12.0
Not Rated	41	9.4	228.1	14.4
Crossover	75	39.3	523.4	6.4

German corporate bond issues	Total number of issuers	Total issue volume (€ million)	Average issue size (€ million)	Average time to maturity (years)
All samples	12,568	5,197.9	413.6	6.6
Corporate	4,193	3,183.5	759.2	7.1
Financial	8,375	2,014.4	240.5	6.4
Investment Grade	10,432	4,804.0	460.5	6.3
High Yield	296	134.2	453.5	6.8
Withdrawn	124	54.3	114.2	8.4
Not Rated	1,240	141.4	114.0	9.0
Crossover	124	63.9	515.6	7.8

Source: data collected on Bloomberg.

Due to the unprecedented monetary policy measures implemented throughout the sample period, the yield for corporate bonds as an asset class generally declined. This is in line with the general trend throughout Europe. In fact, corporate loan rates fell to historically low levels across all issuer types and credit categories (**Figure 2.32** and **2.33**, respectively). Throughout the time frame we looked at, business issuers offered greater yields than financial issuers, which reflected investors' anticipation of bank bailouts. Between 2008 and 2010, when investors learned about an implicit safety net as troubled banks in numerous European nations were rescued in a concerted public effort, the disparity between the yields of non-financial and financial issuers grew significantly. Indeed, due to the troubled situation, the gap is much more significant in Italy than in France or Germany. Only around 2011–2014, as a result of the crisis in sovereign debt, the rise in non-performing loans, and the passage of the new European Bank Recovery and Resolution Directive, has this spread shrunk. While the first two variables indicated a higher chance of financial trouble for banks, the latter increasingly shifted the expense of potential bank distress on loan holders (bail-in). More recently, both corporate and financial issuers' yields started increasing again, due to the unstable situation created by the pandemic.

Additionally, as spotted in **Figure 2.33**, as a result of quantitative easing, the yield differential between high-yield and investment grade issues dramatically decreased, which is consistent with the general trend at the European level. Once more, two causes may be attributed to this result: Investors' increased appetite for high-yield bonds and sub-investment grade issuers' increased demand for market-based sources of funding in the wake of the bank credit constraint brought on by the sovereign debt crisis. The yields started diverging again in 2020, as a consequence of the uncertainty dictated by the pandemic.

In an attempt to shed light on the extent of the repercussions of the extraordinarily situation driven by the pandemic on the returns of investors in corporate debt, we take a closer look at investment grade issues in 2021 by Italian, French, and German non-financial firms with maturities ranging from 5 to 10 years. In particular, we compare the average total return offered by 21 bonds by Italian issuers, from their

Figure 2.32 Italian, French, and German corporate bond issues (2006–2021): average effective yields for different issuer types

Source: data collected on Bloomberg.

Figure 2.33 Italian, French, and German corporate bond issues (2006–2021): average effective yields for different rating classes

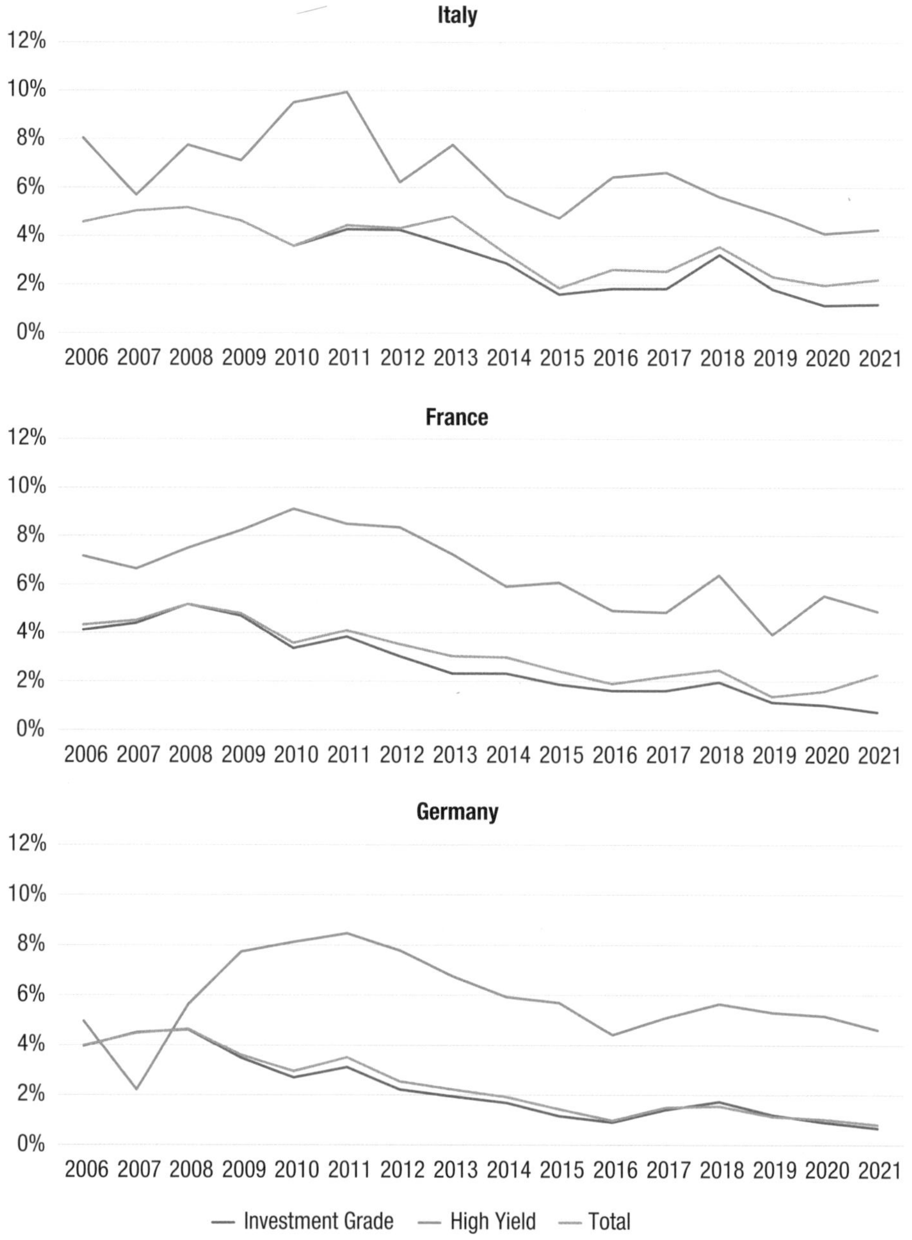

Source: data collected on Bloomberg.

Figure 2.34 2021 issuers: average total return of investment grade corporate bonds (5–10 year maturity) by Italian, French, and German non-financial firms

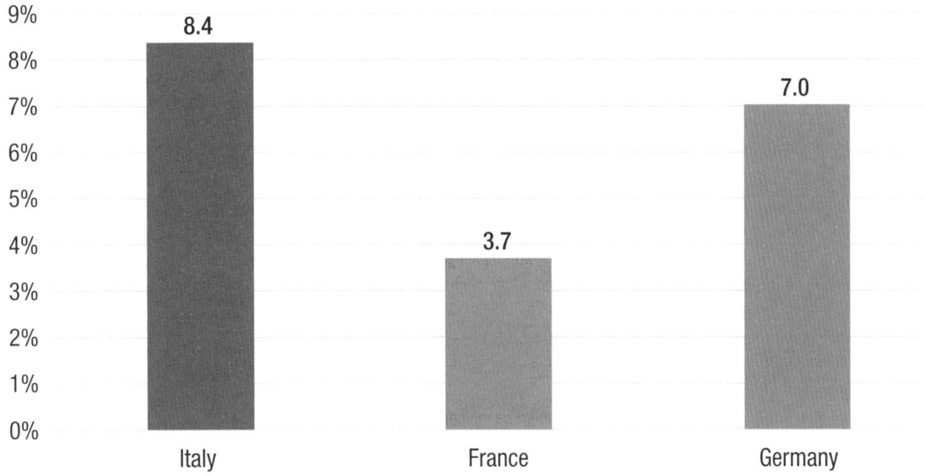

Source: data collected on Bloomberg.

issue date up to the end of 2021, with returns on 73 German and 17 French issues. Figure 2.34 shows that, in absolute terms, the total returns generated by Italian corporate debt were higher than those of French and German firms.

Specifically, investors focusing on investment grade issues by Italian non-financial firms in 2021 with 5–10 years maturities would have achieved on average an 8.4% total return. Instead, investors who opted for similar issues by French or German companies would have obtained 3.7% and 7.0%, respectively. All corporate debt has been especially appealing to investors in light of relative performances with respect to domestic sovereign issues, offering on average total returns that were higher than domestic government bonds.

2.5 Conclusions

The analysis of the Italian IPO market reveals a number of key trends and structural differences compared to other European markets such as Germany and France. First, Borsa Italiana accounts for a significant proportion of the total number of IPOs in the period between 2006 and 2021, representing 50% of the total. However, it only represents 26% of aggregate IPO volume. This suggests that the Italian market is characterized by smaller deal sizes compared to other European markets, and it is in line with the country's economic framework and the structural differences across Italian, French, and German markets.

Similarly, the AIM plays a significant role in the Italian IPO scene, accounting for 82% of transactions and approximately 19% of IPO volume. This is a higher proportion compared to France, where it represents 30% of IPO flow and 3% of IPO volume, and Germany where it collects, respectively, the 12% of the newly listed companies and the 4% of the IPO volume. This highlights that the Italian AIM market is more active compared to other European markets. Furthermore, the Italian AIM market is also more underpriced than its main market counterpart. It seems that shares are offered at a discount due to information problems and, in some cases, also due to a lack of liquidity. However, overpricing occurs too, making the AIMs generally more mispriced than the main market. This issue is common in comparable countries, such as Germany and France, but it seems to be less evident in Italy than abroad.

The Italian IPO market is mainly dominated by funds headquartered abroad, while only the 9% of funds are in Italy. Foreign funds are mostly located in Luxembourg (39%), the United States (29%), and the UK (9%). European countries (Italy and Luxembourg excluded) covered the 12% of invested funds. Only when deals are limited and their size is small, the proportion of shares allocated to Italian investors grows. As a consequence, when IPO volume and deal size picks up, foreign investors take the lead. Indeed, the presence of foreign investors compared to Italian investors is more significant in deals supporting larger companies (91%) compared to smaller ones (77%).

Taking into account both the domestic vs. foreign investors division and the institutional vs. retail comparison in newly issued stock, it seems that the major limit to the domestic investment base can be found in the lack of a solid institutional pillar. Our analysis also confirms the lack of a large private pension investment pillar in Italy, which currently contributes only residually to institutional demand. As such, this represents a huge unexploited potential as well as a drag on the full development of the domestic equity market. Furthermore, from the network analysis of IPOs in Italy in 2020 and 2021, it emerged that the most connected investors are not the ones that invested the highest amounts, but rather the ones that invested smaller amounts in many different companies. Conversely, the companies that attracted the highest numbers of investors were the ones that raised the highest amount of capital in IPO.

Additionally, the market is dominated by investors following the growth and the blended and strategies but, during the considered period (2006–2021), their significance reversed, ending with a dominance of the former. Indeed, in 2006, investors following the blended strategy accounted for 76% of capital invested and funds operating under the growth strategy covered 10% of the market, while in 2021, they, respectively, accounted for 37% and 49%. The increased presence of growth investors indicates the belief of investors that companies in the stock exchange face high risk but are rich in potential.

The limits of domestic investment demand are reflected also in the Italian debt market: The share of Italian debt investors averages only 4% of the investor base. The inadequacy of the domestic capital market has favored the attraction of a significant stream of capital from Luxembourg and the United States, which together represent half of the investment base in Italy. In Italy, high-yield issues have been increasing steadily since 2015, peaking in 2021, when they accounted for approximately one-third of the issues. The trend is common across Europe. Moreover, in Italy as well as in Europe, the differential between investment grade and high-yield issues has been decreasing steadily between 2011 and 2020, and only since 2020 it started diverting again. While the former trend is mainly due to quantitative easing policies, investors' increased appetite for high-yield bonds and sub-investment grade issuers' increased demand for market-based sources of funding, the latter is a consequence of the increase in uncertainty due to the pandemic.

References

AIFI (2022). *Annuario del private equity, venture capital e private debt 2022*. Bancaria Editrice.

Bajo, E., Chemmanur, T.J., Simonyan, K., & Tehranian, H. (2016). Underwriter networks, investor attention, and initial public offerings. *Journal of Financial Economics*, 122(2), 376–408. https://doi.org/10.1016/j.jfineco.2015.12.001

Banca d'Italia (2022). *Annual report for 2021*. Available at: bancaditalia.it.

Bonanno, G., Caldarelli, G., Lillo, F., Micciché, S., Vandewalle, N., & Mantegna, R.N. (2004). Networks of equities in financial markets. *The European Physical Journal B*, 38(2), 363–371. https://doi.org/10.1140/epjb/e2004-00129-6

Cappiello, L., Holm-Hadulla, F., Maddaloni, A., Mayordomo, S., & Unger, R. (2021). *Non-bank financial intermediation in the euro area: Implications for monetary policy transmission and key vulnerabilities*. ECB Occasional Paper Series, No. 270. Available at: ecb.europa.eu.

Caselli, S., Gatti, S., Chiarella, C., & Gigante, G. (2017). *Does investing in Italian capital markets pay? The past decade perspective*. Bocconi University BAFFI-CAREFIN Centre, Position Paper. Available at: equitalab.eu.

CONSOB (2022). *Annual report 2021*. Available at: consob.it.

Fitch (2016). *EMEA capital market monitor*. Credit Market Research.

Garlaschelli, D., Battiston, S., Castri, M., Servedio, V.D.P., & Caldarelli, G. (2004). The scale-free topology of market investments. *Physica A: Statistical Mechanics and its Applications*, 350(2–4), 491–499. https://doi.org/10.1016/j.physa.2004.11.040

Holm-Hadulla, F., Musso, A., Nicoletti, G., & Tujula, M. (2022). *Firm debt financing structures and the transmission of shocks in the euro area*. ECB Economic Bulletin, 4/2022. Available at: ecb.europa.eu.

Mediobanca (2019a). *Calepino dell'azionista*. Available at: areastudimediobanca.com.

Mediobanca (2019b). *Indices and data on investments in listed securities*. Available at: areastudimediobanca.com.

Preqin (2022). *2022 Preqin global private debt report*.

Prometeia (2014). *Loans and private debt funds: Products features and market trends*.

Société Générale (2016). *Banking on negative rates*. Cross Asset Research.

3 Capital Markets Issuers: Equity Securities

by *Carlo Chiarella*
CUNEF Universidad

The bond between corporate financing and growth is well established in the finance literature. In particular, well-developed equity capital markets are at the cornerstone of economic growth. They provide firms with the funds they need for investment. They allow investors to diversify and share risk. They reduce information asymmetries among investors by enhancing information transfer and processing, and they discipline management, thereby mitigating agency conflicts for shareholders.

It is a broadly shared opinion that one of the key factors contributing to the fragility of the Italian economy is the undercapitalization of its companies with respect to their European counterparts. In particular, the high level of leverage that is typical of Italian companies, represents a crucial weakness of the system. One that amplifies the impact of adverse macroeconomic shocks. As a consequence, standing on relatively less robust legs, the Italian economy often ends up more severely affected by adverse economic shocks than other countries.

Therefore, the process of strengthening the Italian economy must necessarily pass through the development of equity capital markets to help companies raise the funds they need to rebalance their capital structure by increasing their capitalization, to grow their size, and to free their full potential. Equity capital, in fact, favors investments in innovation and R&D, as well as the attraction and retention of talent.

Considering the above arguments and given the importance of bringing together companies and equity capital, this chapter offers a comprehensive analysis of the Italian market for equity capital, with a special focus on IPOs, the motivations behind the listing process of Italian issuers and their shareholders' base. The remainder of the chapter is organized as follows. As a starting point for the discussion, the next section introduces the financing needs and the capital structure preferences of Italian companies. Then, a complete overview of key trends in equity capital offerings is provided, including a detailed description of the issuers. This is followed by the discussion of why Italian companies go public and their ownership characteristics. Final remarks and policy recommendations conclude the chapter.

3.1 The Capital Structure and Financing Needs of Italian Companies

Italian companies come in different sizes and operate in different sectors. Nevertheless, the way in which they collect financial resources and finance their operations is not indifferent to their growth and robustness, especially in the case of the smallest ones. In this respect, two fundamental forces are at play when weighing corporate funding decisions and alternative sources of financing. On the one hand, there is equity capital that is seen as a form of protection against adverse events and prevention of default. On the other hand, there is the tax advantage of debt that stems from the deductibility of interest expenses.

At the international level, the European Union considers capital markets and market-based corporate finance as the key for the relaunch of the economy and has dedicated more and more attention to strengthen capital market circuits, with a special focus on small and medium-sized firms (SMEs).[1] Nonetheless, in Italy, the overwhelming dominance of traditional bank lending has made companies, particularly SMEs, especially dependent on bank lending as their primary form of financing.

[1] Two examples are the High-Level Forum on the Capital Markets Union launched in 2020, and the Technical Expert Stakeholder Group on SMEs constituted in 2021. Their recommendations indicate a number of policy and regulatory/supervisory actions useful to increase the financial flexibility of European firms and to reform European capital markets to make them more functional for the relaunch of the Eurozone economy.

More specifically, **Figure 3.1** provides some insight on the funding preferences of Italian companies by comparing across major European economies the total debt to equity of domestic non-financial firms, and the total credit they receive from the banking sector as a percentage of GDP. The picture that emerges from this comparison suggest that companies in Italy are less capitalized and can only partially rely on bank finance to fill their funding gap. While Italian companies are the most indebted, bank credit supply in Italy is lower than in Germany or France. This makes the system intrinsically vulnerable. It ties, in fact, the investment and production capacities of Italian companies to the health of the banking sector and vice versa.

Exacerbating the dependence on bank lending and the lack of flexibility in terms of sources of financing, many of the relief measures set up by the government to alleviate the heavy economic effects of the first wave of the COVID-19 pandemic concentrated on traditional bank lending, further eroding companies' equity base. This is, for example, the case of moratoria

Figure 3.1 **Corporate funding preferences across major European economies**

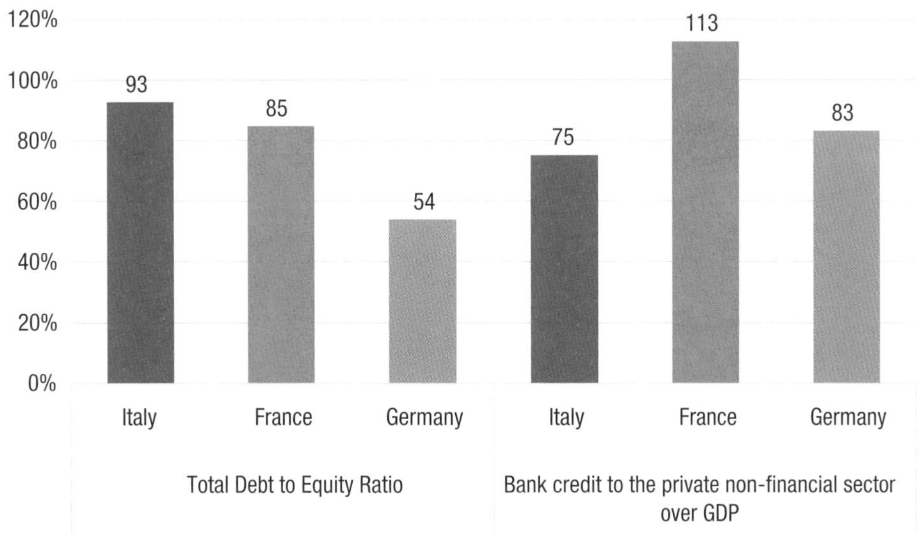

Source: FRED and Bank of International Settlements.

on maturing debt, or State guarantees to banks extending new financing to corporations. In the immediate term, the use of the banking channel ensures vital support to many companies, but in the short to medium term, an increase in corporate indebtedness can lead to higher default risk (Crouzet & Tourre, 2021) and can be a deterrent of investment (Hennessy et al., 2007; Demmou et al., 2021) and a drag on economic growth (Kalemli-Ozcan et al., 2018; Brunnermeier & Krishnamurthy, 2020). Indeed, with monetary policy keeping interest rates at historic rock bottom levels for a prolonged period, the nonfinancial corporate debt over GDP in the euro area rose at 111.2% in 2021 (see **Figure 3.2**).

This high level of corporate debt by historical standards also poses risks to the financial system. If credit risk is not properly priced, banks, governments, and investors will be left exposed should the viability of the borrowers be challenged by unexpected adverse shocks. Indeed, AFME (2021) estimates that €324 billion of the debt in the EU is unsustainable, of which 57% is attributable to SMEs. The resulting equity gap according

Figure 3.2 Corporate debt as a percentage of GDP

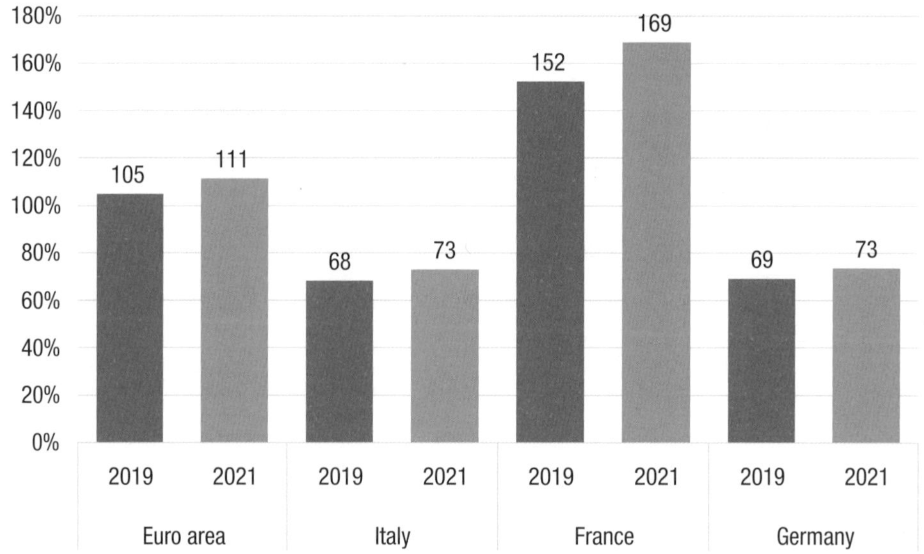

Source: Bank of International Settlements.

to AFME is around €1 trillion, or 2–3% of the European gross domestic product according to similar estimates by Ebeke et al. (2021).

Tackling the risks associated with this mounting debt burden is an onerous task. Italian companies need to strengthen their financial profile, relying more on equity capital funding to achieve more robust capital structures that ensure both the liquidity necessary for immediate survival and the appropriate solidity to grow with minor risks. This requires a determined and capillary action of capitalization. In one of the first studies that tried to quantify the impact of COVID-19 lockdown measures on firm leverage and possible financial distress in a large sample of Italian companies, Carletti et al. (2020) estimate an equity shortfall of approximately €117 billion, or about 7% of GDP. According to their forecasts, overcoming just the equity shortfall of only financially distressed companies with negative book value of equity would require an equity injection of at least €31 billion. This is in line with more recent estimates by Caselli et al. (2022b) showing that at least €14 billion of the outstanding debt of Italian companies is unsustainable and needs restructuring, and that the additional equity capital required to rebalance the capital structure of Italian companies in financial distress in line with a B-credit rating is about €36.8 billion.

Unfortunately, the current development of equity capital markets in Italy, notwithstanding recent fiscal and legislative efforts, sharply contrasts with the central role this market should have. The role that listed companies have in terms of overall impact on the economic system is limited, as shown in **Table 3.1**. According to Caselli et al. (2022a), there were only 377 companies listed on Borsa Italiana in 2020, compared to 905 companies listed on Euronext Paris, and 495 listed on Deutsche Börse. Their market capitalization accounted for 36.7% of the country's GDP, significantly less than in Germany or France where listed companies accounted for 55.5% and 131.5%, respectively. The comparison suggests that fewer Italian companies decide to go public than in Germany or France, and that their stock market capitalization as a percentage of GDP is the lowest among the countries considered. While the gap with France may be explained by the bank centrism of the Italian corporate funding model compared to the more market-oriented French economy, it is important

Table 3.1 **The contribution of listed companies to the economy**

Country	Number of listed companies in domestic stock exchange	Market capitalization of listed companies as a % of GDP	Total revenue of listed companies as a % of GDP	Listed companies' contribution to the domestic tax revenue	Listed companies' contribution to domestic workforce	Listed companies' share of investments from abroad	Listed companies' share of trademarks
Italy	377	36.7	30.9	47.2	5.4	6.6	7.2
Germany	495	55.5	61.7	40.1	15.3	8.3	15.7
France	905	131.3	78.0	71.9	30.5	31.0	21.1

All data are for 2020, except for the contribution to taxes that refers to 2019.

Source: Caselli et al. (2022a).

to note that Italy lags far behind Germany that also relies mostly on bank finance. A similar pattern is observable for companies' revenues, which account for 30.9% of GDP in Italy, 61.7% in Germany, and 78% in France. Italian listed companies contribute to about half of the domestic tax revenue, but they account for only 5.4% of the country's workforce, attract only 6.6% of investments directed to Italy from abroad, and control only 7.2% of the domestic trademarks.

The underdevelopment of the Italian equity markets has deep repercussions on the structure of the country's business environment, which is populated by small and micro family-owned firms. If we look at the Fortune 500 ranking, in 2021, only six Italian companies made the cut, one half of which are financial intermediaries (i.e., Assicurazioni Generali, Banca Intesa, and Unicredit) and the other half are companies developed within the public system (i.e., ENI, ENEL, and Poste Italiane). In 2011, Italy had 10 companies in the ranking and 8 in 2001. These numbers are not only a long way from the United States and China but also form other major European economies: 27 companies in Germany, 16 in France, and 9 in Spain.

According to the latest available census of businesses conducted by ISTAT in 2019, 99.5% of Italian firms have less than 50 employees and most companies do not employ more than 5 people. Moreover, these firms employ more than two-thirds of the entire workforce. Over 70% of firms are family-owned and have a highly concentrated ownership structure, with the largest shareholder controlling approximately 70% of the company, on average, and the top three shareholders controlling more than 93%. This is reflected in the composition of corporate boards, where 56% of appointed directors are family members when the company is fully owned by the family, and 48% otherwise.

3.2 Equity Capital Markets Funding: Key Trends

In the period going from 2006 to 2021, Italian companies have raised on Borsa Italiana €38.2 billion on 335 IPOs, €140.4 billion on 477 follow-on offerings, and €25.7 billion on 70 convertible offerings, for an aggregate amount of €204.3 billion on 882 deals. At the end of the period, the market capitalization of Italian companies totaled €757 billion, standing at 43% of GDP. **Figure 3.3** breaks down deal flow by year, in terms of aggregate deal value and number of offerings. Not surprisingly, equity offerings are cyclical, closely tracking the ups and downs of market conditions.

A closer look at the structure of the market in **Figure 3.4** reveals that follow-on offerings, which include mainly rights issues, but also accelerated book-buildings (ABB), bought deals and fully marketed deals, prevail over IPOs and convertible offerings both in terms of number of deals and deal value. In particular, follow-on offerings account for 54.1% of the number of deals and 68.7% of their aggregate value. By comparison, IPOs, which account for 38% of the number of deals, only contribute to 18.7% of the aggregate offering value. This suggests that the Italian equity market is dominated mostly by already listed-firm and is less appealing for not-yet-listed firms that may not reach the critical mass necessary to access capital markets, or that may be more reluctant to allow outside investments and acquiescence to market discipline.

In line with this argument, new admissions have been bleak also in 2022. Borsa Italiana registered 20 new admissions down from 49 in 2021: only four of them on the Euronext Milan and all the others on the Euronext Growth Milan.[2] Addressing this problem, by promoting both capital markets and market-based corporate finance, is the main objective of a specific task force that has been set up under the coordination of the Italian Minister for Economy and Finance, as discussed in the introduction of this book. Its first step in this direction has been the publication of the *Green Book on the Competitiveness of the Italian Capital Markets as a Support*

---

[2] Following the sale of Borsa Italiana by the London Stock Exchange Group and its inclusion in Euronext, since 2021 the MTA and AIM markets have been relabeled Euronext Milan and Euronext Growth, respectively.

Figure 3.3 **Italian equity capital markets annual deal volumes (2006–2021)**

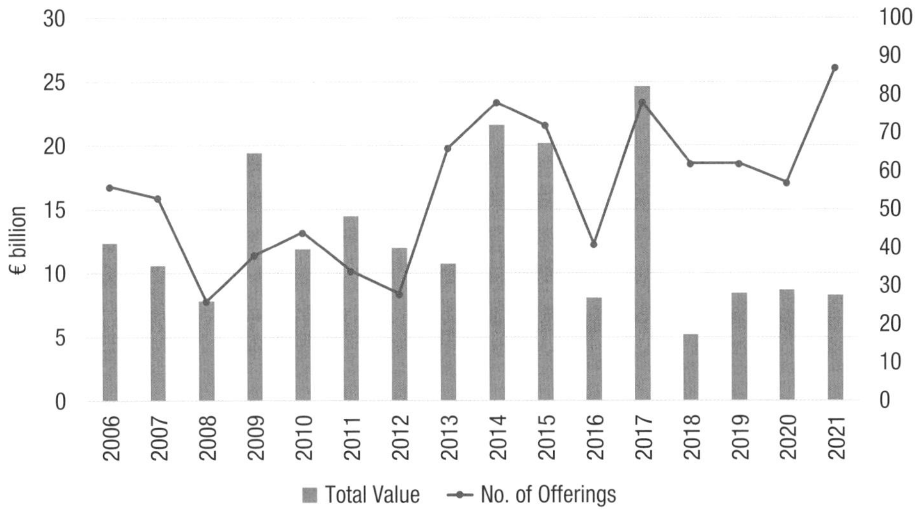

Source: EquitaLab.

Figure 3.4 **Italian equity capital markets transactions (2006–2021)**

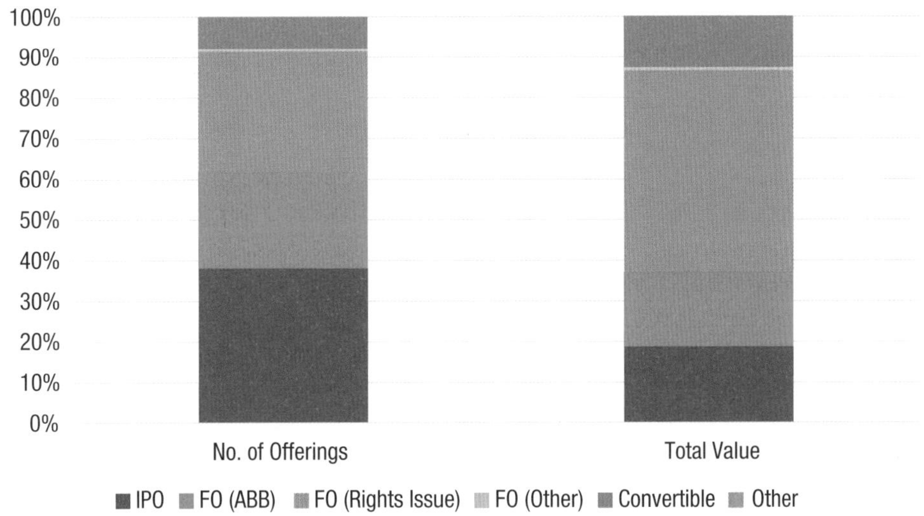

Source: EquitaLab.

for Growth (MEF, 2022), calling for a vigorous institutional effort to reimagine and to rebuild the capital market infrastructure in an attempt to make listing more attractive for Italian companies, and especially for smaller ones.

Indeed, the onerous access of companies to the market is further corroborated by the larger size of follow-on and convertible offerings compared to IPOs. **Table 3.2** provides some summary statistics of deal value across different types of deals. Overall, the average offering is worth €231.7 million, but more than half of the deals are for an amount smaller than €50 million and only a handful, approximately 10%, exceed €500 million. The value of the median deal is, in fact, just €38.5 million. IPOs are smaller on average than follow-on or convertible offerings. The average deal value is €114.2 million for IPOs, while it reaches €178 million for ABBs, €378.6 million for rights issues and €372.2 million for convertible offerings. Two-thirds of IPOs are for amounts smaller than €50 million, and IPOs contribute for about one-half of the deals below that lower threshold. On the contrary, ABBs and rights issues account jointly for approximately two-thirds of the deals in the size ranges between €50 million and €500 million.

Table 3.2 Italian equity capital markets transactions' size (2006–2021)

	All	IPO	FO (ABB)	FO (Rights Issue)	Convertible
Average deal value (€ million)	231.7	114.2	178.0	387.6	372.2
Number of deals per size range:					
<€50 million	480	236	69	156	16
€50–€100 million	84	24	40	16	4
€100–€250 million	146	40	59	29	17
€250–€500 million	83	20	28	23	12
>€500 million	84	14	15	37	16

Source: EquitaLab.

The industrial sector is the one that provides by far the largest contribution to overall transaction volume, both in terms of number of offerings and total deal value. **Figure 3.5** shows the sectorial breakdown of equity capital markets transactions in Italy, based on the industry of the issuer. The industrial sector accounts for 70.5% of the number of deals and 41.6% of the aggregate deal value. This gap is explained by the fact that the average offering size for industrial issuers is €136.5 million, much smaller than in the case of banks (€866.7 million) or utilities (€564.3 million). Within the industrial sector, a large portion of the offerings come from companies in the computer and electronics general industry group, or automotive, professional services, healthcare, retail consumer products, machinery, and real estate and property.

Figure 3.5 **Italian equity capital markets transactions' sectorial breakdown (2006–2021)**

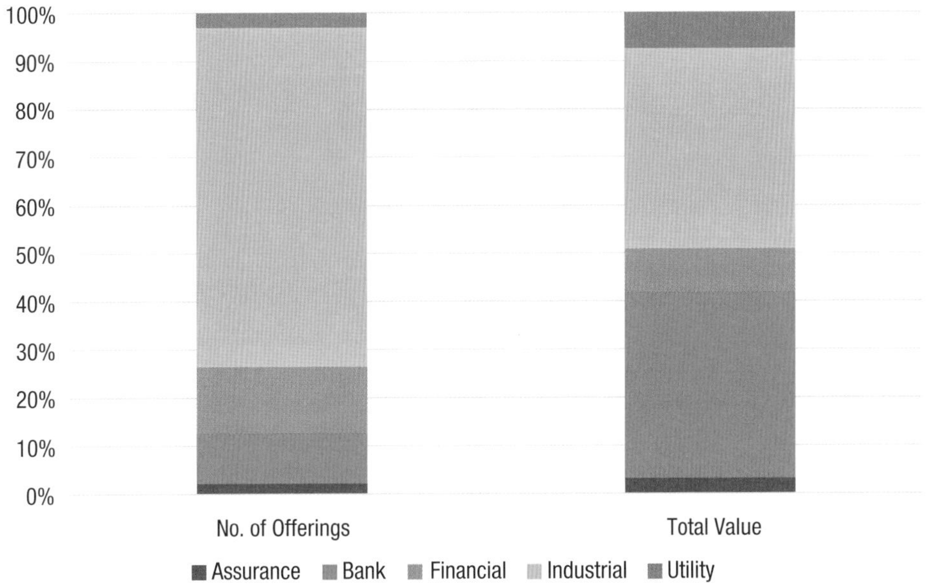

Source: EquitaLab.

Table 3.3 Italian equity capital markets offerings' characteristics (2006–2021)

Averages	All	IPO	FO (ABB)	FO (Rights Issue)	Convertible
Floating (% outstanding shares)	27.2	33.5	7.6	42.1	2.3
Primary shares (%)	65.0	79.5	15.2	100.0	–
Secondary shares (%)	28.0	20.4	83.8	–	–

Source: EquitaLab.

Table 3.3 provides further insight into the characteristics of offerings by Italian companies in equity capital markets, reporting the average proportion of the company shares that are offered to investors and the extent to which these are existing shares sold by shareholders or newly issued stocks. The average offering typically involves less than one-third of the shares of the company, about 27.2%, and the median one even less, 19.7%. A smaller stake is usually floated in IPOs than in rights issues, consistent with the relatively smaller deal value of this type of offering. Then, the proportion of existing shares sold by shareholders to newly issued stocks suggests that the fundraising function of equity capital markets dominates the mere transfer of ownership. On average, 65% of the shares offered in a deal are newly issued and only 28% of existing shares are involved. The primary component of the offering is even more prominent in IPOs, where it almost reaches 80% of the shares. This is consistent with the view of the listing as a means to obtain additional financial resources to support company growth. The opposite applies to ABBs, which preeminently involve existing shares of shareholders that wish to sell their stake in the company. For these deals, the secondary component accounts on average for 83.8% of the offering.

Further zooming in on the accessibility of the market, and to put figures in the international context, **Figure 3.6** compares the number and the value of IPOs on Borsa Italiana between 2014 and 2021, with those on Euronext Paris and Deutsche Börse. During the period, Borsa Italiana has seen 43 IPOs for a total value of €18.4 billion on its general MTA (Euronext Milan) market and 190 listings for a total of €4.2 billion on the AIM

Figure 3.6 **IPOs on Borsa Italiana, Euronext Paris, and Deutsche Börse (2014–2021)**

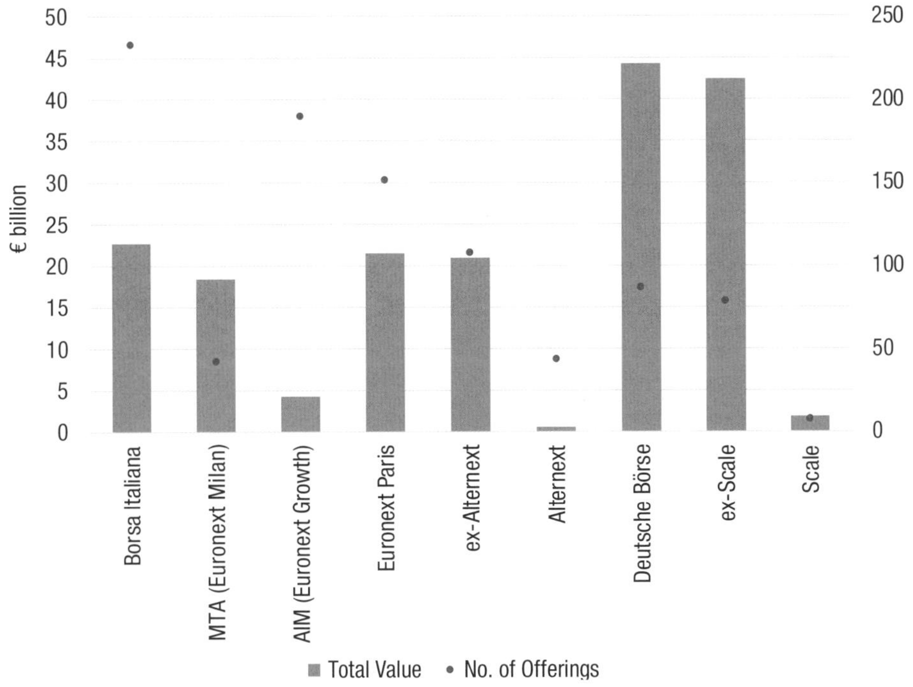

Source: EquitaLab.

(Euronext Growth) market, or an aggregate of 233 listings for €22.6 billion. This is equivalent to 10.7% of the total number of IPOs across all exchanges in the EU and 6.6% of their value. By comparison, 152 companies listed on Euronext Paris during the same period, for a total value of €21.5 billion, and 87 on Deutsche Börse, for a value of €44.2 billion.

Notably, if the analysis is confined to the main markets only, excluding the offerings on AIM (Euronext Growth), Alternext and Scale, IPOs in France (108) and Germany (78) outnumber those observed in Italy (43) by a factor of two or more. Yet, in terms of values, IPOs in France and Italy are roughly comparable, at €20.8 billion and €18.7 billion, respectively. The total for Germany is instead more than twice as much, at €42.4 billion, which suggests that the typical offering size is similar in Italy and Germany, but much smaller in France.

On top of this, drawing further attention on the necessity to improve capital market efficiency, Borsa Italiana has historically also experienced more frequent withdrawals of planned IPOs and delistings relative to other major European exchanges. In a study by EquitaLab comparing capital markets in Italy and the UK, Caselli et al. (2016) report that between 2009 and 2015, the number of companies listed in Italy has dropped on average by 10 each year, and that the rate of withdrawn IPOs (over all announced IPOs since 2006) has reached 40.7%, well above the corresponding rate in other major exchanges.[3]

More recently, as regards delisting, 2022 has seen 19 tender offers for an amount of about €3 billion and 21 delistings, 13 on the main market and 8 on the Euronext Growth Milan for a total further loss of about €28 billion of market capitalization. While other markets in continental Europe, notably Germany, have experienced similar trends, delisting has been particularly severe in Italy. Among the causes of this retreat from the stock exchange, which reduces even the size and the strength of equity capital markets, is that key shareholders often believe that prices in the market do not properly reflect the fundamentals of listed companies.

These numbers suggest that Borsa Italiana may be less accessible than other major European equity markets and therefore less efficient for the financing of smaller companies, which are precisely the backbone of the Italian economy. **Figure 3.7** sheds some light on this point by comparing the distribution of the size of IPOs across different markets. As regards Borsa Italiana, the average IPO is worth €97 million, but €427 on the MTA (Euronext Milan) and 22.3 in on the AIM (Euronext Growth). In fact, while 90% of the listings on AIM (Euronext Growth) are for less than €50 million, about 57.6% of those on MTA (Euronext Milan) are for more than €100 million. By contrast, the average IPO is for €193.4 on Euronext Paris (excluding Alternext), where 72% of the IPOs are for less than €50 million, and €536.94 on Deutsche Börse (excluding Scale) with 34.4% of the IPOs in excess of €100 million. The larger average offering size in Italy and Germany confirms higher barriers of entry for smaller companies to access

[3] At the time Borsa Italiana was part of the London Stock Exchange Group. The rate of IPO withdrawals was 30.3% for the UK market.

Figure 3.7 **Deal size of IPOs on Borsa Italiana, Euronext Paris, and Deutsche Börse (2014–2021)**

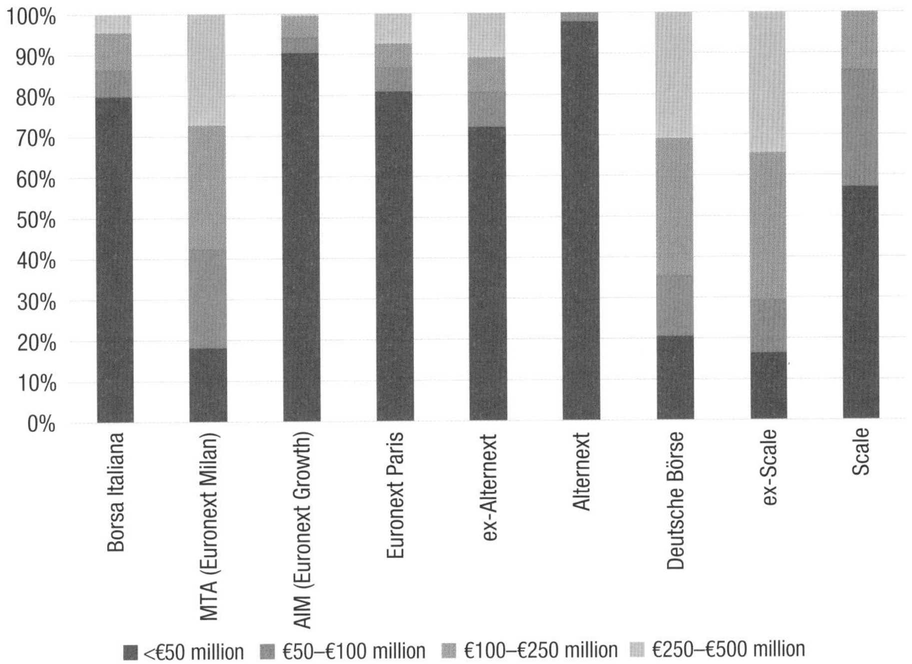

Source: EquitaLab.

to equity capital markets than in France, where the economy is more market-based.

Table 3.4 offers additional information about the characteristics of IPOs in different markets, comparing the average proportion of the company shares that are offered to investors and the extent to which these are existing shares sold by shareholders or newly issued stocks. The average IPO on Borsa Italiana typically involves about one-third of the shares of the company, 38.7% on MTA (Euronext Milan) and 32.7% on AIM (Euronext Growth), and in line with offerings on Euronext Paris and Deutsche Börse. Then, the proportion of existing shares sold by shareholders dominates newly issued stocks on the AIM (Euronext Growth), suggesting that the fundraising function of equity capital markets dominates in this market. On average, 95% of the shares offered in an IPO are newly

Table 3.4 Offering characteristics of IPOs on Borsa Italiana, Euronext Paris, and Deutsche Börse (2014–2021)

Averages	Borsa Italiana	Euronext Milan (MTA)	Euronext Growth (AIM)	Euronext Paris	Euronext Paris (Main)	Euronext Paris (Alternext)	Deutsche Börse	Deutsche Börse (Main)	Deutsche Börse (Scale)
Deal value (€ million)	97.0	427.0	22.3	141.2	193.4	13.2	508.4	536.9	226.0
Floating (%)	33.8	38.7	32.7	32.3	33.6	29.3	35.3	35.2	35.8
Primary (%)	85.8	44.7	95.2	88.5	85.5	95.9	61.9	60.3	77.6
Secondary (%)	14.2	55.3	4.9	14.4	14.7	4.1	38.1	39.7	22.5

Source: EquitaLab.

issued and only 4.9% of existing shares are involved. The primary component of the offering is also prominent in IPOs on Euronext Paris and Deutsche Börse main markets, where it almost reaches 85.5% and 60.3% of the shares, respectively. The opposite applies to IPOs on MTA (Euronext Milan), which preeminently involve existing shares of shareholders that wish to sell their stake in the company. Inconsistent with the view of an IPO as a means to obtain additional financial resources to support company growth, for listings on MTA (Euronext Milan) the primary component accounts on average for only 44.7% of the offering, while the secondary component stands at 55.3%.

A natural question is then to ask what the typical characteristics of the companies listed in Italy are. In a recent study by EquitaLab, Caselli et al. (2021) analyze a sample of 295 Italian companies listed on Borsa Italiana MTA (Euronext Milan) between 2007 and 2019. The number of companies observed each year ranges between a minimum of 129 in 2015 and a maximum of 164 in 2009. Industrial companies account for the majority of the observations in the sample, at approximately 70%, as reported in **Figure 3.8**.

Figure 3.8 The sectoral composition of Italian listed companies

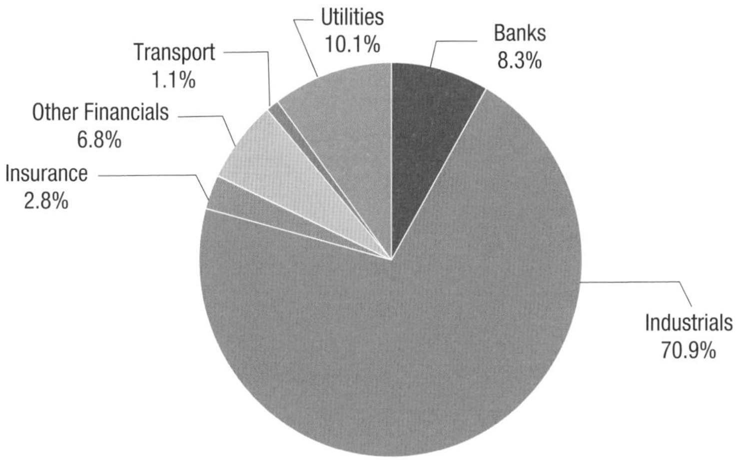

Companies are classified according to the Refinitiv general industry classification.

Source: Caselli et al. (2021).

Banks, insurance companies, and other financial institutions represent approximately 18% of the listed companies in the sample. The remainder is split between utilities and transportation. The distribution of observations across industries remains stable over time. Every year, the most represented sector is the industrial one, followed by utility companies. Banks are the only exception. From seven observations for this industry in 2007, the figure more than doubled (to 15) in 2019.

Table 3.5 presents summary statistics of company financials for these firms. As regards size, they range from minimum revenues of €1.6 million and to maximum €73 billion, with an average value of €2.5 billion and a median of €417 million. Total assets range instead from €13.7 million to maximum €926.8 billion. The average company has a market capitalization of €1.7 billion, but the median one does not reach €200 million of capitalization. The number of employees grows at an average rate of 3%. This numbers indicate unequivocally that listed companies in Italy

Table 3.5 Italian listed companies: summary statistics of selected company financials

	Obs.	Mean	St. Dev.	Min.	Med.	Max.
Total assets (€ million)	1,103	18,869.19	93,363.52	13.72	892.12	926,827.50
Revenues (€ million)	1,825	2,607.97	7,506.77	1.58	422.16	73,100.00
Return on equity	1,825	0.05	0.14	−0.66	0.06	0.41
Return on (net) assets	1,825	0.09	0.11	−0.41	0.08	0.40
Change in number of employees	1,825	0.03	0.09	−0.20	0.01	0.38
Market capitalization (€ million)	1,825	1,660.15	5,080.79	0.01	187.88	52,200.00
Tobin's Q	1,094	0.57	0.69	0.01	0.35	6.07
Stock Beta	1,825	0.90	0.39	0.10	0.86	2.30
Stock return (monthly, %)	18,548	−0.24	9.9	−30.47	−0.17	29.57
Trading volume (monthly, million)	18,908	62.40	327.00	–	2.47	5,660.00

Source: Caselli et al. (2021).

are large and mature firms. These are also relatively profitable and financially robust companies. On average, firms report a positive ROE (5%), with a standard deviation of 14%, and a positive RONA (9%), with a standard deviation of 11%. Their stock market beta is at 0.90 and the Tobin's Q is at 0.57, but with a standard deviation of 0.69.

3.3 Why Do Italian Companies Go Public?

In 2017, a study by CONSOB (Giordano and Modena, 2017) show that Italian firms that are listed on Borsa Italiana are more profitable, grow faster, and invest more than comparable private firms. More specifically, they compare 51 medium-sized listed companies with their non-listed peers (matched by industry and size) over the period 2002–2011 and find that listed firms: (i) report higher rates of growth in terms of revenues; (ii) are more profitable; (iii) have better access to debt capital markets and bank loans, which allows them to invest more than non-listed firms whose investments are constrained by their cash flow generation; and (iv) are more resilient in times of economic recession or financial crisis.

These results suggest the staying private is costly, as companies grow at a slower pace. This also has negative consequences for economic growth more in general, as shown by Geranio & Appendini (2013) at the country level. Nonetheless, if we look at the development of the Italian equity capital market, we observe that Italian firms seem relatively less prone to go public than their international peers.

There are a number of studies in finance literature trying to identify the factors that motivate companies to go public or remain private. Among them, Amihud & Mendelson (1988) show that the liquidity of listed stocks induces firms to go public. Similarly, Zingales (1995), Mello & Parsons (1998), and Stoughton & Zechner (1998) argue that decisions to go public are driven by the goal of helping shareholders who wish to sell their shares and exit the firm. According to Welch (1989), the fact that listed firms find it easier to access funding motivates the decision to go public. Finally, Jensen & Meckling (1976), Pagano & Roell (1998), Holmstrom & Tirole (1993), and Bolton & Von Thadden (1998) propose an alternative explanation grounded on the increased discipline that public ownership imposes on management. In the Italian context, Pagano et al. (1998) study a sample of companies in pre- and post-IPO stages. They show that Italian companies tend to go public in order to rebalance their capital structure rather than to finance growth.

Against this backdrop, in a study by EquitaLab focused on the Italian equity capital markets, Caselli et al. (2018) examine the determinants of the decision to go public or stay private on the basis of company interviews and an empirical study of the pre-IPO characteristics of the companies that go public compared to those that do not.

With the aim of introducing the most relevant factors that encourage or discourage Italian companies from going public, the study starts with a detailed account of a round of extensive one-on-one interviews with the executive managers of a focus group of eight companies listed on Borsa Italiana and their closest private competitors conducted in the Fall of 2017. The focus group included firms in different sectors, including consumer goods and services, industrial products and services, and healthcare. Each listed company in the group was matched with the closest comparable that was still private event though it was eligible for an IPO. The objective was to form a qualitative sample that was broad enough to represent the productive economy as well as Italian areas of excellence, while preserving comparability of among listed and private companies.[4]

First, all company managers of listed companies indicated that even though a broader and deeper investor base and the possibility for a better valuation may have supported the case for a listing abroad, they refrained from pushing this option owing to the challenges. In particular, they mentioned the difficulties of gaining sufficient international recognition and supporting the liquidity of the stock, as well as the higher administrative and regulatory costs.

Then, as regards the motives for undertaking an IPO, **Figure 3.9** reports the reasons that listed companies highlighted when asked about the

[4] The listed companies in the focus group include Ferragamo, IVS, Masi, Recordati, IMA, Cerved, Safilo, and Piquadro. Their private counterparts are Valentino, Argenta, Antinori, Teamsystem, De Rigo, and three additional undisclosed companies. For more information, see Caselli et al. (2018).

Figure 3.9 Reasons for undertaking an IPO

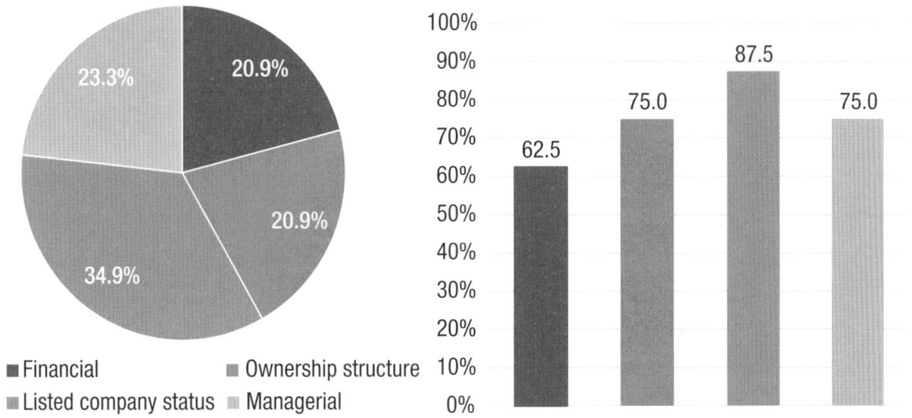

The bar chart reports the proportion of interviews in which each type of reason was cited, while the pie chart represents the frequency with which the different motive types were mentioned as a percentage of all company responses.

Source: Caselli et al. (2018).

drivers of their decision to go public, grouped into four main categories: financial, managerial, related to the ownership structure of the company, or associated with the achievement of the status of listed company. The more recurrent reasons for going public related to the achievement of the listed status. They were raised in seven of the eight interviews (see the bar chart), and they accounted for approximately 35% of all replies (see the pie chart). Within this category, a number of specific aspects were emphasized by company managers: gains in term of visibility, credibility and transparency, the enhancement of the financial culture across the organization an easier use of stock as currency for M&A activities, and a greater ability to attract and retain talent with stock-option plans.

Reasons for going public associated with the company's ownership structure or its management were cited in six interviews and accounted for 20.9% and 23.3% of the company responses, respectively. The former ones included the exit of financial sponsors, the sale of partial stakes by founders, and a general rebalancing of the ownership structure. The latter ones ranged from the improvement in terms of transparency and rigor of planning and control processes, to the strengthening of the company's bargaining power relative to customers and suppliers, and the development of more efficient communication channels between the company and its stakeholders, including institutional channels. Financial motives were mentioned in five interviews and accounted for 20.9% of all replies. These related to the need to fund external growth through mergers and acquisitions, the need to rebalance and optimize the capital structure of the company, and the need to fund medium- to long-term investment projects.

Notably, the private companies in the focus group did not perceive the listed status as an advantage. Although these firms recognized that they might not have the visibility enjoyed by their listed competitors, the same opportunities for external growth, or the same ability to attract and retain talent, they made several arguments in support of their private status, as reported in **Figure 3.10**.

Figure 3.10 Pros and cons of being private rather than public

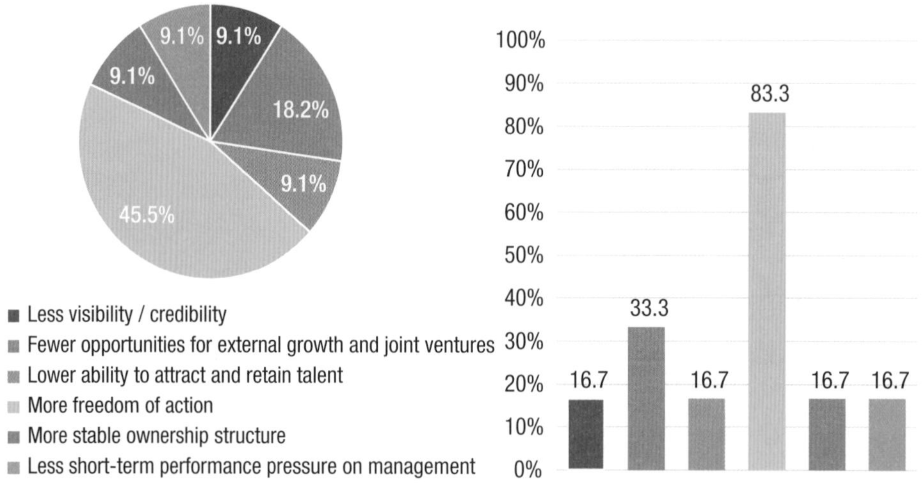

The bar chart reports the proportion of interviews in which each type of reason was cited, while the pie chart represents the frequency with which the different motive types were mentioned as a percentage of all company responses.

Source: Caselli et al. (2018).

In particular, they pointed out that staying clear of market scrutiny provided them with more freedom of action compared to their listed competitors. This freedom included the ability to embark on more innovative projects, more flexibility in redesigning their business models, more stable ownership structures, and less short-term pressure on management to perform.

More specifically, **Figure 3.11** summarizes the reasons that kept private companies from going public. In this case, the most frequently cited reasons had to do with the drawbacks of the listed status, which were brought up in six of the eight interviews (see the bar chart) and accounted for approximately 47.6% of all replies. These included the concern that market short-termism would not adequately value (or incentivize) managerial focus on long-term objectives, the worry that the benefits of a public listing would be entirely offset by the liquidity of stocks due to a small market capitalization, the desire to avoid high levels of disclosure while

Figure 3.11 Reasons for remaining private

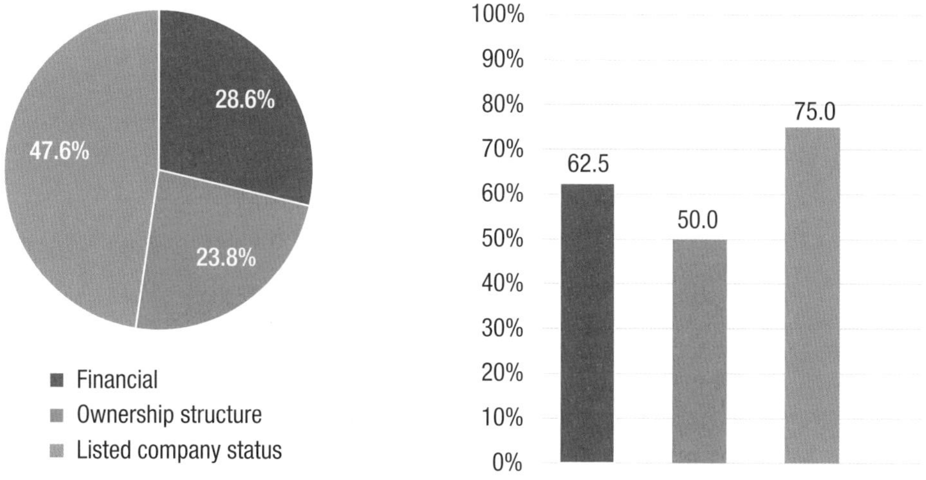

The bar chart reports the proportion of interviews in which each type of reason was cited, while the pie chart represents the frequency with which the different motive types were mentioned as a percentage of all company responses.

Source: Caselli et al. (2018).

restructuring the business model, and the cost associated with the listing process and investor relations.

Financial motives were mentioned in five interviews and accounted for 28.6% of all replies, while reasons associated with the company's ownership structure were cited in four interviews and accounted for 23.8% of all responses. The former ones included the desire of keeping the financial structure of the company sound and balanced, the availability of alternative sources of funding to support growth, such as financial sponsors, and unfavorable market conditions that did not guarantee a valuation of the company in line with the expectations of the shareholders. The latter ones ranged from concerns about dilution of control, to financial sponsors' and anchor investors' aversion to or lack of interest in going public.

Then, Caselli et al. (2018) further analyze the decision to go public or remain private by comparing the pre-IPO characteristics of firms that have listed their shares on Borsa Italiana with the characteristics of a set of comparable companies that remained private. This helps shed some light on what are the pre-IPO company characteristics that can explain why the arguments in favor of a listing may eventually prevail over those against it, and vice versa.

The analysis focused on 22 IPOs of non-financial nor State-owned companies that listed on Borsa Italiana MTA (Euronext Milan) between 20017 and 2017. In most cases (11), the IPO involved both newly issued shares and shares sold by shareholders (OPSV). Only new shares were offered in three cases, while only existing shares (OPV) were offered in eight cases. The total value of shares offered in the sample period exceeds €9 billion. The IPOs range in size from €33 million to €2.5 billion, with an average of €414.2 million. More than two-thirds of the listings took place in the post-2012 period, with the most IPOs recorded in 2015. They involved existing shares sold by current shareholders more often than newly issued shares, and most of these shares were allocated to institutional, rather than retail, investors. Among OPSVs, the number of new shares issued exceeded the number of shares sold by existing shareholders in only 5 out of 11 listings. Regardless of the type of transaction, less than one in five shares went to retail investors, on average. No shares at all were allocated at all to retail investors in 4 out of 22 listings.

Each IPO company is matched with its closest comparable, based on industry and size in the year prior to the listing, among all IPO-eligible firm that did not go public. These are the companies fitting at least one of the following criteria: operating revenues in excess of €100 million, total assets in excess of €200 million, or more than 1,000 employees.[5] **Table 3.6** reports the mean values of a broad set of company financials retrieved from AIDA for IPO firms and IPO-eligible firms that did not go public. On average, IPO companies are larger than that of their non-IPO counterparts, especially in terms of the number of employees. However, they are generally also younger firms still in their growth phase (see number of employees) and operating with a more leveraged capital structure. These findings are consistent with the rationale that the decision to go public is driven by the need to fund growth and to rebalance the firm's capital structure. Notably, this result holds whenever the listing involves newly issued shares (OPSV and OPS), but not when it only involves the sale of existing shares (OPV). In the latter case, the IPO serves as a way out for existing shareholders and does not affect the company's finances. In fact, OPVs seem to be common among companies that have not yet reached their mature stage, as they report high growth but no profitability.

Deeply embedded in the decision to go public or to stay private are also the implications of a listing on control rights. In this respect, the presence of a single large blockholder controlling with direct ownership more than 50% of the shares is more frequent among IPO-eligible firms that did not go public (17 out of 22) than for IPO companies (12 out of 22). Vice versa, 4 out of 5 companies that report no single blockholder with a with a direct ownership stake larger than 25% are IPO-firms. The proportion is 6 out of 9 among companies with no controlling blockholder. This evidence is consistent with the rationale that one of the determinants of why firms

[5] These are more restrictive criteria than the ones applied, for example, by Geranio and Appendini (2013), who treat all firm with at least €50 million in revenue or at least 150 employees as IPO eligible.

Table 3.6 Pre-IPO company financials (averages): IPO firms vs. IPO-eligible comparable firms

	Total (44)	No-IPO (22)	IPO (22)	OPSV (11)	OPS (8)	OPV (3)
Size						
Employees	1,996.6	869.5	3,072.4*	4,506.5**	2,206.3***	124.0
Total assets (€ million)	787.0	392.0	1,180.0	844.0	1,990.0**	262.0
Growth						
Age	21.1	26.7	15.5**	19.1	13.1*	8.7
Employees (3-year CAGR, %)	12.4	–1.0	26.6*	12.1***	9.8**	15.8***
Total assets (3-year CAGR, %)	10.1	6.7	13.7	6.8	2.4	17.5
Profitability						
EBITDA margin	5.5	10.3	1.6	15.1	17.8	–9.9***
Return on assets (%)	6.2	7.8	4.6	8.3	8.8	–19.9***
Return on equity (%)	10.2	10.6	9.8	16.2	19.3	–3.9*
Capital structure and credit capacity						
Leverage (%)	21.5	16.2	26.9*	37.0***	16.5	17.6
Cash flows (% of total assets)	7.5	9.2	5.8	7.0	11.9	–14.7***
Tangible assets (% of total assets)	19.9	22.2	7.6	9.6	24.9	27.9
Current ratio	1.75	1.35	2.22	1.16	1.11	8.33***
Capital intensity						
Working capital (% of total assets)	14.3	16.0	12.6	21.7	6.2	–3.9
Capex (% of total assets)	–5.1	–3.6	–6.9	–7.4	–6.8	–5.8

*, **, and *** indicate that the mean for IPO firms, or a specific type of IPO firms, is different from the mean computed across non-IPO firms at the 10%, 5%, and 1% levels of statistical significance, respectively.

Source: Caselli et al. (2018).

may decide to stay private is that the current shareholders do not wish to lose control over the company.

Against this backdrop, in further analyses, Caselli et al. (2018) link these firm characteristics with the decision to go public, the type of listing, and the resulting allocations to retail and institutional investors, in the context of different regression models. Consistent with the rationale that the decision to go public is driven by the need to fund growth and to rebalance the capital structure of the company, they find that a greater likelihood of undertaking an IPO is associated with a larger company size, faster growth (in the number of employees), and more leverage. More specifically, the coefficient estimates of a Logit regression of an indicator variable taking the value of 1 for companies that listed the following year on firm characteristics suggest that a one–standard deviation increase in firm size, growth, or leverage increases a company probability of embarking on an IPO by approximately, 15%, 34%, and 14%, respectively.

Similarly, Caselli et al. (2018) show that the fraction of an offering involving new shares is larger when the firm needs financing to grow. Pre-IPO growth in the number of employees is positively associated with the amount of newly issued shares offered and negatively associated with the number of shares sold by existing shareholders. Then, consistent with the argument that market short-termism may be a concern for smaller firms, we find that firm size and firm age are positively associated with the proportion of the offering focused on retail shareholders. These are also often firms with strong, widely recognized brands.

Summing up, firms go public when their characteristics are such that the arguments in favor of a listing prevail over the arguments against it. This is consistent with the view that when weighing the pros and cons of a listing, companies are well aware that achieving their goals depends on meeting investors' expectations. Only companies that fully meet investors' requirements can reap the benefits of going public. All others will only bear the costs. Indeed, as of now, only larger firms access the market. For them the arguments against going public are milder, since the cost of complying with market regulation and meeting investor demands is smaller. On the contrary, going public by means of an IPO represents the peak of their growth process and an occasion to gain visibility and recognition of their standing or allows some of the shareholders to liquidate their investments. For smaller firms that need funds to support their high rates of growth or reduce their leverage, going public represents instead a necessary step toward reaching an optimal size and creating value for shareholders. However, only a few of them eventually gain access to market funding given the drawbacks of market scrutiny and the cost of meeting investor expectations.

With this in mind, the listing process should be simplified and, the regulatory and administrative costs associated with a public listing should be reduced to allow more medium-sized companies to access deeper and more efficient equity capital markets. The EU proposal of the Listing Act EU is a first encouraging step in this direction.[6] It envisages shorter prospectuses, with a maximum length of 300 pages for IPOs and 50 pages for follow-on public offerings or admissions to trading on regulated exchanges, drafted only in English and made available in electronic format. These will also be standardized in terms of format, structure, and contents. Alongside, the proposal prompts a simpler process for the control and approval of the prospectus by the supervising national authorities and introduces an exemption from the publication of the prospectus for follow-on offerings as long as the securities being offered are similar to the ones already listed. The minimum free float requirement is also reduced from 25% to 10%, giving more flexibility to issuers whose existing shareholders want to maintain control stakes in their firms.

3.4 The Ownership Structure of Italian Companies

A first historical overview of ownership, control, and corporate governance for all companies traded on the Milan Stock Exchange from 1900 to 2000 is provided by Aganin & Volpin (2005). They find that family firms and pyramidal groups are both prominent in corporate governance and

[6] See in particular the Proposal for Directive of the European Parliament and of the Council amending Directive 2014/65/EU to make public capital markets in the Union more attractive for companies and to facilitate access to capital for small and medium-sized enterprises and repealing Directive 2001/34/EC.

prevalent in corporate ownership. In line with this result, in a more recent study conducted on a large sample of both listed and private companies in the period 2005–2016, Baltruinate et al. (2019) confirm the prominence of family ownership and report high levels of ownership concentration, large overlaps between ownership and control, and an extensive degree of managerial localism.

These findings are consistent with both legal origin theories (La Porta et al., 1998; Glaeser & Shleifer, 2002) and political theories (Roe, 2000; Rajan & Zingales, 2004; Pagano & Volpin, 2005) of financial development in the law and finance literature. Indeed, Aminadav & Papaioannou (2020)'s study corporate control by tracking controlling shareholders for 42,720 listed firms from 127 countries over the period 2004–2014. They reveal that government and family control are pervasive in civil-law countries, where ownership is more concentrated, while ownership is relatively more dispersed in common-law countries. Italy is no exception. In the 244 firms of their sample, 69.5% are controlled by a shareholder with more than 20% of the voting rights, 36.1% are family-controlled, and 3.8% are government controlled. On average, the one, three, and five largest shareholders account for 44%, 58.8%, and 63.1% of the voting rights, respectively. Only 4.9% of widely held firms have no shareholder with more than 5% of the voting rights, while 25.6% of them have at least one such shareholder.

More recently, in a study by EquitaLab on the ownership characteristics of shareholders in Italian listed companies, Caselli et al. (2021) confirm that Italian listed companies are characterized by a high degree of ownership concentration and the existence of controlling shareholders or at least a pervasive presence of shareholders with substantial voting power.

The study focuses on 295 Italian companies listed on Borsa Italiana between 2007 and 2019. Detailed information on their ownership structure is retrieved from CONSOB for each company at the end of each year. This includes all stakes by ultimate shareholders that own at least 2% directly or indirectly, as well as their voting rights.

Summary statistics of the ownership characteristics of Italian listed companies are reported in **Table 3.7**. More than half of the companies in the sample (56%) have a controlling shareholder and 84% have at least one fulcrum shareholder. In line with the thresholds typically used in the

Table 3.7 Ownership characteristics of Italian listed companies: summary statistics

	Obs.	Mean	St. Dev.	Min.	Med.	Max.
Sum of voting rights	1957	60.79	18.17	2.00	64.37	90.14
Number of shareholders	1957	3.39	2.19	1.00	3.00	15.00
Number of shareholder types	1957	2.01	0.85	1.00	2.00	5.00
Number of shareholder nationalities	1957	1.48	0.50	1.00	1.00	2.00
Presence of a controlling shareholder	1957	0.56	0.50	0.00	1.00	1.00
Presence of a fulcrum investor	1957	0.84	0.36	0.00	1.00	1.00
Dispersed ownership	1957	0.06	0.25	0.00	0.00	1.00
Ownership concentration: top	1957	45.91	20.41	2.00	51.31	89.00
Ownership concentration: top-3	1957	56.96	19.07	2.00	61.59	89.83
Ownership concentration: top-5	1957	59.54	18.30	2.00	63.14	89.83

Summary statistics of ownership variables are computed across observations grouped by company-year.

Source: Caselli et al. (2021).

literature (see, for example, Aminadav et al., 2020), these are defined as shareholders in control of more than 50% and 20% of a company's voting rights, respectively. Dispersed ownership accounts for less than 6% of the observations. Each company has on average more than three different shareholders with an ownership stake of above 2%, up to a maximum of 15. The number of different shareholder types per company is two on average and can reach up to five. Ownership concentration, measured on the basis of the total share of voting rights of the largest five shareholders, is high on average, 60%, and can reach up to 89.8%.

Based on the information contained in the CONSOB files, the analysis then extends to examine more in depth the identity of the shareholders and the characteristics of the shareholders base. Following Federo et al. (2020), all shareholders appearing on the CONSOB files are classified into one of the following six mutually exclusive categories based on information collected manually from their public filings and webpages:

- corporation;
- family;
- government;
- institutional investor;
- founder; and
- venture capital or private equity fund.

In addition, shareholders are also categorized based on their nationality as domestic (i.e., Italian) or foreign, with the latter accounting for only a very small part of the shareholder base, or about 30% of the observations. **Table 3.8** reports the whole population of shareholders observations, grouped together according to the above criteria.

Families and founders account for approximately 60% of the shareholders in our sample. They are most likely the clearest examples of long-term investors who can support the firm even in troubled times. What's more, they can provide management with a sufficiently farsighted view to implement successful long-term investment plans.

The second most prominent shareholder group is that of institutional investors, venture capital, and private equity funds. Together, they represent about 25% of the shareholders in our sample, which is mostly populated by asset managers. This is consistent with the significant growth of the asset management industry in recent decades, which has led to a large-scale intermediation of equity ownership. While the group is heterogeneous in terms of investment goals and horizons, they can play an active role in corporate governance by engaging in coordinated behavior (Bushee, 1998; Edmans & Manso, 2011; Schnatterly & Johnson, 2014; Gantchev & Jotikasthira, 2018; Glaum et al., 2018; Lee et al., 2018; Crane et al., 2019; Cvijanovic et al., 2021).

Then, some of the largest Italian champions see the presence of the State as a relevant shareholder. While the presence of the State should not necessarily be detrimental to the performance of owned firms, its indirect influence on the appointment of top management teams could have

Table 3.8 The shareholder base of Italian listed companies: who they are

	Corp.	Family	Gov.	Inst. Inv.	Founder	VC&PE	Dom.	Foreign	Tot.
Ultimate shareholders									
Obs.	188	135	52	282	576	45	900	378	1,278
(%)	(14.71)	(10.56)	(4.07)	(22.07)	(47.07)	(3.52)	(70.42)	(29.58)	(100)
By shareholder and company									
Obs.	235	202	79	828	647	81	1,262	810	2,072
Mean	3.9	3.9	5.7	2.33	3.6	2.5	3.67	2.42	3.2
St. Dev.	3.0	3.3	3.6	1.91	2.2	2.0	2.69	2.03	2.5
Min.	1	1	1	1	1	1	1	1	1
Med.	3	3	5	2	3	2	3	2	2
Max.	13	13	13	13	8	11	13	12	13
By shareholder and year									
Obs.	791	614	338	1,031	2,122	139	3,720	1,214	5,034
Mean	1.2	1.3	1.3	1.9	1.1	1.5	1.25	1.49	1.3
St. Dev.	0.5	0.9	1.3	1.9	0.5	1.1	0.93	1.46	1.1
Min.	1	1	1	1	1	1	1	1	1
Med.	1	1	1	1	1	1	1	1	1
Max.	6	8	10	17	6	7	12	17	17

Grouping by shareholder and company provides an indication of the number of years of ownership by a given shareholder in a particular company. Grouping instead by shareholder and year gives an indication of the number of companies per shareholder each year.

Source: Caselli et al. (2021).

an impact on the final performance of the participated firms. This poses an important and pressing question, as the aftermath of the COVID-19 pandemic led to an intensified role of the State in the equity capital of the firms (Caselli, 2020).

The grouping of observations at the shareholder-company level provides an indication of the number of years of ownership by a given shareholder in a particular company. Table 3.8 shows that the average holding horizon per shareholder during the sample period is 3.2 years. It ranges from 2.3 years for the institutional investors category to 5.7 years for the government, and it is longer on average for domestic than foreign shareholders (3.6 vs. 2.4 years).

Then, the grouping of observations by shareholder and year gives an indication of the number of companies per shareholder each year. **Table 3.8** shows that the shareholders in the sample can report ownership stakes above 2% in up to 17 different companies at the same time, as in the case of institutional investors.

Table 3.9 reports observations grouped instead by shareholder, year, and company, where each firm also assigned to its industry according to the Refinitiv general industry classification. This provides further insight into the prevalence of different shareholder types across different industries. For example, corporate ownership is prevalent in companies operating in the insurance and transportation sectors. Institutional investors are ubiquitous, but their presence is stronger in banks. Government is present particularly in utilities and transportation companies, and industrial companies is where ownership by families and founders is more common.

Taking a different perspective, then, **Table 3.10** reports the summary statistics on the voting rights of each shareholder type. While the average share of voting rights controlled by any shareholder in the sample is about 18%, this figure varies significantly across shareholder types. Not surprisingly, the ownership stakes of family shareholders are the largest, accounting on average for 34.3% of the voting rights, while those of institutional investors fall short of 8% and are the smallest. The same holds also for domestic compared to foreign shareholders (21.5% vs. 9.6%).

Table 3.9 The shareholder base of Italian listed companies: breakdown by sector

	Corp.	Family	Gov.	Inst. Inv.	Founder	VC&PE	Dom.	Foreign	Tot.
Obs.	923	793	448	1,933	2,325	205	4,665	1,962	6,627
(%)	(13.93)	(11.97)	(6.76)	(29.17)	(35.08)	(3.09)	(70.39)	(29.61)	(100)
Banks	121	62	16	325	135	4	392	181	573
(%)	(21.12)	(10.82)	(2.79)	(41.01)	(23.56)	(0.70)	(68.41)	(31.59)	(100)
Industrials	504	560	166	1,382	1,885	160	3,204	1,453	4,657
(%)	(10.82)	(12.02)	(3.56)	(29.68)	(40.48)	(3.44)	(68.80)	(31.20)	(100)
Insurance	76	16	10	50	28	2	140	40	182
(%)	(41.76)	(8.79)	(5.49)	(27.47)	(15.38)	(1.10)	(78.02)	(21.98)	(100)
Other Fin.	90	58	7	141	172	26	362	132	494
(%)	(18.22)	(11.74)	(1.42)	(28.54)	(34.82)	(5.26)	(73.28)	(26.72)	(100)
Transport.	21	9	11	11	3	-	53	2	55
(%)	(38.18)	(16.36)	(20.00)	(20.00)	(5.45)	-	(96.36)	(3.64)	(100)
Utility	111	88	238	114	102	13	512	154	666
(%)	(16.67)	(31.21)	(35.74)	(17.12)	(15.32)	(1.95)	(76.88)	(23.12)	(100)

Source: Caselli et al. (2021).

Table 3.10 The shareholder base of Italian listed companies: voting rights of different shareholder types

	Corp.	Family	Gov.	Inst. Inv.	Founder	VC&PE	Dom.	Foreign	Tot.
Obs.	923	793	448	1,933	2,325	205	4,665	1,962	6,627
Mean	20.05	34.26	19.89	7.58	20.38	11.34	21.47	9.58	17.95
St. Dev.	22.58	25.78	18.24	13.66	21.85	16.49	22.92	15.52	21.69
Min.	2.00	2.00	2.00	2.00	2.00	2.00	2.00	2.00	2.00
Med.	7.51	41.44	12.50	3.97	3.97	5.04	9.39	4.90	6.66
Max.	82.17	84.00	72.50	89.00	87.56	78.80	88.99	89.00	89.00
Banks									
Obs.	121	62	16	235	135	4	392	181	573
Mean	6.85	15.61	25.36	14.32	11.03	5.34	14.11	8.55	12.35
Industrials									
Obs.	504	560	166	1,382	1,885	160	3,204	1,453	4,657
Mean	24.73	39.84	18.13	6.33	21.80	9.54	23.54	9.44	19.14
Insurance									
Obs.	76	16	10	50	28	2	142	40	182
Mean	9.02	15.68	32.35	13.00	26.75	3.04	17.36	5.00	14.64
Other Fin.									
Obs.	90	58	7	141	172	26	362	132	494
Mean	18.04	25.00	18.84	9.70	13.51	25.61	15.92	13.62	15.31
Transport.									
Obs.	21	9	11	11	3	–	53	2	55
Mean	25.97	20.12	57.57	6.52	34.26	–	28.77	4.59	27.89
Utilities									
Obs.	111	88	238	114	102	13	512	154	666
Mean	21.25	22.87	18.51	3.98	16.00	8.09	18.47	9.79	16.47

Source: Caselli et al. (2021).

Breaking down the sample by industry, **Table 3.10** also shows that the average share of voting rights controlled by any shareholder is larger in industrial or transportation companies (19.1% and 27.9%, respectively) than in other industries. Industrial companies, in particular, are where corporate and family shareholders control larger shares of voting rights on average, while transport, together with insurance and banks, is where government has larger stakes.

Taking the analysis back at the company level, **Table 3.11** confirms that families and founders control on average a larger share of the voting rights (13.9% and 24.2%, respectively) and are significantly more likely to be fulcrum shareholders (25% and 37%, respectively). Not surprisingly, a higher share of the voting rights in the hands of one type of shareholder corresponds to lower shares for the other categories. As regards the international profile of shareholders, the median and average percentage of voting rights of foreign investors is very low; 2% and 10%, respectively. More specifically, only 7% of the overall sample (namely 129 observations) are controlled by an international shareholder.

Table 3.11 Ownership characteristics of Italian listed companies: breakdown by shareholder type

	Obs.	Mean	St. Dev.	Min.	Med.	Max.
Corporate						
Sum of voting rights	1,957	9.46	19.68	<2.00	<2.00	89.83
Number of fulcrum investors	1,957	0.15	0.36	0.00	0.00	2.00
Rank	1,975	1.67	0.88	1.00	1.00	5.00
Family						
Sum of voting rights	1,957	13.88	23.86	<2.00	<2.00	84.00
Number of fulcrum investors	1,957	0.25	0.45	0.00	0.00	2.00
Rank	1,957	1.42	0.73	1.00	1.00	4.00

(Continued on next page)

(Continued)

	Obs.	Mean	St. Dev.	Min.	Med.	Max.
Government						
Sum of voting rights	1,957	4.55	13.99	<2.00	<2.00	88.15
Number of fulcrum investors	1,957	0.09	0.33	0.00	0.00	2.00
Rank	1,957	1.45	0.77	1.00	1.00	4.00
Institutional investor						
Sum of voting rights	1,957	7.49	15.16	<2.00	2.19	89.00
Number of fulcrum investors	1,957	0.06	0.24	0.00	0.00	2.00
Rank	1,957	2.04	0.67	1.00	2.00	5.00
Founder						
Sum of voting rights	1,957	24.21	29.05	<2.00	5.99	88.25
Number of fulcrum investors	1,957	0.37	0.55	0.00	0.00	3.00
Rank	1,957	1.43	0.69	1.00	1.00	4.00
VC & PE						
Sum of voting rights	1,957	1.19	6.42	<2.00	<2.00	78.80
Number of fulcrum investors	1,957	0.02	0.12	0.00	0.00	1.00
Rank order	1,957	2.38	0.92	1.00	2.00	5.00
Domestic						
Sum of voting rights	1,957	51.18	24.35	<2.00	57.66	89.50
Number of fulcrum investors	1,957	0.83	0.56	0.00	1.00	3.00
Rank	1,957	1.07	0.26	1.00	1.00	2.00
Foreign						
Sum of voting rights	1,957	9.60	17.64	<2.00	2.22	89.00
Number of fulcrum investors	1,957	0.11	0.31	0.00	0.00	2.00
Rank	1,957	1.75	0.43	1.00	2.00	2.00

Summary statistics of ownership variables are computed across observations grouped by company-year. Variable Rank captures the position in the ranking of shareholders based on their voting rights, with Rank equal to 1 being the highest.

Source: Caselli et al. (2021).

3.5 Conclusions

Italy can rely on an unparalleled world of SMEs, districts, and supply chains. With banks under constant pressure of Basel Capital requirement rules, the implementation of MREL regulations, the recent request by ECB to prudentially revise internal credit risk models and the need to optimize credit risk and balance sheet structure, it is essential that these companies develop alternative sources of funding to avoid relying excessively on debt financing. More specifically, Italian companies need to become less reliant on debt and more prone to exploit the potential of equity capital markets.

The picture that emerges from the analysis of the Italian equity capital markets in this chapter sheds light on the need and urgency to promote the use of the stock market. But the transition by Italian companies to a more balanced funding structure requires the combination of three key elements: a favorable tax treatment, a streamlined rules for listing (which does not necessarily mean simplified), and a well-diversified group of institutional investors able to provide funds for the different stages of the life of the company.

As regards the first point, the issue is that the taxation of liabilities does not provide any educational or selective mechanism, but only a cap on the deductibility of interest that is anchored to an indicator (the EBITDA) that is not related in any way to the structure of liabilities as a whole, or the cost of capital. In this respect, reshaping taxation could be very useful to level the difference between debt capital and risky capital and promote the concept of greater quality of capital, which is functional to a more appropriate structure of companies in relation to their current state in the development cycle.

Second, even if the regulatory framework is aimed at ensuring homogeneous regulation all across Europe, national authorities maintain some degree of discretion in their approaches and bear different legal responsibilities. Some use their supervisory function to control formal compliance with regulation and procedures, verifying, for example, that the risk factors in the prospectus are compatible with the status of a listed company. Others instead consider their mandate in broader terms and also verify in greater detail the substance of the disclosure offered to investors. As a result, even if the temporal framework in which different national authorities act is for all the same, as regulated by European laws, some tend to request additional disclosure and information more frequently, thus exploiting in full the maximum days allocated to the process. This also explains why the prospectus is longer and more complex in some countries than in others. In this respect, rationalizing the listing rules to simplify the process and reduce the costs associated with it could help smaller companies go public. As of now there is, in fact, almost no proportionality to the offering size, which reduces the base of companies that are eligible for an IPO. Even if they fall short of setting up a unified capital market infrastructure with a single supervisory authority and common listing requirements, both the EU Listing Act and the MEF Green Book represent an encouraging further push toward the objective of harmonizing the listing rules, the simplification of information requirements, and a reduction of listing costs for both IPOs and follow-on offerings.

Lastly, the strength of the equity market is indissolubly tied to the depth and composition of its investor pool. The equity market is in fact not only a formidable source of funding for companies, but it is also a great means of diversification for investors. With a disproportionate share of Italian wealth invested in underperformed and illiquid real estate assets, it is no surprise that companies have had to rely mostly on the banking system for funding their investments. Attracting investors to the capital market is ultimately as important as enticing companies. Indeed, improving the efficiency of the stock market, supporting high-quality research, and promoting a healthy asset management industry are all necessary steps to attract deeper pools of capital that will make the benefits of gaining access to the market for companies more than offset the costs associated with it.

References

AFME (2021, January). *Recapitalising EU businesses post COVID-19: How equity and hybrid markets instruments can drive recovery.* Available at: afme.eu

Aganin, A. & Volpin, P. (2005). The history of corporate ownership in Italy. In Morck, R.K. (ed.), *A History of Corporate Governance around the World: Family Business Groups to Professional Managers* (pp. 325–366). Chicago: University of Chicago Press.

Amihud, Y. & Mendelson, H. (1988). Liquidity and asset prices: Financial management implications. *Financial Management,* 17(1), 5–15. https://doi.org/10.2307/3665910

Aminadav, G. & Papaioannou, E. (2020). Corporate control around the world. *The Journal of Finance,* 75(3), 1191–1246. https://doi.org/10.1111/jofi.12889

Baltrunaite, A., Brodi, E., & Mocetti, S. (2019). *Ownership structure and governance of the Italian firms: New evidence and effects on firm performance.* Questioni di Economia e Finanza (Occasional Papers) No. 514, Bank of Italy. Available at: bancaditalia.it

Bolton, P. & Von Thadden, E.L. (1998). Blocks, liquidity, and corporate control. *The Journal of Finance,* 53(1), 1–25. https://doi.org/10.1111/0022-1082.15240

Brunnermeier, M. & Krishnamurthy, A. (2020). Corporate debt overhang and credit policy. *Brookings Papers on Economic Activity,* 2020(2), 447–502. https://doi.org/10.1353/eca.2020.0014

Bushee, B.J. (1998). The influence of institutional investors on myopic R&D investment behavior. *The Accounting Review,* 73(3), 305–333. Available at: jstor.org

Carletti, E., Oliviero, T., Pagano, M., Pelizzon, L., & Subrahmanyam, M.G. (2020). The COVID-19 shock and equity shortfall: Firm-level evidence from Italy. *The Review of Corporate Finance Studies,* 9(3), 534–568. https://doi.org/10.1093/rcfs/cfaa014

Caselli, S. (2020). *La grande tentazione: Perché non possiamo rinunciare a banche e mercati.* Milan: Bocconi Editore.

Caselli, S., Gatti, S., Chiarella, C., & Gigante, G. (2016). *Benchmarking the UK market: A way to create an efficient and effective capital market in Italy?.* Bocconi University BAFFI-CAREFIN Centre, Working Paper. Available at: equitalab.eu

Caselli, S., Gatti, S., Chiarella, C., & Gigante, G. (2018). *Why do Italian companies go public? An empirical analysis of the period 2006-2016.* Bocconi University BAFFI-CAREFIN Centre, Working Paper. Available at: equitalab.eu

Caselli, S., Gatti, S., Chiarella, C., Gigante, G., & Negri, G. (2021). *Ownership characteristics of shareholders in Italian listed companies: Do they really matter for firm performance?*. Bocconi University BAFFI-CAREFIN Centre, Working Paper. Available at: equitalab.eu

Caselli, S., Gatti, S., & Zava, M. (2022a). *Capital markets scorecard*. Bocconi University/Equita Quarterly Columns Series on Capital Markets, n. 2. Available at: equitalab.eu

Caselli, S., Gatti, S., Chiarella, C., Clerici, M., Asaro, F., & Botti, F. (2022b). *Growing corporate debt and the zombie company effect*. Bocconi University/Equita Quarterly Columns Series on Capital Markets, n. 3. Available at: equitalab.eu

Crane, A.D., Koch, A., & Michenaud, S. (2019). Institutional investor cliques and governance. *Journal of Financial Economics*, 133(1), 175–197. https://doi.org/10.1016/j.jfineco.2018.11.012

Crouzet, N. & Tourre, F. (2021). *Can the cure kill the patient? Corporate credit interventions and debt overhang*. Working Paper. https://dx.doi.org/10.2139/ssrn.3954581

Cvijanovic, D., Dasgupta, A., & Zachariadis, K. (2021). *The Wall Street stampede: Exit as governance with interacting blockholders*. ECGI Finance Working Paper No. 632/2019. Available at: ecgi.global

Demmou, L., Calligaris, S., Franco, G., Dlugosch, D., McGowan, M.A., & Sakha, S. (2021). *Insolvency and debt overhang following the COVID-19 outbreak: Assessment of risks and policy responses*. OECD Working Paper. https://doi.org/10.1787/18151973

Ebeke, C., Jovanovic, N., Valderrama, L., & Zhou, J. (2021). *Corporate liquidity and solvency in Europe during COVID-19: The role of policies*. IMF Working Paper WP/21/56. Available at: imf.org

Edmans, A. & Manso, G. (2011). Governance through trading and intervention: A theory of multiple blockholders. *The Review of Financial Studies*, 24(7), 2395–2428. https://doi.org/10.1093/rfs/hhq145

European Commission (2022). Proposal for a Directive of the European Parliament and of the Council amending Directive 2014/65/EU to make public capital markets in the Union more attractive for companies and to facilitate access to capital for small and medium-sized enterprises and repealing Directive 2001/34/EC. Available at: eur-lex.europa.eu

Federo, R., Ponomareva, Y., Aguilera, R.V., Saz-Carranza, A., & Losada, C. (2020). Bringing owners back on board: A review of the role of ownership type in board governance. *Corporate Governance: An International Review*, 28(6), 348–371. https://doi.org/10.1111/corg.12346

Gantchev, N. & Jotikasthira, C. (2018). Institutional trading and hedge fund activism. *Management Science*, 64(6), 2930–2950. https://doi.org/10.1287/mnsc.2016.2654

Geranio, M. & Garcia Appendini, E. (2013). Come sarebbe l'Italia con 1000 società quotate?. *Economia & Management*, 3, 95–115.

Giordano, L. & Modena, M. (2017, September). *Implicazioni e possibili motivazioni della scelta di non quotarsi da parte delle medie imprese italiane*. CONSOB Discussion Papers, No. 7. Available at: consob.it

Glaeser, E.L. & Shleifer, A. (2002). Legal origins. *The Quarterly Journal of Economics*, 117(4), 1193–1229. https://doi.org/10.1162/003355302320935016

Glaum, M., Landsman, W.R., & Wyrwa, S. (2018). Goodwill impairment: The effects of public enforcement and monitoring by institutional investors. *The Accounting Review*, 93(6), 149–180. https://doi.org/10.2308/accr-52006

Hennessy, C.A. & Whited, T.M. (2007). How costly is external financing? Evidence from a structural estimation. *The Journal of Finance*, 62(4), 1705–1745. https://doi.org/10.1111/j.1540-6261.2007.01255.x

High Level Forum on the Capital Markets Union (2020, June). *A new vision for Europe's capital markets: Final report of the high-level forum on the Capital Markets Union*. Available at: finance.ec.europa.eu

Holmström, B. & Tirole, J. (1993). Market liquidity and performance monitoring. *Journal of Political Economy*, 101(4), 678–709. https://doi.org/10.1086/261893

ISTAT (2020). *Censimento permanente delle imprese 2019*. Available at: istat.it

Jensen, M.C. & Meckling, W.H. (1976). Theory of the firm: Managerial behavior, agency costs and ownership structure. *Journal of Financial Economics*, 3(4), 305–360. https://doi.org/10.1016/0304-405X(76)90026-X

Kalemli-Özcan, Ș., Laeven, L., & Moreno, D. (2018). *Debt overhang, rollover risk, and corporate investment: Evidence from the European crisis*. Working Paper No. w24555, National Bureau of Economic Research. https://doi.org/10.3386/w24555

La Porta, R.L., Lopez-de-Silanes, F., Shleifer, A., & Vishny, R.W. (1998). Law and finance. *Journal of Political Economy*, 106(6), 1113–1155. https://doi.org/10.1086/250042

Lee, J.M., Park, J.C., & Folta, T.B. (2018). CEO career horizon, corporate governance, and real options: The role of economic short-termism. *Strategic Management Journal*, 39(10), 2703–2725. https://doi.org/10.1002/smj.2929

MEF (2022). *La competitività dei mercati finanziari italiani a supporto della crescita*. Available at: dt.mef.gov.it

Mello, A.S., & Parsons, J.E. (1998). Going public and the ownership structure of the firm. *Journal of Financial Economics*, 49(1), 79–109. https://doi.org/10.1016/S0304-405X(98)00018-X

Pagano, M., Panetta, F., & Zingales, L. (1998). Why do companies go public? An empirical analysis. *The Journal of Finance*, 53(1), 27–64. https://doi.org/10.1111/0022-1082.25448

Pagano, M. & Röell, A. (1998). The choice of stock ownership structure: Agency costs, monitoring, and the decision to go public. *The Quarterly Journal of Economics*, 113(1), 187–225. https://doi.org/10.1162/003355398555568

Pagano, M. & Volpin, P.F. (2005). The political economy of corporate governance. *American Economic Review*, 95(4), 1005–1030. Available at: jstor.org

Rajan, R.G. & Zingales, L. (2004). *Saving capitalism from the capitalists: Unleashing the power of financial markets to create wealth and spread opportunity*. Princeton: Princeton University Press.

Roe, M.J. (2000). Political preconditions to separating ownership from corporate control. *Stanford Law Review*, 53(3), 539–606. https://doi.org/10.2307/1229469

Schnatterly, K. & Johnson, S.G. (2014). Independent boards and the institutional investors that prefer them: Drivers of institutional investor heterogeneity in governance preferences. *Strategic Management Journal*, 35(10), 1552–1563. https://doi.org/10.1002/smj.2166

Stoughton, N.M. & Zechner, J. (1998). IPO-mechanisms, monitoring and ownership structure. *Journal of Financial Economics*, 49(1), 45–77. https://doi.org/10.1016/S0304-405X(98)00017-8

Technical Expert Stakeholder Group (TESG) on SMEs (2021). *Empowering EU capital markets for SMEs: Making listing cool again*. Available at: commission.europa.eu

Welch, I. (1989). Seasoned offerings, imitation costs, and the underpricing of initial public offerings. *The Journal of Finance*, 44(2), 421–449. https://doi.org/10.1111/j.1540-6261.1989.tb05064.x

Zingales, L. (1995). Insider ownership and the decision to go public. *The Review of Economic Studies*, 62(3), 425–448. https://doi.org/10.2307/2298036

4 Capital Markets Issuers: Debt Securities

by *Giulia Negri*

Luxembourg School of Business
and SDA Bocconi School of Management

In the last 15 years, following the onset of the financial crisis in 2008, the subsequent sovereign debt crisis, and the COVID-19 pandemic, the landscape of corporate funding in Italy has significantly changed. Capital markets have become an increasingly important source of funding for Italian companies, who have realized the importance of developing alternative financing options and the danger of relying excessively on bank lending.

The transition from bank funding to disintermediated, market-based alternatives is driven by different concurring factors. On the one hand, the experience of the financial crisis gave banks and their regulators a better understanding of the risks that can derive from excessive leverage, while the ensuing recession increasingly weighed on their balance sheets with the souring of non-performing loans (NPLs). This led to some retrenchment by banks, as their efforts were primarily directed to deleveraging while cleansing their balance sheets, rather than supporting economic growth through the provision of credit. As a result, companies faced the reduced supply of credit through the traditional banking channel and faced the stark reality of the risks of relying on only one funding source. To diversify funding strategies, demand for non-bank finance intensified. In the light of this, companies started to progressively substitute bank loans with corporate bonds, with investors stepping in to fill the corporate funding gap resulting from the contraction in bank lending.

On the other hand, the disintermediation of corporate funding is favored by the monetary policy adopted by central banks, which has contributed to a decline in long-term bond yields, prompting investors to head for the riskier ends of the corporate bond market. As a result, with yield-starved investors looking more favorably on relatively more risky assets, bond markets became available for a larger number of companies. Nonetheless, the diversification of corporate funding has been accompanied by structural change flowing from, for example, technological innovation that facilitates new forms of intermediation such as peer-to-peer lending.

This development is extremely welcome, especially within the Italian economic environment, which displayed financial weaknesses during the crisis due to its historical and almost exclusive reliance on conventional bank credit. However, the transition of Italian companies to a more balanced funding structure is far from complete. The post-crisis fallback of bank lending was only partially offset by an increase in bond financing. On the one hand, the domestic debt capital market was mostly confined to companies with the highest credit rating and therefore inadequately developed to completely fill the corporate funding gap resulting from the credit crunch. On the other hand, access to more developed foreign markets, dominated by foreign investors, was mainly restricted to Italian companies with sufficient critical mass or enough international recognition to attract investors interest. This meant that the majority of small and medium-sized companies (SMEs), which play a vital role in the Italian economy, were left out of this form of financing. Excessive bank dependence has therefore represented in the postcrisis period an obstacle to the growth of Italian firms and a drag on the economy.

At the same time, investors do not just seek for the highest credit rating bond, but in recent years, their interest shifted from "pure return" to a "clean return" under the logic of investing in sustainable assets, that is companies that adopt sustainable practices. This increasing interest had a twofold effect. On the one side, companies started to issue bonds linked to a performance defined as "sustainable," such as Green Bonds, or Sustainability-linked Bonds. On the other side, this pushed the European Commission to create a framework to help investors identify if and how an asset is sustainable.

The rest of the chapter is structured as follows: Section 4.2 presents the debt context from a macro-economic point of view with reference to the European and the Italian landscape, Section 4.3 presents the corporate debt context, concentrating on bonds issuances from 2006 through 2021, minibonds, and NPLs. Section 4.4 presents the trends for one of the hottest topics in capital markets: ESG Bonds, and finally, Section 4.5 illustrates the research findings of Caselli et al. (2019) about the factors impacting the likelihood of issuing a bond and the cost drivers of bond issuance.

4.1 Macroeconomic Debt Context

Debt funding is crucial to Italian companies. As of December 31, 2022, the leverage ratio for the listed Italian companies was 1.30. Most importantly, debt funding is pivotal at a country level in Italy, as the Italian government debt historically exceeds the country GDP. To understand the current level of the debt exposure and the current bond issuances of Italian listed companies, it is necessary to adopt a more comprehensive view and look at the trend of the real GDP in Italy in the last period.

Figure 4.1 represents the growth rates of the real GDP since the burst of the Global Financial Crisis of 2007 until 2021 for a sample of selected countries (France, Italy, Germany, and Spain) and for the European Union. It can be seen that the trend of the change rate of the real GDP of the past 15 years has been discontinuous across the five areas. At the European Union trend, the change for the year 2021, 11.8%, represents one of the highest growths of the period, outperformed only by the change between 2007 and 2008, after the collapse of 2007. The lowest point is represented by the change between 2014 and 2015 (–13.4%).

As it can be already gathered from the previous figure, the COVID-19 pandemic hit hard on public spending. This is visible from Figure 4.2, that presents the deficit/surplus of the same selected areas 2017 through 2021.

At a European Union level, it is possible to say that the pandemic toll heavily impacted government spending. The European Union deficit was slightly lower than 0 in the period 2017–2019, where the lowest value was –0.8% in 2017. Due to the unforeseeable spending of 2020 and 2021, the deficit got worse and it reached record levels of 6.7% in 2020 and 4.6% in 2021.

Figure 4.1 Growth real GDP

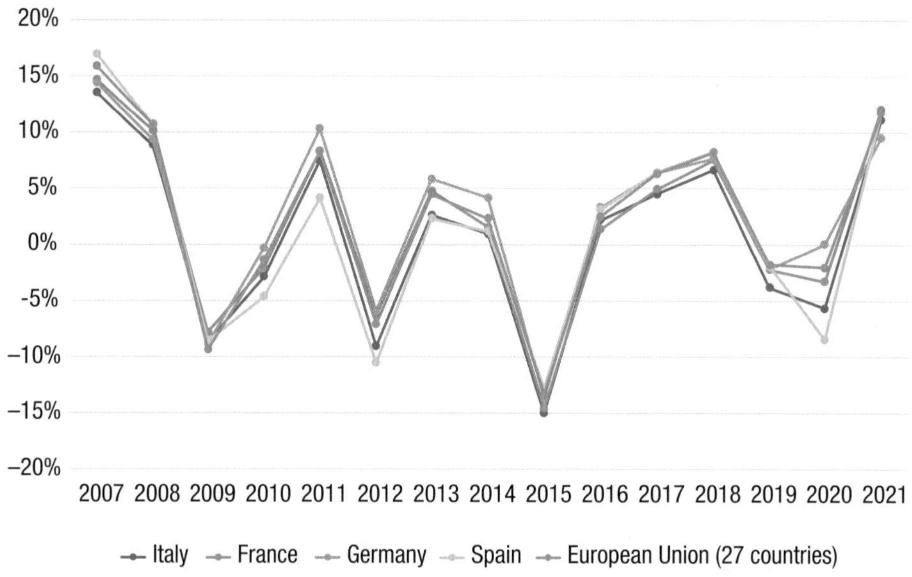

Source: World Bank.

Taking a closer look at the individual countries, it can be seen that in the pre-pandemic years, Germany preserved a situation of surplus, reaching the highest level for the period considered in 2018 with 1.9%, while in 2020 and in 2021, it reached a deficit of around –4%, where 2020 was the worst year of the series with a deficit for 4.3%. A sharp increase in the deficit level can be seen for the other countries taken into consideration, France, Italy, and Spain. Spain was the one that recorded the highest level of deficit in 2020, more than 10% (10.1%), and the worst level across all countries of the European Union. Italy recorded a deficit larger than 9% (9.5%), mildly better than Spain, but performing worse than France (9%). In 2021, the government deficits reduced for all areas represented. In particular, with reference to Italy, the deficit improved and reached 7.2%, despite still being larger than the Spanish and the French level, 6.9% and 6.5% respectively.

Figure 4.2 Government deficit/surplus (% of GDP)

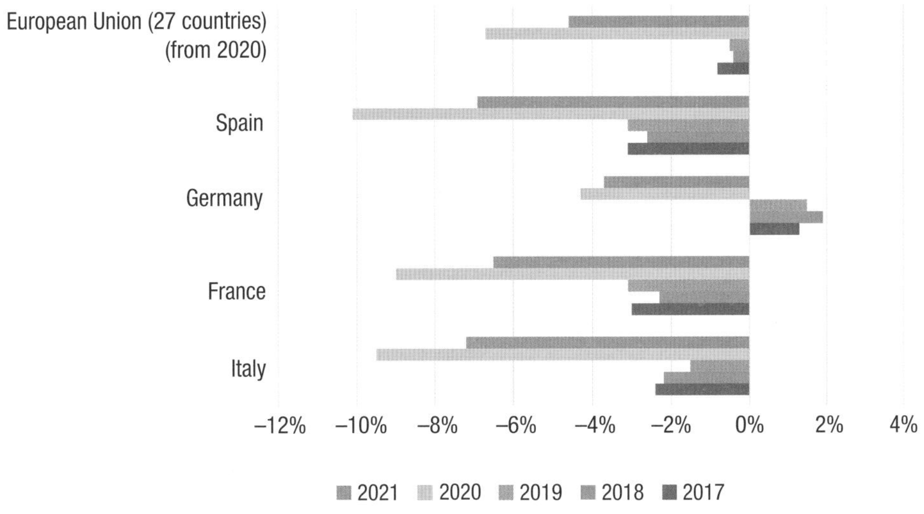

Source: Eurostat.

As a complementary note, it is worth mentioning that in 2020, the average deficit of the European Union (27 Member States) was 6.7%, and there was only one country with a government spending surplus, Denmark (surplus was 0.2%).

4.2 The Italian Debt Market

This section presents the current features of the Italian debt market, first introducing the trend in bond issuances of the period 2006–2021, and then presenting data about minibonds and NPLs.

Before delving into the core features of the Italian debt market, it is important to understand that the disintermediation is not the only element that has been changing in the last year. Italian listed companies are also changing to whom they ask for their financing. This is proved by a piece of research by Accornero et al. (2018), that was conducted on a sample of 500 debt offerings. This study shows that foreign investors are the largest subscribers of debt securities issued by Italian non-financial listed

Figure 4.3 **Breakdown of investors in debt securities issued by Italian non-financial companies by nationality and type, 2013 vs. 2017**

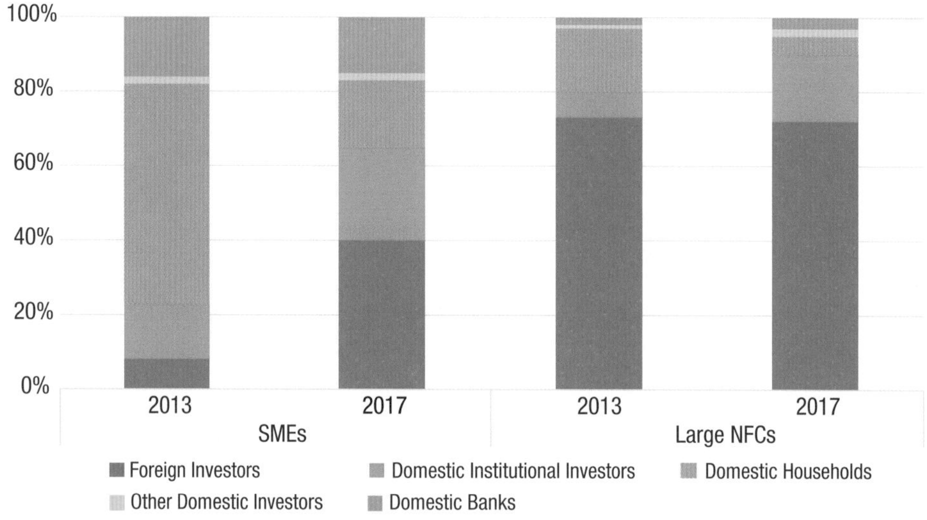

Source: Bank of Italy; Accornero et al. (2018).

firms (**Figure 4.3**). It can be seen that domestic institutional investors and domestic banks play a minor role. This means that companies are left out of this form of financing due to the structural lack of a strong domestically focused investor base. In Italy, debt securities issued by non-financial companies end up crowded out by the huge volumes of bank and public debt offerings.

4.2.1 Bond issuance

Figure 4.4 presents the trend from 2018 through the third quarter of 2022. It can be seen that in 2019, prior to the COVID crisis, the outstanding debt for non-financial companies' ratio was 65%, while at the end of 2020, it peaked at almost 74%. This sharp increase is most likely generated by two effects: The first is the increase in the financial needs of corporations for the year 2020 (i.e. the numerator of the ratio) and the second one is generated by the decrease in the GDP level (i.e. the denominator of the ratio).

Figure 4.4 Non-financial corporations debt outstanding to GDP (left-hand scale) and leverage (right-hand scale)

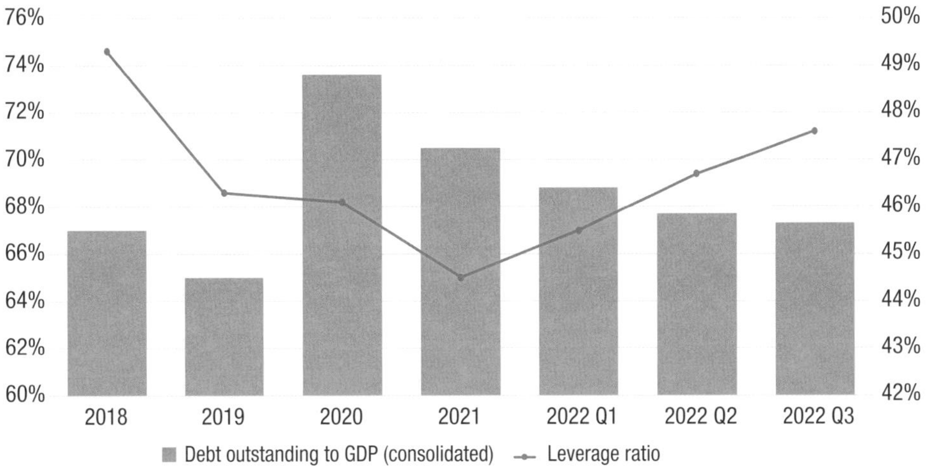

Leverage is expressed as a percentage of total Liabilities and Equity.

Source: ECB.

In 2021, the ratio slightly decreased and reached 71% and then kept on improving throughout the first three quarters for 2022 until it reached 67%, coming back to the pre-pandemic level of 2018, despite being still larger than the minimum value it had in 2019.

After a helicopter view on the trend on the debt market in the Italian landscape, it is possible to analyze some of the components of the financial leverage, namely bonds.

In the last years, the interest of Italian listed companies for bonds increased. This is due to the very advantageous conditions at which firms could access corporate debt markets, as it can be seen by **Figure 4.5**, which compares the spread yield to worst for investment grade and high-yield bonds. Because of an extraordinarily loose monetary policy, yields on corporate bonds dropped to historic lows in the last ten years (with the exception of the first months of 2020). In this landscape, the appetite for risk of yield-starved investors probably contributed to the compression of the spread between high-yield and investment grade issues, making

Figure 4.5 Yield to worst: corporate bond indices

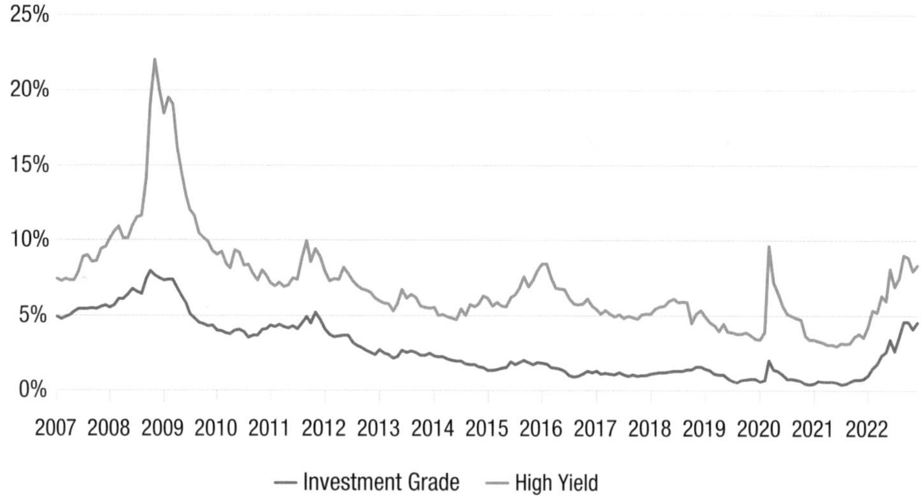

Source: Bloomberg.

market debt funding more viable and more attractive to a broader range of potential issuers.

Over the period 2006–2021, Italian non-financial companies issued 576 bonds overall, accounting for 6% of the 9,324 bonds issued by European non-financial companies. Across the whole period, the average maturity is 9.15 years. For 93% of them, namely 8,647, the coupon type was fixed, while for 7%, namely 677, the coupon type was floating.

Italy ranks at the fourth position of the countries where most issuers are headquartered, the first three being the United Kingdom (2,242 issues; accounting for 24%), Germany (1,868 issues; accounting for 20%), and France (1,864 issues; accounting for 20%). At an aggregate level, European companies issued an aggregate value of $6,465,942.52 million, while Italian companies issued a total of $458,692.73 million.

Figure 4.6 reports the industry breakdown both for Italy and for Europe. At Italian level, the most represented sector is Utilities and Power, weighing for one-third of all issuances; at European level, Consumer

Figure 4.6 Bond issuers (2006–2021): industry representation

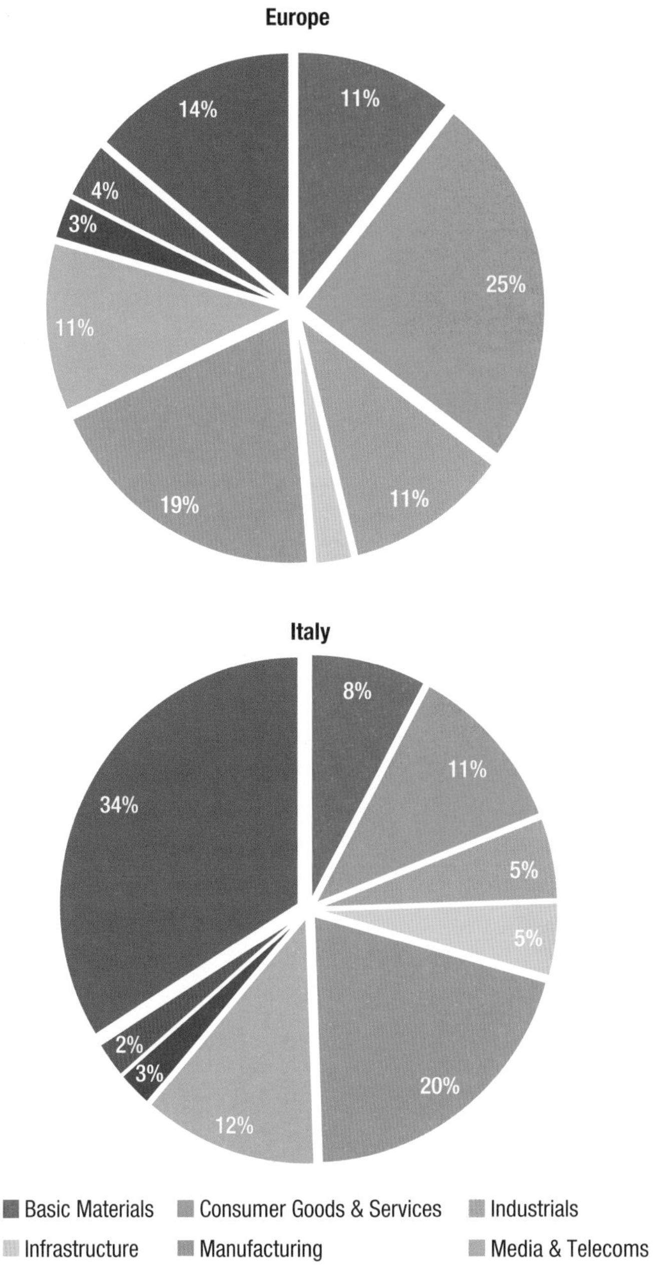

Source: EquitaLab; Bondradar.

Goods & Services is mostly represented accounting for one fourth of the overall sample.

Figure 4.7 presents the trend in terms of volume and value across Italian and European issuers in the period 2006–2021. The figure reports the number of bonds issued in the two areas and the average value by area.

Talking about the volume of issues, it can be seen how 2020 and 2021 reached two among the highest levels of the period, in line with the European level. In Italy, 51 bonds were issued in 2020 (+21% with respect to 2019), and 64 bonds were issued in 2021 (+25% with respect to 2020), setting the overall record for the Italian bond issuances of the whole period. These spikes are in line with what presented above in **Figure 4.4**, that indicated an increase in the debt outstanding for non-financial companies, hence confirming why the debt-to-GDP ratio increased.

Figure 4.7 Trend of volume (left-hand scale) and value (right-hand scale) of bonds issued in Italy and in Europe

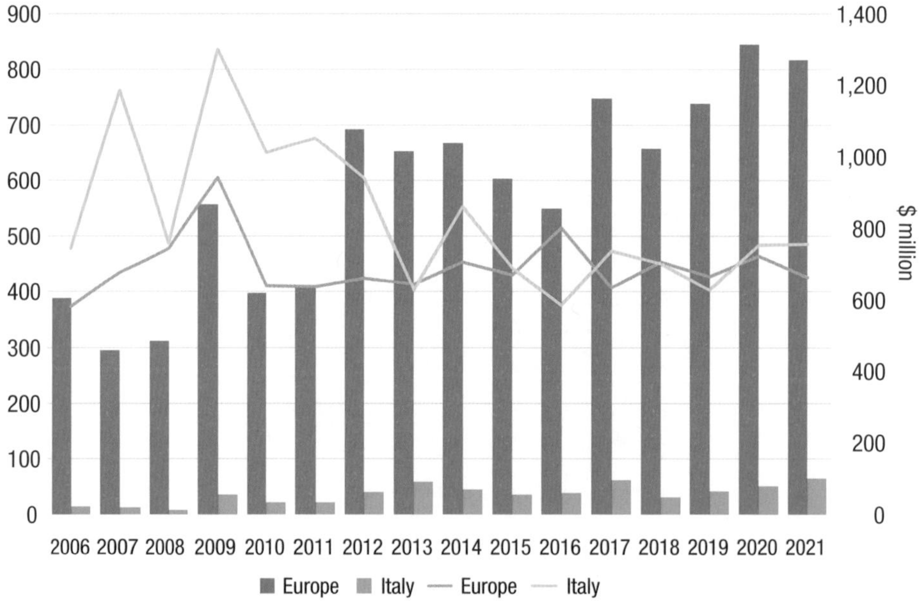

Source: EquitaLab; Bondradar.

Concerning the European market, it can be seen that 2020 is the record year in terms of number of issuances, 845 (+14% with respect to 2019) and 816 in 2021 (–3% with respect to 2020).

If the Italian issuers play a lesser role from the volume point of view, from a value point of view, Italian issuers play a front-row role.

Across the 16 years from 2006 through 2021, only in 4 years, the Italian average value of issued bond is lower than the European one (namely in 2013, 2016, 2018, and in 2019). This confirms the need of Italian companies to rely on debt and, at the same time, the current disintermediation wave that is linking more and more Italian non-financial companies with capital markets.

From a value perspective, the time series can be separated into two sub-periods: before 2012 (included) and after 2013 (included). In the years prior to 2013, Italian bonds are on average much larger than European ones (with the exception of 2008). The record years in Italy were 2009 and 2007. In 2007, and from 2009 through 2011, the average value is larger than $1 billion, for the sake of clarity it is worth mentioning a few companies that issued bonds over those years. In that period, ENEL issued more than $33 billion in bonds, while ENI issued more than $13 billion in bonds, just to name a few.

After 2013, the trend of the average value gets stagnant and more aligned to the rest of Europe, with few exceptions represented by then Wind in 2014 (see **Table 4.1** reporting the ten biggest bonds by size issued by non-financial companies).

Figures 4.8 and **4.9** report the ranking for the bonds issued by Italian and by European companies, respectively. Most securities enjoy a positive rating, namely investment grading, both in Italy and in Europe. However, in Italy, the trend of investment grade is non-constant over time, and as a consequence, the years from 2013 through 2015 see a larger portion of high-yield securities, with 2014 being the worst performing year of the time series with more than one half of the bond issues rated as High Yield.

As it can be seen in **Figure 4.9**, European bonds are generally better rated than Italian ones. The swing effect noted in the Italian representation is not that evident in the European landscape despite 2013 and 2014 present more than 30% of bonds as High Yield.

Table 4.1 **Largest bonds by size issued by Italian non-financial corporations (2006–2021)**

Year	Issuer	Currency of issuance	Value USD equivalent (m)
2009	ENEL	EUR	3,571.45
2012	ENEL	EUR	3,298.35
2014	Wind	EUR	2,856.00
2014	Wind	USD	2,800.00
2010	ENEL	EUR	2,697.03
2014	Wind	EUR	2,415.00
2010	Wind	EUR	2,363.98
2009	ENEL	GBP	2,309.94
2009	Fiat Chrysler	EUR	2,233.55
2009	ENEL	EUR	2,150.06

Source: EquitaLab; Bondradar.

Figure 4.8 **Rating of bonds issued by Italian companies**

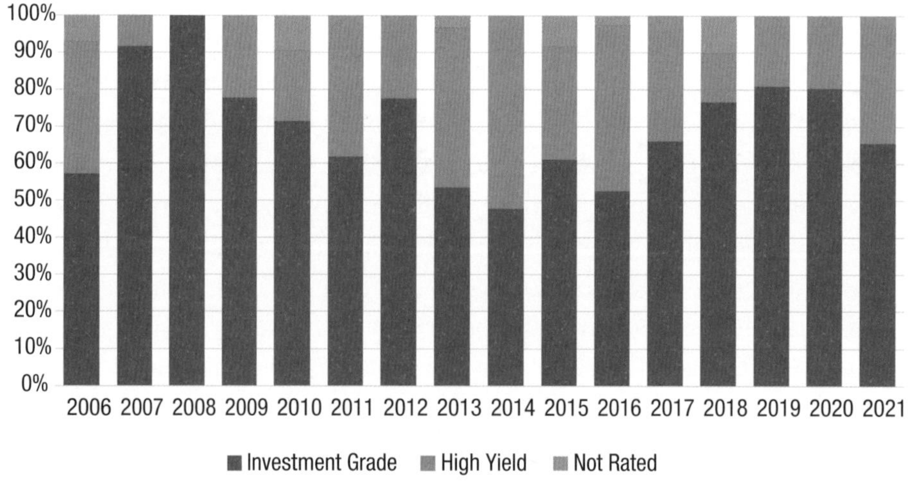

Source: EquitaLab; Bondradar.

Figure 4.9 **Rating of bonds issued by European companies**

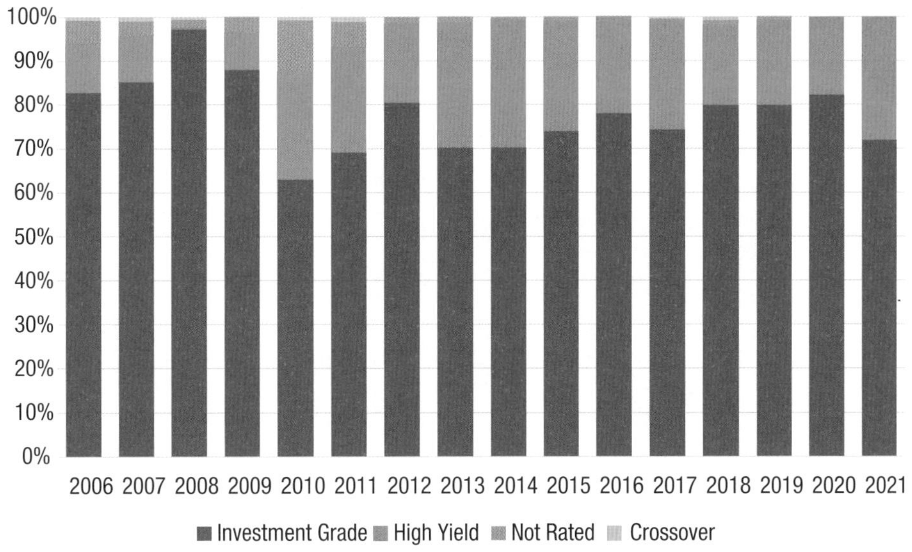

Source: EquitaLab; Bondradar.

4.2.2 The minibond trend in Italy

Disintermediation gained ground also among SMEs. Indeed, since their introduction in 2013 through September 2022, 329 minibonds have provided access to debt capital markets to a considerable number of SMEs. The number of issues grew year after year, reaching a record of 57 new offerings in 2017 (**Figure 4.10**). Moreover, after the rising trend of issuers of minibond in the first years, the initial enthusiasm decreased after it reached a first spike in 2014 with an aggregate value of €521 million and a second one in 2018 with an aggregate value of €460 million. Looking at the average size of the minibonds, an expectedly opposite trend can be seen in 2019 as it was one of years with one of the lowest number of minibond issued, and yet it was the year with the highest average value per issue, €15.37 million.

As per the maturity of the minibond, throughout the whole period, it is 5.4 years on average, and the shortest average maturity is recorded

Figure 4.10 Volumes and values (€ million) of minibonds issued by Italian companies

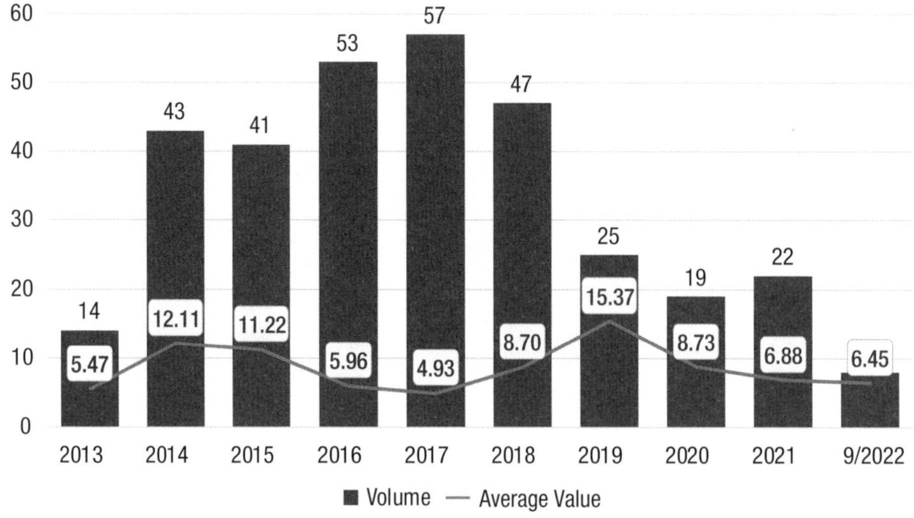

Source: EquitaLab.

in 2017 (3.3 years), and the furthest average maturity is recorded in 2019 (8.1 years). As per the capital repayment, for 56% of the minibonds issued from 2013 through September 2022, the capital repayment is amortized, while for the outstanding 46%, the capital repayment is under the form of a bullet. The 329 minibonds considered in the analysis were issued by a total of 269 companies. About 226 issued only one minibond, whereas 43 companies issued more than one minibond; more precisely 30 of them issued 2 minibonds, ten issued 3, two companies issued 4, and just one company issued 5 minibonds.

4.2.3 Non-performing loans

Figure 4.11 presents the trend of NPLs from 2014 through 2021. At first glance, it can be seen that the portion of NPLs is decreasing overall. At a European Union, the maximum level was reached in 2014 with an 11.71%. This value has been progressively decreasing to 2.5% in 2021. The Italian

Figure 4.11 **Gross non-performing loans (% of gross loans)**

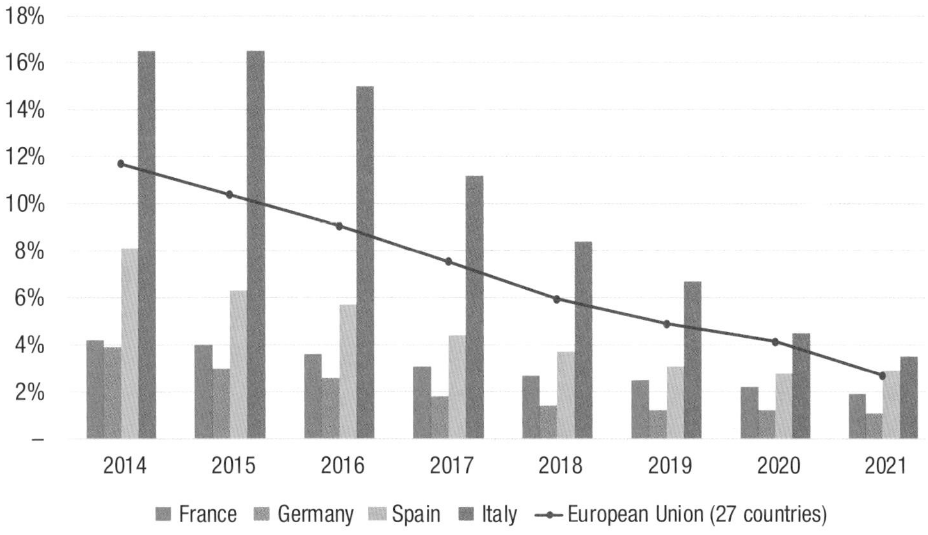

Source: Eurostat; ECB.

portion of NPLs out of gross loans is much higher than the EU average, the maximum level was reached in 2014 and 2015 where the percentage was 16.50%. In more recent years, the level is steadily decreasing and reached 3.5% in 2021. The figure also shows the level of NPLs for France, Germany, and Spain. Among the selected areas, Germany is the best performing one with a maximum level of 3.90% in 2014, whereas Spain and France both presented larger percentages of NPLs over the time analyzed (8.10% for Spain in 2014; 4.20% for France in 2014), that was still considerably lower than the EU average.

4.3 ESG Bonds

The COVID-19 pandemic accelerated the focus on sustainability and sustainable finance that started some years prior in response to the increasing trend of temperature. Sustainable debt instruments have raised financing for many sustainable development projects in different countries over the past years and are crucial in the transition to a low-carbon and more inclusive economy. Since the pandemic hit, the social dimension has gained much more importance, bringing in social bond issuances as a result. Given the new sense of urgency in addressing climate change and societal issues, the solid growth in green, social, sustainability, and sustainability-linked bonds is likely to continue. At the same time, the European Union is introducing new regulatory frameworks to make sure that Europe takes the lead in a sustainable finance direction.

With the increasing interest both from a regulatory perspective and, as a consequence, from capital markets many debt securities have now been labeled as "green" or "social." In order to shed some light on the existing taxonomy of sustainable-related debt instruments, some definitions need to be presented (PwC Luxembourg, 2021; ICMA, 2021):

- *Green Bonds.* There are four types of Green Bonds:
  - Standard Green Use of Proceeds Bond: a standard recourse-to-the issuer debt obligation.
  - Green Revenue Bond: a nonrecourse-to-the issuer debt obligation in which the credit exposure in the bond is to the pledged cash flows of the revenue streams, fees, taxes etc., and whose use of proceeds go to related or unrelated green project(s).
  - Green Project Bond: a project bond for a single or multiple green project(s) for which the investor has direct exposure to the risk of the project(s) with or without potential recourse to the issuer.
  - Green Securitized Bond and Covered Bond: a bond collateralized by one or more specific green project(s), including but not limited to Covered Bonds, Asset-Backed Securities (ABS), Mortgage-Backed Securities (MBS), and other structures. The first source of repayment is generally the cash flows of the assets.
- *Social Bonds* are any type of bond instrument where the proceeds will be exclusively applied to finance or refinance in part or in full new and/or existing social projects. Different types of Social Bonds exist in the market. Following the logic applied to Green Bonds, Social Bonds can be classified into the following four categories:

- Standard Social Use of Proceeds Bond: a standard recourse-to-the-issuer debt obligation aligned with the Social Bond Principles (SBP) (ICMA, 2021).
- Social Revenue Bond: a non-recourse-to-the-issuer debt obligation aligned with the SBP in which the credit exposure in the bond is to the pledged cash flows of the revenue streams, fees, taxes, etc., and whose use of proceeds go to related or unrelated social project(s).
- Social Project Bond: a project bond for a single or multiple social project(s) for which the investor has direct exposure to the risk of the project(s) with or without potential recourse to the issuer, and that is aligned with the SBP.
- Social Securitized and Covered Bond: a bond collateralized by one or more specific social project(s), including but not limited to covered bonds, ABS, MBS, and other structures; and aligned with the SBP. The first source of repayment is generally the cash flows of the assets. This type of bond covers, for example, covered bonds backed by social housing, hospitals, schools.

• *Sustainability Bonds* are bonds where the proceeds will be exclusively applied to finance or refinance a combination of both green and social projects.
• *Sustainability-Linked Bonds* are any type of bond instrument for which the financial and/or structural characteristics (typically their interest coupon) can vary depending on whether the issuer achieves predefined Sustainability/ESG objectives.

For the sake of clarity, it is worth mentioning that in the document as well as in the analysis, all the above categories have been grouped together, and labeled as "ESG Bonds."

In Europe, in the time frame from 2006 through 2021, 1,147 ESG bonds have been issued, across all sectors (including, *inter alia*, financial companies) for an aggregate value of $1.06 trillion.

Figure 4.12 presents the trend of the volume and of the value of ESG bonds issued. It can be seen that despite the analysis starting in 2006, the first ESG bonds of the sample dates 2012. Since 2012, the number and the aggregate of ESG bonds rocketed until it reached a record in 2021 with 484 ESG securities issued corresponding to half of a trillion USD ($487 billion).

Figure 4.12 ESG bonds trends in volume and value ($ million) in Europe

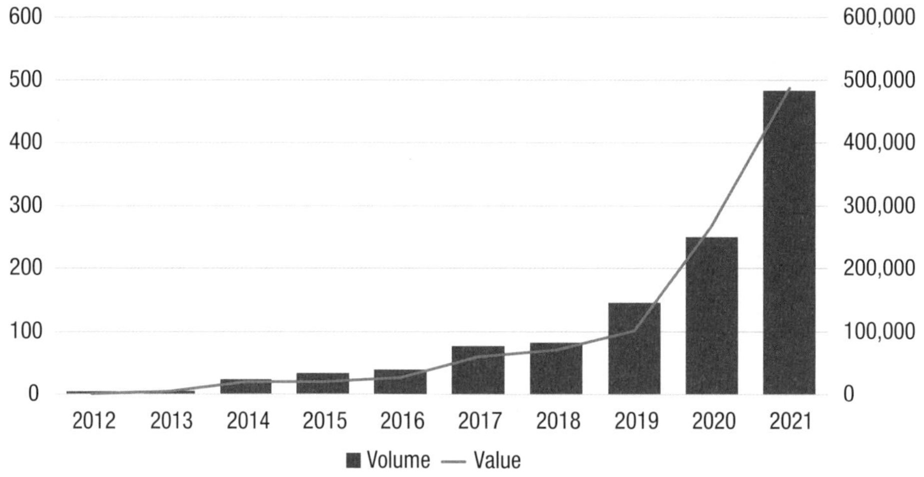

Source: EquitaLab; Bondradar.

Across the whole period, there is a yearly average growth rate in value for 140%, and a yearly average growth rate in the volumes for 84%, standing for an increase in the average value that each ESG bond has as well.

As for the average maturity of ESG Bonds, it is 9.7 years and it is quite constant throughout the whole period (maximum being 10.26 in 2019, and minimum being 5.07 in 2013).

From industry and country perspectives, **Figure 4.13** presents an industry breakdown and **Figure 4.14** presents a country breakdown.

It can be seen that corporate and financial companies overall represent three quarters of all ESG Bonds (75%). The remaining quarter is split among Local Government Agencies (e.g., Regions), States, and European Commission agencies (referred to in the pie chart as "Supra").

From a geographical perspective, the three countries where companies that issued ESG Bonds are mostly located in France, Germany, and UK, that on aggregate are 45%, for a total of 511 securities. Italy ranks as seventh with 7% of companies that have issued an ESG bond (namely, 85).

Figure 4.13 ESG bonds issued in Europe (2006–2021): industry breakdown

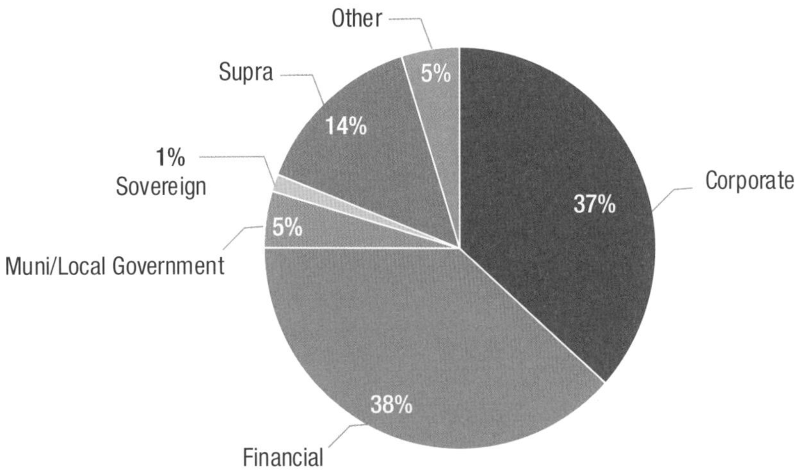

Source: EquitaLab; Bondradar.

Figure 4.14 ESG bonds issued in Europe (2006–2021): country breakdown

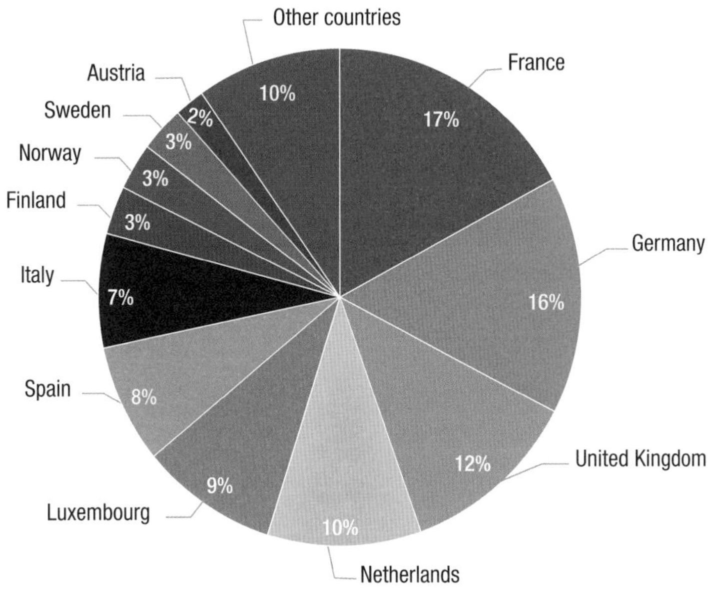

Source: EquitaLab; Bondradar.

4.4 The Determinants and the Costs of Bond Issues for Italian Non-Financial Companies

4.4.1 Research rationale

The final section of the chapter is dedicated to the empirical analysis promoted by Equita SIM and Bocconi in 2019 about the access to the corporate bond market by Italian firms. More specifically, they study what drives the choice of issuing a bond for the first time (inaugural offering) and the determinants of the pricing of that bond at launch. The goal is to shed light on the factors that foster or hinder corporate funding disintermediation by identifying the main differences between issuers and non-issuers, as well as among various issue types. To this end, they collect data from Dealogic DCM Manager on corporate bonds offerings by Italian listed and non-listed firms in domestic and international markets. The analysis is focused on first-time (inaugural) issuers only, as this should allow Authors to better identify their characteristics. Consistent with other studies that adopted the same approach, such as Datta et al. (2000), Hale & Santos (2008), and Accornero et al. (2015), they define inaugural issues as all those offerings by companies that had not issued any bond in the previous 10 years. The analysis excludes banks and financial services companies, because their funding needs differ from those of non-financial companies, so they may access market funding on alternative grounds. The final sample consists of 102 inaugural bond offerings. Among these, 12.5% have multiple tranches, bringing the total of different tranches in the sample to 124. The analysis of the choice of accessing the bond market for the first time is carried out at the issue level, while to study the determinants of pricing the analysis is carried out at the tranche level. **Figure 4.15** shows the distribution of the inaugural issues over the sample period. Consistent with increasing disintermediation and the low yields following QE, which facilitated access to debt capital markets for a broader range of firms, inaugural issues are concentrated in the post-2012 period.

The sample can be considered as representative of the entire population of Italian non-financial companies, as it encompasses issuers from

Figure 4.15 Inaugural issues by Italian non-financial companies

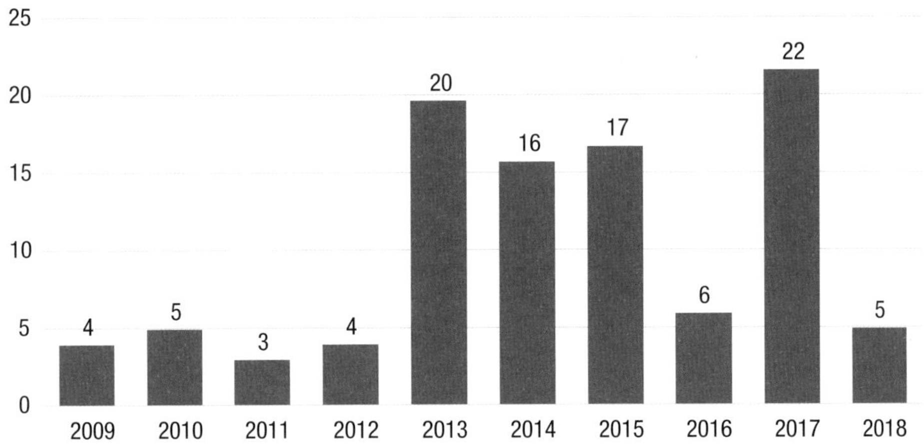

Source: Dealogic.

20 different industry groups. **Figure 4.16** provides a representation of the sectorial breakdown of these issuers. Companies belonging to the sectors of Utility & Energy, Transportation, or Telecommunications account for approximately one-third of the sample. As for the rest of the sample, it has a good level of heterogeneity both industry-wise and in terms of the financing needs that issuers try to meet by accessing the debt market. This is reported by **Figure 4.17**, that shows the reported use of proceeds for the offerings in question.

Among the more specific purposes specified by the issuers, debt refinancing seems to play an important role, in line with a trend that sees non-financial companies increasingly replacing bank debt with market funding.

Concerning the issue characteristics, almost two-thirds (62%) of the offerings in the sample are investment-grade rated, while the remaining part (38%) is rated as High Yield. Despite the fact that none of them are directed at retail investors, 58.9% are offered as public issues and 41.1% as private placements. In addition, 10.5% of the offerings are addressed to the domestic market, while 79% target euro area markets.

Figure 4.16 Inaugural issues by Italian non-financial companies (2009–2018): breakdown by sector

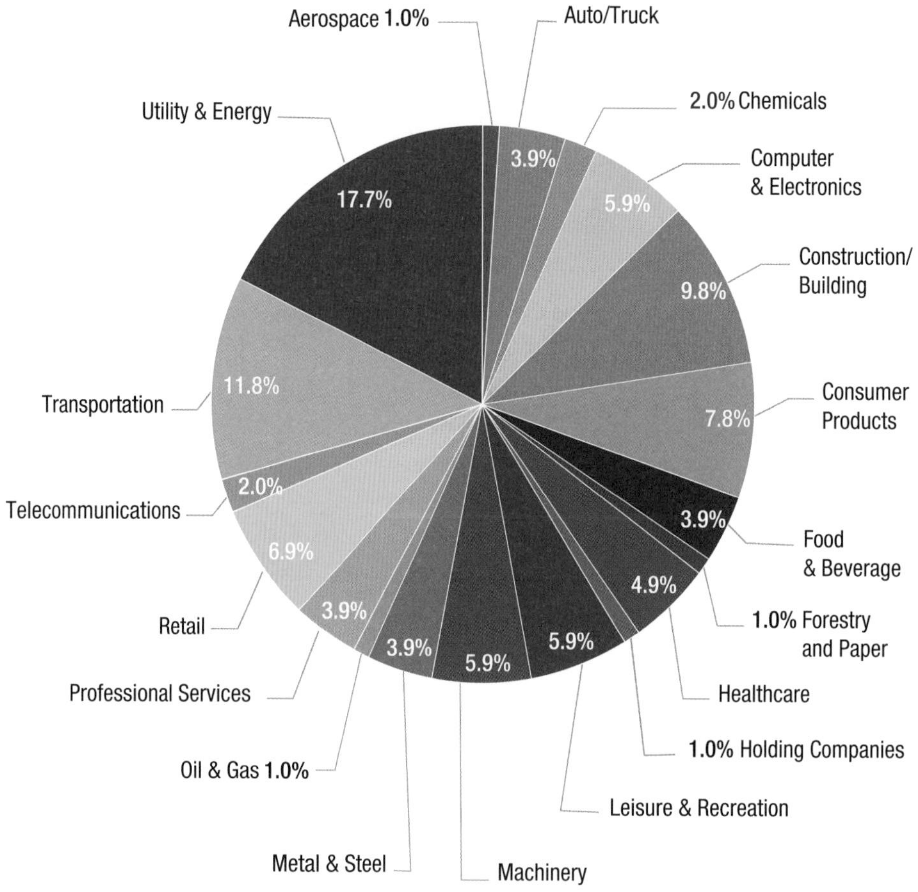

Source: Dealogic.

Figure 4.18 shows relative markets of listing. Luxembourg and Ireland are favorite destinations, though it is worth mentioning that most issues have multiple listing markets. Concerning the listing currency, the issues represented in the sample are predominantly denominated in Euros (88.7%); only 11.3% are in US dollars. Approximately half are registered (52.4%),

Figure 4.17 Inaugural issues by Italian non-financial companies: reported use of proceeds, non-exclusive categories

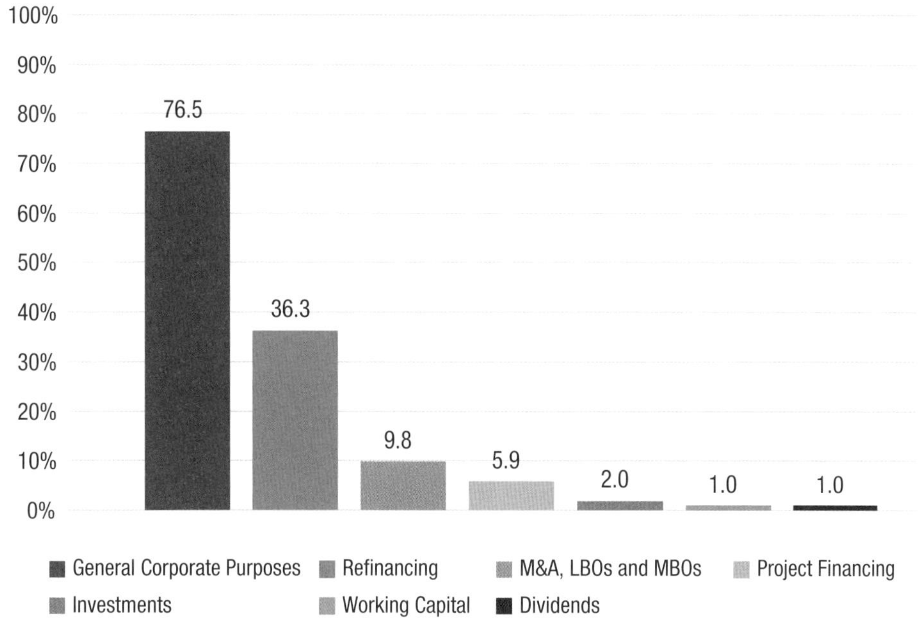

Source: Dealogic.

while the majority of the issues are registered fixed rate (90.32%), senior (98.2%), unsecured (67.5%), and callable (60.8%).

To further corroborate the representativeness of the sample, **Table 4.2** provides summary statistics in terms of issue characteristics. The size of the issues in the sample ranges from a minimum of €5 million up to approximately €1.6 billion, while the average issue size is €329 million (and median is €215 million). On average, each issue involves three or more banks, with gross fees ranging from 0.2% to 2% of the deal's value. Only one tranche per issue is generally offered, but in a few cases multiple tranches are issued, with a maximum of five. Maturities range from a minimum of 4 years to almost 30 years. The average number of years to maturity is approximately 7.5. Coupon rates, spreads, and yields vary considerably within the sample, which suggests a certain degree of heteroge-

Figure 4.18 Inaugural issues by Italian non-financial companies: markets (non-exclusive) of listing

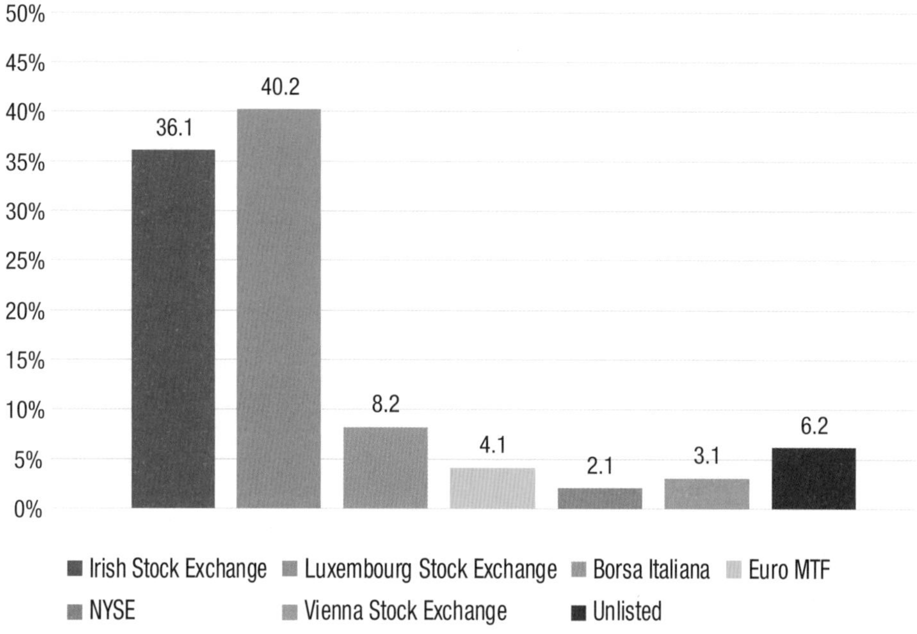

Source: Dealogic.

neity among issues with respect to credit risk. This implies that more and more companies regardless of their creditworthiness are able to access the debt capital markets. Moreover, the decline of coupon rates, spreads, and yields over time reflects the effect of expansionary monetary policies and quantitative easing on the cost of accessing debt capital markets. Also, the time to complete the issue varies considerably within the sample. However, rather than depending solely on the characteristics of the offering, the time that elapses between the filing and the settlement of the issue depends on the market where it is listed. In this respect, they find that in general issues are more expedited where regulation is less demanding and markets are considered as more efficient, such as Luxembourg or Ireland.

Table 4.2 Inaugural issues by Italian non-financial companies: descriptive statistics, all tranches

Variable	Obs.	Mean	St. Dev.	Min	Med	Max
Issue-level variables						
No. of banks	102	3.61	2.70	1	3	11
No. of bookrunners	102	3.34	2.58	1	3	12
No. of tranches	102	1.22	0.58	1	1	5
Deal value (€ million)	102	329	362	5	215	1,570
Gross fee (€ million)	102	2.43	2.96	–	1.26	15.70
% of Deal value	102	0.71	0.64	0.2	0.35	2.00
Tranche-level variables						
Years to maturity	124	7.45	3.56	4.37	7.00	29.59
Rating	64	BB/BB+	2.9 no.	CCC+	BB+	A-
Coupon (fixed rate, %)	81	4.64	2.18	0.50	4.50	12.00
Pre-2012	10	5.08	0.91	3.75	5.13	7.00
Post-2012	71	4.58	2.30	0.50	4.37	12.00
Spread to benchmark (bp)	43	404	247	100	332	1,134
Pre-2012	7	239	61	155	257	316
Post-2012	36	436	256	100	401	1,134
Spread to swap (bp)	24	202	104	60	184	514
Pre-2012	6	222	51	145	225	290
Post-2012	18	196	116	60	172	514
Yield to maturity (%)	70	4.77	2.41	0.68	4.56	12.67
Pre-2012	8	5.40	0.75	4.61	5.28	7.00
Post-2012	62	4.66	2.53	0.68	4.34	12.67
From filing to settlement (days)	90	21.04	90.43	–	7	794
Luxembourg Stock Exchange	32	6.53	2.38	–	7	12
Irish Stock Exchange	24	9.54	8.04	–	7	38
Unlisted	28	10.64	20.90	–	3	98

4.4.2 Drivers underlying the choice of non-financial companies to issue bonds

To study the determinants of the choice of accessing the bond market for the first time, they look at the differences between issuers and non-issuers. To this end, they collect financial data from Bureau Van Dijk Amadeus on all Italian non-financial companies, incorporated under the legal status of S.r.l. or S.p.A., with total assets larger than €10 million (last reported).

They then match each first-time issuer with its closest comparable non-issuer belonging to the same peer group, as defined according to Amadeus' industry and size classification. In particular, they pair up each first-time issuer with its closest comparable in terms of annual sales in the year prior to the issue. **Table 4.3** provides summary statistics on these companies in terms of age, total assets (and rate of growth in the year before the issue), sales (and rate of growth in the year before the issue), leverage (computed as the ratio between long-term financial debt

Table 4.3 Summary statistics for first-time issuers and comparable non-issuers (in the year prior to the issue)

	First-time issuers		Non-issuers		Differences	
	Mean	St. Dev.	Mean	St. Dev.	Diff.	T-stat
Age	28.47	28.02	29.96	25.35	−1.49	(−0.34)
Total assets (€ million)	2,353.89	4,010.00	1,504.26	3,605.83	849.63	(1.33)
Asset growth	0.09	0.40	0.10	0.59	−0.01	(−0.13)
Sales (€ million)	1,346.01	2,071.79	921.70	1,857.84	424.31	(1.29)
Sales growth	0.10	0.47	0.05	0.30	0.06	(0.79)
Financial leverage	0.21	0.16	0.09	0.14	0.11***	(4.58)
Return on assets	0.06	0.05	0.04	0.09	0.02	(1.62)
Return on equity	0.09	0.19	0.08	0.19	0.01	(0.17)
Investment rate	0.27	0.72	0.32	1.26	−0.05	(0.27)

*, **, and *** indicate that the coefficients are different from 0 at 10%, 5%, and 1% levels of statistical significance, respectively.

and total assets), return on assets (computed as the EBIT reported in the year before the issue over total assets), return on equity (computed as the net income reported in the year before the issue over the book value of equity), and investments (proxied by the growth in fixed assets net of depreciation and amortization expenses in the year before the issue). As expected, first-time issuers are large, mature, and profitable companies. The average company reports total assets of more than €2.3 billion and sales larger of €1.3 billion. This organization is nearly 30 years old and has positive growth trends, both in terms of assets (+9% the year prior to the issue), sales (+10% the year prior to the issue) and investments (+27% the year prior to the issue). No significant difference emerges between issuers and their comparables, apart from greater financial leverage. Indeed, issuers report an average leverage of 21% in the year prior to the offering, while the respective figure for their comparable is 14%. This finding is consistent with the issuers recurrently reporting debt refinancing as their intended use of proceeds (see **Figure 4.17**) and may suggest a pecking-order among sources of debt. In this framework, companies would rank bank debt first in order of preference, and then tap debt markets on a residual basis as an alternative source of funding.

To better assess whether the decision to issue a bond for the first time is determined by pre-issue characteristics of the firms analyzes and taken into consideration, Authors model the choice of accessing the bond market as a dichotomous variable that takes the value of 1 for companies that issued a bond and 0 otherwise. They then link the decision to issue a bond to its determinants by means of a probit model. The determinants of the probit models are the company characteristics reported in the year prior to the issue, including the age of the company, its size (computed as the logarithmic transformation of its total assets), growth (in terms of total assets), leverage, return on assets, and rate of investment. This approach is similar to the one adopted by Accornero et al. (2015) to study first-time corporate bond issuers in Italy. **Table 4.4** shows the results of the analysis under alternative model specifications, focusing on different groups of variables.

The estimation of the model indicates that size and leverage are the key characteristics that drive the issuer's decision to launch a bond, rather

Table 4.4 Probit model estimations: coefficients and year-clustered robust standard errors (in parenthesis)

	I	II	III	IV
Age	−0.0027236	−0.0019688	−0.0015914	−0.0016025
	(0.0040916)	(0.0033983)	(0.0033383)	(0.0033293)
Size	0.4368095***	0.374299***	0.3625392***	0.3647086***
	(0.0736445)	(0.0891235)	(0.0891327)	(0.0887714)
Growth	-0.0017064	0.0166445	0.0107996	-0.2153883
	(0.2129543)	(0.2091434)	(0.2115168)	(0.4460608)
Leverage		2.41807***	2.467171***	2.497409***
		(0.7904562)	(0.8187685)	(0.8324293)
Return on assets			2.658473	2.816041
			(2.35366)	(2.468451)
Investment rate				0.1240493
				(0.1631475)
Constant	−5.843847***	−5.373184***	−5.369887***	–
	(0.9205141)	(1.081372)	(1.153082)	(1.150214)
N. obs	126	126	126	126
Pseudo R2	0.11	0.16	0.18	0.18

*, ** and *** indicate statistical significance at the 10%, 5%, and 1% level, respectively.

than finding funding in more traditional bank loans. Indeed, larger and more leveraged companies are more likely to be first-time issuers. More specifically, according to model specification IV, one standard deviation-large increase either in size or in leverage, would escalate the probability of a bond issue by approximately 15.5% and 12.8%, respectively, and all else being held equal. The positive relation between company size and the probability of bond issuance is consistent with the high fixed costs of the latter and high information asymmetries preventing smaller enterprises from accessing the market (see Cantillo & Wright, 2000; Denis & Mihov,

2003; Mizen & Tsoukas, 2013). As a matter of fact, the information asymmetry between larger, more reputable issuers and investors is narrower, facilitating the placement of the securities to a broader investor base. In addition, larger company size is associated with larger issues. In fact, the Spearman correlation between a company's total asset and the value of its bond issue is 0.497, statistically significant at the 1% level. This favors the liquidity of the securities, making them more appealing for investors, and better justifies the fixed costs of a bond issue. Moreover, larger company size is linked to higher leverage, consistent with a greater ability to generate cash flows and an enhanced borrowing capacity. Across the sample of issuers and non-issuers, the Spearman correlation between a company's total assets and its leverage ratio is 0.357, statistically significant at the 1% level. Therefore, the positive relation between the probability of bond issuance and leverage is consistent with the proven borrowing capacity (Denis & Mihov, 2003) of larger and more indebted firms, as well as the need to rebalance their financial structures.

4.4.3 The drivers of bond pricing at the issue

As the analysis concerns first-time issuers, in order to discover what motivates companies to access bonds in the first place, it is necessary to address the question of which factors are relevant in determining corporate bond pricing. To do so, authors investigate with an OLS regression the key fundamental variables that can explain primary market pricing of the inaugural bonds in the sample. This approach is similar to the one adopted by Gabbi & Sironi (2002) to study the issuance spreads of Eurobonds.

The sample considers all the tranches offered in the first-time. The dependent variable is either a tranche yield to maturity at launch (available only for fixed rate issues) or its spread to benchmark (available for fixed and floating rate issues, but with more missing observations). Independent variables include the following set of issue characteristics:

- High Yield, a dummy variable equal to 1 for tranches with a rating below BBB- and 0 otherwise.

- Rating, a continuous variable that assigns a numerical (progressive) value to different rating classes, with higher values being associated with better credit quality as in Corielli et al. (2010).
- Domestic, a dummy variable equal to 1 for tranches offered only domestically and 0 for international tranches (including Euro).
- Private Placement, a dummy variable equal to 1 for private placements and 0 for public issues.
- Multiple Tranches, a dummy variable equal to 1 if the offering involves multiple tranches and 0 otherwise.
- Offering Size, a continuous variable representing the logarithmic transformation of the total deal value in euro.
- Secured, a dummy variable equal to 1 if the tranche is secured and 0 otherwise.
- Callable, a dummy variable equal to 1 if the bond is callable and 0 otherwise.
- Luxembourg, a dummy variable equal to 1 if the tranche is registered in Luxembourg and 0 otherwise.
- Number of Bookrunners, a continuous variable indicating the number of bookrunners placing the bond.
- Float, a dummy variable equal to 1 for floating and variable rate tranches and 0 for fixed rate tranches.

Table 4.5 shows the results of our analysis under alternative model specifications, focusing on different groups of variables. The estimation sample varies considerably across different specifications due to data availability, making the interpretation of the coefficients less robust. However, a few clear relations emerge. First, non-investment grade tranches are associated with higher yields and higher spreads to benchmark, consistent with the higher level of credit risk involved. According to model specification III, on average, all else being equal, the yield at launch on investment grade tranches is 1.37% lower than for high-yield ones, and the spread to benchmark is lower by almost 200 bps. The same holds true if the High Yield dummy is replaced by the continuous variable capturing the different rating classes (unreported). In this case, a rate downgrading corresponds on average, all else being equal, to a 0.2% increase in the yield

Table 4.5 Linear regression model estimation: coefficients and year-clustered robust standard errors (in parenthesis)

	Yield to maturity (%)			Spread to benchmark (bp)		
	(I)	(II)	(III)	(I)	(II)	(III)
High Yield	2.484***	1.836**	1.376**	381.078***	291.924**	198.168**
	(0.748)	(0.702)	(0.481)	(80.48)	(93.58)	(66.81)
Domestic	0.099	−0.264	−2.798***			
	(1.205)	(0.924)	(0.817)			
Private Placement	−0.435	-0.859	−0.412			
	(0.723)	(1.175)	(1.031)			
Multiple Tranches	−0.723	−0.689	−1.532**	32.44	45.491	-7.436
	(0.709)	(1.026)	(0.641)	(81.929)	(64.835)	(89.23)
Offering Size		−0.348	0.052		−56.195**	-88.324
		(0.442)	(0.383)		(22.793)	(60.21)
Secured		1.1	1.553**		137.622	181.382**
		(0.826)	(0.516)		(74.284)	(63.41)
Callable		1.062	0.895*		39.779	4.82
		(0.594)	(0.433)		(73.671)	(52.459)
Luxembourg			−0.632			23.046
			(0.543)			(103.796)
No. Bookrunners			−0.187*			0.989
			(0.095)			(4.621)
Float rate				−71.706	−181.935***	−199.245***
				(83.667)	(40.923)	(49.756)
Constant	4.095***	10.5	3.638	216.571***	1,306.200**	1992.933
	(0.353)	(8.527)	(7.245)	(19.027)	(439.761)	(1,173.467)
Observations	70	63	54	43	43	36
R-squared	0.31	0.419	0.527	0.57	0.661	0.768

*, **, and *** indicate statistical significance at the 10%, 5%, and 1% level, respectively.

at launch and a rise by 21 bps of the spread to benchmark. Yet investors seem to be more concerned with the probability of default than with the loss given default. Indeed, secured tranches are associated with higher yields and higher spreads to benchmark. This suggests that while collateral mitigates losses in case of default, and to some extent can also affect the ratings, its impact is limited in terms of pre-venting default. Secured tranches may then proxy for higher credit risk, everything else being equal, if, for example, their frequency is higher in the lower end of the investment grade class or in the lower end of each rating class.

In addition, tranches offered only domestically or tranches that form part of a multiple offering are linked to lower yields. As expected, proximity with investors reduces information asymmetry, which leads to a lower cost for accessing the market. Yet lower borrowing cost can be the result of the domestic market representing a smaller liquidity pool, which is accessible only to stronger issuers. In the same vein, structuring larger issues in multiple tranches allows companies to cater to different investor types, while enhancing the credit quality of the more senior tranches.

Finally, floating rate tranches are associated with lower spreads to benchmark. However, this specific result should not be generalized, as it is most likely specific to the time frame adopted for the analysis. Fixed and floating rates reflect, to a different extent, the slope of the yield curve. If long-term rate expectations are significantly higher than short-term ones, then the spread to benchmark of floating rate tranches will be lower than that of fixed rate tranches and vice versa.

4.5 Conclusions

In the light of the data presented in this chapter, it can be gathered that, generally speaking, debt is an important component for Italian listed companies, and that the disintermediation between banks and non-financial companies is taking ground. The importance of debt as a funding resource is reflective of a broader macroeconomic context, Italy being a country where historically government debt has a big role in terms of GDP. The COVID-19 pandemic has played a stress-test role both on companies and on governments' finances. This is evident in the Debt outstanding-to-GDP ratio that sees a steep increase most likely generated by the increase in the financial needs of corporations for the year 2020, and by the decrease in the GDP level.

At a bond level, the demand keeps on increasing both at a Europe and at an Italian level. At an aggregate level, European companies issued 9,324 bonds in the period 2006–2021 for a cumulative value of around $6.5 billion. Italy ranks fourth among the European countries where most bonds are issued. In the overall period analyzed (2006 through 2021), the most active issuers belong to the Utilities and Power sector, weighing for one-third of all issuances, and the aggregate value of bonds issued by Italian companies was half a trillion USD. If in terms of volume, Italy accounts just for 6% of all issued bonds, in terms of average value, Italian issuers are in line with European trends, as the average size of bonds issued by an Italian company is larger than the size of European ones in 12 years out of the 16 observed.

In addition to bonds, Italian companies are also engaged in the issuance of minibonds, that have seen their record year in 2017 with 57 offerings. From 2017 onwards, there is a slight decline in the choice of issuing minibonds, even if the decline in value is compensated by the average of minibonds, that has increased in the latest years with a record in 2019 where the average minibond collected €15.37 million.

Talking more specifically of the health of the debt structure, it can be seen how the NPLs portion of gross loans decreased over time and reached 3.5% in 2021 from 16.50% recorded in 2014 and in 2015. Regardless this strong improvement in the health of the Italian debt securities, Italy is still one of the worst performing countries at a European Union level, where the overall percentage of NPLs for 2021 is 2.70%.

In addition to the ever-increasing importance of the issuance of debt securities in general, capital markets have been paid attention to sustainable finance as an answer to the current effects of the climate change, and in response to a society more and more careful about social and individual needs. This has generated concrete attention from the side of the regulators and of capital markets with the introduction of green bonds, Social Bonds, Sustainability Bonds, and Sustainability-linked Bonds, collectively called ESG Bonds. Data show a strong increase in the issuance of ESG

Bonds from all kinds of companies across Europe, reaching an aggregated value larger than $1 trillion at the end of 2021, where half of it is just referred to 2021 for a total volume of 1,147 ESG Bonds, where around 500 were issued in 2021. The countries were most ESG securities issuers are located are France, Germany, and the UK, accounting altogether for 45% of the bonds issues, whereas Italy ranks seventh with 7% of the ESG bonds issued.

All the above together with the findings of Caselli et al. (2019) indicate that companies have changed their approach to the bond market. If in the past debt funding was seen as a residual source, it has been progressively chosen by an increasing number of issuers. This reflects an increased corporate understanding of the importance of developing alternative financing options and the danger of relying excessively on bank lending. Indeed, the transition from bank funding to disintermediated, market-based alternatives represent an extremely welcome development in the corporate funding for Italian companies, which displayed financial weaknesses during the crisis due to their historical and anomalously almost exclusive reliance on conventional bank credit.

The findings of Caselli et al. (2019) identified the most likely determinants and costs of corporate bond issues in the Italian market, leveraging a fairly diversified sample with offering sizes ranging from €5 million to €1.6 billion. They noted a relevant number of issues addressed to the Euro area markets (79%); most of these had a single tranche and were coordinated by more than three bookrunners. In order to compare first-time issuers to similar companies that had not tapped into the corporate bond market, they matched the two types of companies using sales figures (relating to the year prior to the issue). By comparing the two groups, they highlighted how the only statistically significant difference across a wide array of financials is attributable to financial leverage (which is higher among first-time issuers). With the intent of explaining concretely the trend for corporate bond market in Italy, Caselli et al. (2019) also estimated a probit model to understand the main drivers of the probability of becoming a first-time issuer. Across the variety of parameters tested, size and leverage proved to be the only significant determinants, and both results are consistent with previous findings published in the literature.

Lastly, thanks to an OLS specification, Authors explored the determinants of bond pricing (always focusing on first-time issuers). The study shows how "high-yield" is the only characteristic which positively impacts the price, both the yield to maturity and the spread to benchmark, across all six models (three for each dependent variable). For the other numerous characteristics considered in the research, statistically significant results emerged either in some specifications only (e.g. Domestic Placement and Model III) or in none at all (e.g. Private Placement).

Overall, these results do paint a picture of an evolving market, caught in the tension between new forces driving the demand and supply of debt capital. On the demand side, there is the need to fill the corporate funding gaps resulting from the retreat by banks from lending sums up with companies' desire to diversify their sources of debt funding. On the supply side, the reduction of bank credit in response to higher capital requirements is offset by more appetite from yield-seeking investors. Everything, then, leads toward a progressive transition from bank funding to disintermediated, market-based alternatives. Yet, moving from the macro picture to the micro level of the economy, the findings of the research show that company size can be an obstacle to debt market funding. With this in mind, policy needs to focus on promoting the development of a larger and stronger domestically focused investor base that ensures that SMEs can also take full advantage of the beneficial effects of debt funding diversification.

References

Accornero, M., Finaldi Russo, P., Guazzarotti, G., & Nigro, V. (2015). *First-time corporate bond issuers in Italy*. Questioni di Economia e Finanza, Bank of Italy Occasional Papers no. 269. Available at: bancaditalia.it

Accornero, M., Finaldi Russo, P., Guazzarotti, G., & Nigro, V. (2018). *Missing investors in the Italian corporate bond market*. Questioni di Economia e Finanza, Bank of Italy Occasional Papers no. 450. Available at: bancaditalia.it

Banca d'Italia (2022). *Annual report for 2021*. Available at: bancaditalia.it

Cantillo, M. & Wright, J. (2000). How do firms choose their lenders? An empirical investigation. *The Review of Financial Studies*, 13(1), 155–189. https://doi.org/10.1093/rfs/13.1.155

Caselli, S., Gatti, S., & Gigante, G. (2019). *The Italian corporate bond market: What is happening to the capital structure of Italian non-financial companies?*. Equita SIM Position Paper. Available at: equitalab.eu

Corielli, F., Gatti, S., & Steffanoni, A. (2010). Risk shifting through non-financial contracts: Effects on loan spreads and capital structure of project finance deals. *Journal of Money, Credit and Banking*, 42(7), 1295–1320. Available at: jstor.org

Datta, S., Iskandar-Datta, M., & Patel, A. (2000). Some evidence on the uniqueness of initial public debt offerings. *The Journal of Finance*, 55(2), 715–743. https://doi.org/10.1111/0022-1082.00224

Denis, D.J. & Mihov, V.T. (2003). The choice among bank debt, non-bank private debt, and public debt: Evidence from new corporate borrowings. *Journal of Financial Economics*, 70(1), 3–28. https://doi.org/10.1016/S0304-405X(03)00140-5

European Commission (2018). *Identifying market and regulatory obstacles to the development of private placement of debt in the EU*. https://doi.org/10.2874/097215

Gabbi, G. & Sironi, A. (2002). Which factors affect corporate bonds pricing? Empirical evidence from Eurobonds primary market spreads. *The European Journal of Finance*, 11(1), 59–74. https://doi.org/10.1080/13518470032000143422

Hale, G. & Santos, J.A. (2008). The decision to first enter the public bond market: The role of firm reputation, funding choices, and bank relationships. *Journal of Banking & Finance*, 32(9), 1928–1940. https://doi.org/10.1016/j.jbankfin.2007.12.016

ICMA (2021, June). *Social bond principles: Voluntary process guidelines for issuing social bonds*. Available at: icmagroup.org

Mizen, P. & Tsoukas, S. (2013). What promotes greater use of the corporate bond market? A study of the issuance behavior of firms in Asia. *Oxford Economic Papers*, 66(1), 227–253. https://doi.org/10.1093/oep/gpt005

PwC Luxembourg (2021). *Green, social and sustainability (linked) bonds: The role of a verifier/certifier*. Available at: pwc.lu

Société Générale (2018, October). *In the mood for loans*. Cross Asset Research.

Conclusion

by *Stefano Caselli* and *Stefano Gatti*

There is a weak link that must be made much stronger, and the destiny of our country rides on it during this delicate phase in which development is the central theme. On one hand, we find the extraordinary availability of financial resources, while on the other, we have companies with their financial needs and projects which are facing the risk of uncertainty. The direct link between the two in our country has never been firmly established. The meeting and mediation point has always been represented by the banking system, with its traditional function of collecting deposits and lending money. The financial market alternative that could take its place has never had the same strength or the same centrality, although the values at stake and the advantages would be impressive.

The pandemic followed by the geopolitical crisis have both made consumption uncertain, but by the same token, these phenomena have given new vigor to the saving process. In fact, the financial wealth of Italian families reached €4,800 billion in 2021 and then grew to €5,300 billion in 2022 – a value that represents a multiple of both our GDP and our public debt. About 25% of these resources are liquid and therefore ready to be invested.

Corporates have important challenges and uncertainties to face, but at the same time, the total state-guaranteed funding reached €127 billion in 2022. The issue today is not a retrospective discussion of this amount, which has made it possible to mitigate obvious employment damage, among other things. Instead the question is how to proceed, and above all how to prevent this commitment from turning into further public expenditure. And this, in addition to the question of whether the path of public guarantees should be pursued in the future in the face of a new year of uncertainty.

The answer to these issues may seem simple, but it must be reiterated with determination: just like what happened with banks after the subprime crisis in 2007 and then in 2011, companies must also raise additional capital, which would make them more robust in the face of risk and capable of seizing opportunities to innovate and invest. More capital means more options to play, thanks to a solid, well-organized, and comprehensive financial system. Less capital and a less robust, comprehensive financial system mean exposing ourselves to the cost of future crises, which would require new public intervention and new debt. We cannot afford this. It is a story we have seen play out too many times before. If we think of the €5,300 billion and the excessively weak link that ties savings to the real economy, the solution is to make this connection much more robust. In addition, to protect the savings themselves that cannot expose themselves to the silent risk of inflation or indulge in crypto-temptations without protection, because both destroy their strength.

What is missing for this transition to finally happen? Can an ecosystem favorable to the capital market be established that can overturn the 30-70 structure that has always distinguished our country (i.e., 30% own resources, 70% debt)? Debate at a European level points the way: the DEBRA European Directive (Debt-Equity Bias Reduction Allowance), at the consultation stage, invites individual countries to introduce elements of clear rebalancing in favor of venture capital in companies. Moreover, the recommendations of the High-Level Forum on the Capital Markets Union and the OECD ("Italy Capital Market Review") push towards strengthening the capital market. Last spring, the MEF presented the "Green Paper on the Competitiveness of Italian Financial Markets in Support of Growth" outlining a series of proposals that must be taken up today to move forward decisively on this trajectory.

The individual instruments of the capital market for the development of the country are now largely available (from the fundamental platform of the Italian Stock Exchange to the various types of funds). However, there is a need to level up as far as capital supply- and demand-side actions, and strongly linking the components of this ecosystem. On the demand side, the size of our companies is an unresolved issue. Granted, small size is an essential factor of vitality and resilience of our country that must not be abandoned; but at the same time, we must create space for growth paths that bring out national champions capable of making a dimensional leap.

Italy has only five companies among the 500 largest on earth, fewer and fewer over the last ten years (and unicorns are disappearing). In 2011, Italy had ten companies in the ranking, and eight in 2001. These numbers are not only far behind the United States and China but also trail other European countries on comparison: Germany has as many as 27 companies, France 26, and let's not forget that Spain is also ahead of us with nine companies. If we look at the dynamics of the last 20 years, in addition to China's domineering growth and an inevitable adjustment of relative positions, only 50% of the companies listed in 2001 are still present today, and of these 90% have systematically resorted to M&A activities. Italy has not only seen companies slip in their positions, but worse, our country has not proposed new names or seen the creation of poles thanks to activism in the acquisition sector, except for financial intermediaries.

What is often seen as a subject to be criticized should for once serve as a good example of how an organization can go from small to large and international. In the pyramid that is the ecosystem of Italian companies, the base is formed by micro-companies, shops and retail; the second layer is SMEs; the third consists of major enterprises. But this structure risks having a wider and wider base and an apex that is more and more narrow. This is a wasted opportunity because Italy's forte – having an extraordinary base of micro to small and medium enterprises – must constitute a reservoir, an incubator for success stories. What's more, these companies must become not just unicorns but more importantly stable members of the Fortune 500 ranking.

If we do not embrace these challenges, we are doomed to forgo growth and live on public spending and new debt, which at some point we will pay for using the reserve of our savings, which are very large and liquid. At the level of industrial policy, these choices must find a very clear side. As far as fiscal policy, the government has the historic opportunity to create the right incentives to advance these strategies. The few areas of tax reduction should be used only in the face of clear business choices: growing via M&A, investing in innovation, capitalization, creating conglomerates, and attracting holding companies. The opportunity for the country to make a leap is one of a kind, and you … take charge and jump. However, a serious discussion on designing fiscal policies must happen first.

Some moves in this direction are the path of permanent incentives for business combinations; the design of a true taxation in support of capitalization acting on the side of the company and its shareholders; more aggressive action by banks in granting development finance, but accompanied by an explicit commitment by shareholders to follow up with capital increases; the development of equity investment initiatives supported by the government to encourage the creation of funds in the space between venture capital and private equity.

In addition to the above is the theme that has always been linked to definitively streamlining prospectuses for access to the stock market and simplifying the rules of permanence. Moreover, we also need to consolidate a narrative that gives the theme of business growth its relevance and its centrality for the future of the country. On the supply side, if the issue of the availability of resources is not an obstacle, the power of the market must be unleashed so that it reaches businesses. The choice of PIRs was an important step, as were (cautious) attempts to offer tax advantages to venture capital investments. We must continue along this path by affirming the principle that investment in risk capital does not have a speculative function (a common misunderstanding); rather it is an instrument of economic policy that fosters growth. A tax policy that rewards this investment throughout the different phases of a company's life, focusing on the medium and long term, would be a decisive step to make the link between savings and business more robust.

If we look at the history of our country since 1996, the year of the great fiscal reform that led to the IRES and IRAP taxes, the picture appears contradictory. On the one hand, successive governments have pursued a path of cutting rates (from IRES at 37% to 24% today) and reducing the weight of IRAP (thanks to the 2011–2012 reform that made the cost of employee labor deductible). But this was not accompanied by a real easing of the tax burden on businesses. According to rankings by World Bank and OECD, Italy places worse than 100th with respect to the tax burden it imposes on companies, with fiscal pressure close to 48%. On the other hand, mechanisms to encourage virtuous behaviors have been implemented inconsistently and often with limited effectiveness. The push to capitalize companies has been limited to the ACE scheme, which, except for the extraordinary rate of 2021, has always had minimal effects. The use of debt has been penalized since 2006, with the rule that limits how much interest is deductible, but without distinguishing between bank and market debt. There is no incentive scheme for listing transactions on the stock exchange. (The last one dates back to the "SuperDIT" of the previous century.) The only exception is the tax credit on advisory fees, up to €500,000. Investments have long benefited from the super amortization scheme, but there is no tool to support aggregations, or those who invest incrementally, as was the case with the very effective scheme known as "Tremonti-bis." As a paradoxical example, at present Italian tax rules reward those who have not capitalized their company and want to sell it (thanks to the rule on revaluations of shareholdings) but do not reward those who capitalize on a company or want to buy and invest. Moreover, rewards those who want to give up real estate as an individual.

The path of our country, running between public debt and the risk of recession, is not easy. The time has come to draw up a fiscal framework aligned with growth, responding in a clear way to the need for reform demanded by the markets, the PNRR, and our true sense of citizenship. There are two main fields of action. The first is to make a decisive link between savings and investment and business. The second goes in the direction of differentiating the main tax rate (IRES) not according to general categories (or even worse, electoral ones) or one-off case-by-case classifications, but in a structural way with respect to certain choices made by enterprises in favor of GDP growth and employment.

Our country has always displayed innate caution in promoting actions that go in the decisive direction of development, as Italy is increasingly careful to redistribute rather than create. But the times call for action and require a different speed. A definitive leap in our capital market would leave an important mark in the history of our country.

About the Authors

Stefano Caselli is the Dean of SDA Bocconi School of Management. Since 2012 to 2022 he has been Vice Rector for International Affairs at Bocconi University, where he is Full Professor of Banking and Finance and Algebris Chair in Long-Term Investment and Absolute Return. He is a member of the international advisory board of the School of Transnational Governance at the European University Institute in Florence, the Stockholm School of Economics, and the SGH Warsaw School of Economics. He is the academic co-director of the Equita Research Lab in Capital Markets, devoted to study the impact of financial markets. His research activities focus on the relation between financial and industrial systems, facing issues both of banking structure and regulation and of corporate finance, with a strong interest in the investment banking industry and private equity and venture capital. He has served as a columnist for the weekly supplement *L'Economia* of *Corriere della Sera* and he has a long-standing experience as independent director of financial intermediaries and corporations.

Stefano Gatti is the Antin IP Professor of Infrastructure Finance at the Department of Finance of Bocconi University. He has been the Director of the Full Time MBA at SDA Bocconi School of Management. His main area of research is corporate finance and investment banking. He has published a variety of texts in these areas, including publications in the *Journal of Money, credit and banking, Financial Management*, the *Journal of Applied Corporate Finance*, and the *European Journal of Operational Research.* He has acted as a consultant to several financial and non-financial institutions and for the Italian Ministry of the Economy, the Financial Stability Board, the Asian Development Bank, the Inter-American Development

Bank, and the OECD Group of G20. He is financial advisor of the Pension Fund of Health Care Professions, member of the compliance risk committee of Deutsche Bank and member of the board of directors and board of auditors of Italian industrial and financial corporations.

Carlo Chiarella, Ph.D. in Finance from Bocconi University, is the Director of the Department of Finance and Accounting at CUNEF Universidad and a Fellow at the BAFFI-CAREFIN Centre for Applied Research on International Markets, Banking, Finance and Regulation. His research focuses on corporate finance, especially in the contexts of capital markets, private equity, and mergers and acquisitions. He has authored several articles in these areas including publications in the *Journal of Financial Econometrics*, the *Journal of International Financial Markets, Institutions & Money*, the *International Review of Economics and Finance* and the *International Review of Financial Analysis*.

Gimede Gigante, Ph.D. in Banking and Finance, is the Director of the Innovation and Corporate Entrepreneurship Center at SDA Bocconi School of Management and the Deputy Director of the Bachelor program in Economics and Finance at Bocconi University, where he has served as Course Director of Principles of International Finance since 2017 and as Academic Director of the Bocconi Summer School since 2019. He has held visiting positions at Columbia Business School and the Salomon Center at New York University's Stern School of Business. He is a member of the Harvard Business Review advisory council and a Fellow of the Research Unit on Investment Banking and Structured Finance at the BAFFI-CAREFIN Centre. His main areas of research are international finance, financial markets, corporate valuation, investment banking, fintech, and private equity.

Giulia Negri is the MBA Academic Director and an Associate Professor of Finance at the Luxembourg School of Business. She is a Fellow of Corporate Finance at SDA Bocconi School of Management and a Fellow at the BAFFI-CAREFIN Centre for Applied Research on International Markets, Banking, Finance and Regulation. Her research and teaching activities focus on corporate valuation, mergers and acquisitions, sustainable finance, and private equity and venture capital. She has conducted several consulting projects for small and medium-sized companies with Madison Corporate Finance, an independent financial advisory firm specialized in corporate finance and M&A advisory. She graduated *summa cum laude* at Bocconi University and earned her Ph.D. from the University of St. Gallen.

Marta Zava is an Academic Fellow at the Department of Finance at Bocconi University, Milan, and a Ph.D. Candidate in Economics at the Graduate School of Economics, Finance, and Management (GSEFM) at Goethe University, Frankfurt. At Bocconi University, she teaches the Finance Lab and assists in the teaching of the International Finance course and the Investment Banking course. Her research activities focus on venture capital and banking. She combines financial subjects with innovative methodologies spanning from artificial intelligence to network science and complex systems. Moreover, she currently serves as a board member of the Complex System Society. Previously, she worked as Supervision Analyst at the European Central Bank, holistically covering Banking Supervision topics.